My name is Neale and I have talked with God.

So have you.

You may not think that you have, but you have. You've probably just called it something else. You may have called it the most loving feeling, the most life-affirming thought, the most expansive inspiration you've ever had. Or perhaps, simply, a *blinding flash of insight*, a *brilliant idea*, an *incredible hunch*, a *stroke of genius*, an *amazing coincidence*, *pure serendipity*, or *remarkable intuition*.

Whatever you called it, it's all the same thing. It's all a communication from a source of wisdom and insight within us that is the birthright of every person.

In my case, I called my encounters with this source exactly what I experienced them to be: Conversations with God. They came in the form of an ongoing dialogue, and I kept a record of them. Several million people have read them and had their lives changed. And now, I would like to share with you what I consider to be the most important of these messages—and some powerful suggestions on how to apply them in your own daily life.

WHAT GOD SAID

The 25 Core Messages of Conversations with God
That Will Change Your Life and the World

NEALE DONALD WALSCH

BERKLEY BOOKS, NEW YORK

THE BERKLEY PUBLISHING GROUP
Published by the Penguin Group
Penguin Group (USA) LLC
375 Hudson Street, New York, New York 10014

USA • Canada • UK • Ireland • Australia • New Zealand • India • South Africa • China

penguin.com

A Penguin Random House Company

Berkley trade paperback ISBN: 978-0-425-26885-8

Library of Congress Cataloging-in-Publication Data

Walsch, Neale Donald.
What God said : the 25 core messages of conversations with God that
will change your life and the world / Neale Donald Walsch.—First edition.
pages cm
ISBN 978-0-425-26884-1
1. God—Miscellanea.   2. Spiritual life—Miscellanea.   3. Private revelations.
I. Walsch, Neale Donald. Conversations with God.   II. Title.
BF1999.W22823 2013
133.9'3—dc23
2013020134

PUBLISHING HISTORY
Berkley hardcover edition / October 2013
Berkley trade paperback edition / October 2014

PRINTED IN THE UNITED STATES OF AMERICA

10 9 8 7 6 5 4 3 2 1

Cover art by ableimages/Masterfile.
Cover design by Lesley Worrell.
Interior text design by Laura K. Corless.

Dedicated to all people
who believe in God
and who have yearned to know
more about this Divine Essence
and their relationship to It.

Acknowledgments

Is it possible that there is something we do not fully understand about God and about Life and about Each Other, the understanding of which would change everything? However you conceive of your personal God, is it okay to explore our ideas about God further?

I want to acknowledge every person who has picked up this book. Even if you put it down without reading it. Even if you start to read it and decide not to finish it. And of course, if you read it to its final page. It takes courage to embark upon excursions such as those offered here.

Every word ever written about God has been written by a human being. Those writers are believed to have been inspired by God. The question is: Has God *ever* stopped inspiring human beings? *Could it be possible that God's messages continue to flow to humanity, even today?* My deepest thanks to everyone who is willing to ask these questions, even if you don't agree with the answers I have found. We have met on the Field of Inquiry, and that is a wonderful first step toward each other. We do not have to agree, but if we can disagree *agreeably*, we will have done what *every* person's God has invited. And that can heal the world.

The day is coming to pass
when the enormity of God's love
and of God's gift to humanity
will be fully realized,
and will become a part
of everyone's life.

This outcome is inevitable.
It is simply a matter of time.

1

Okay, you claim to have talked directly with God, so tell us . . . what is God's message to the world?"

The speaker was the world-famous host of one of America's most popular national television morning shows, and he was asking me to answer the biggest question of all time.

"Can you bring it down to a sentence or two?" he added. "We have about thirty seconds."

My mind raced. How could I say something in thirty seconds that would capture the essence of what Deity wants the world to know? Then, in one quick flash, I heard God's answer in my head. I blinked and made an announcement that surprised even me.

"Actually, I can bring it down to *five words*."

The host raised his eyebrows, showing a nanosecond of disbelief, then deadpanned to the camera: "All right then. Ladies and gentlemen, from a man who says he *communes with The Divine*, here is God's message to the world . . . in five words."

I knew that millions were watching in households around the globe. This was my chance to bring God's most important communication to more people than I ever imagined I would, or could,

in my lifetime. Looking straight into the lens I repeated the words
I had just been given to say.

"You've got me all wrong."

A One-in-a-Million Chance

My name is Neale and I should explain.

I have talked with God.

Not just once, in a singular moment of epiphanic revelation, but
many, many times.

So have you.

You may not think that you have, but you have. You've probably
just called it something else. You may have called it a *blinding flash
of insight*. Or a *brilliant idea*. Or an *incredible hunch*, a *good guess*,
a *stroke of genius*, a *coincidence*, *serendipity*, or *women's intuition*.

Whatever you called it, it's all the same thing. It's all a communication from a source of wisdom and insight within us that is the
birthright of every person.

In my case I called my encounters with this source exactly what
I experienced them to be: conversations with God.

Luckily, I wrote down all the exchanges that I had, so I've never
forgotten them. The process started when I sat down at 4:20 in the
morning on a day in the early 1990s and wrote an angry letter to
God, demanding to know why my life wasn't working and how I
could *make* it work.

What followed was an ongoing on-paper dialogue with Deity,
in which I asked the most perplexing or frustrating questions of my
life, and answers were given to me exactly as if I was being given
dictation.

At one point I was told by God: "This will one day become a
book," and so, a few months later, I sent my first handwritten notes

to a stenographer to have them transcribed, then I printed out the document and sent it to a publisher . . . almost as a dare.

I don't know who I was daring . . . myself or God . . . but I knew that I wanted to "test" what I had been given, to see if it had any validity at all, to see if any of it was true.

I was fully aware, of course, that the chances of some publishing house actually printing and distributing a book from a person claiming to be talking directly to God were one in a million. It simply wasn't going to happen.

Wrong.

It happened.

So Now, the Expansion Begins

Now here I am after nine books in the *Conversations with God* series, and I'm doing what I have done every time I sat down to write a book. I'm asking myself: *Why are you writing this book? What are you hoping to accomplish here? Is this book needed?*

Let me answer my own questions so that you can get a sense of what's ahead—and so that you can decide whether or not you want to take this journey.

- I am writing this book because I have been asked many, many times by many, many people to expand upon what God said in the three thousand pages that make up the *Conversations with God* books—and I want to do so in one tidy volume, so that God's message for humanity could be made easily and rapidly accessible.

- What I hope to accomplish with these new, never-before-published expansions of the messages of *Conversations with*

God is make them *immediately usable* in day-to-day life. I want the ideas to be functional and not just conceptual.

• This book is needed for two reasons: (1) Millions of people have read *Conversations with God* (the books in the series have been published in thirty-seven languages), and those readers asked me not only to expand the material but also to tell them which of the many messages are the most important. (2) The messages of *Conversations with God* can change the world if people know how to apply them, and the world is desperately in need of changing right now. Not in fifty years. Not in twenty-five years. Not in ten years. Right now.

The Problem Is Systemic

It's time to be honest here: Nothing is working.

I mean, nothing.

Not a single major system that we have put into place on this planet is functioning correctly. Not our political, not our economic, not our environmental, not our education, not our social, and not our spiritual system. None of them are producing the outcomes that we say we want. In fact, it's worse. They're producing the outcomes that we say we *don't* want.

And not just on a global scale. It gets down to the personal level. It gets right down to you and me. All but the tiniest percentage of the world's people are caught up in struggle. *Daily* struggle. Struggle not merely to be happy, but to *survive*, to *get by*, to just *stay afloat*.

And now, it has gone past even that. Because now, even those people who *are* living the "good life" are not having a good time.

Not even them. Personal happiness seems mysteriously and frustratingly elusive. And even when people achieve it, they can't hold on to it.

Now that's the greatest clue, that's the biggest hint, that's the surest sign that something's amiss. When even those who *should* be happy by any reasonable measure are not, there's got to be a *serious systemic problem* in a society's culture. You can tell that a social formula is askew when even if the formula is working, *it's not*; when even if everything's going right, *something's desperately wrong*.

That's where we are today, and I think it's time for a New Message to guide humanity. I think it's time for a brand-new cultural story to be embraced by our species.

Now if you like your life exactly the way it is, and if you like your world precisely as it presents itself, you may disagree with me. Yet if for no other reason than that, you may want to read on. If you yearn to keep things the same, you should know all there is to know about changes that others (in this case, millions of others) are being invited to consider.

If you agree with me that it's time for some major changes to be made, in the world at large and perhaps in your own life, you have come to exactly the right place.

The messages here were meant to change everything.

Hold On to Your Seat

For quickest reading and maximum impact, I have reduced the core messages of the nine *Conversations with God* books to a thousand words. Then, I've offered significant expansions of them.

Here, then, is the clearest articulation and the most practical application of what I consider to be the most important insights of *Conversations with God*.

Not every statement in the thousand-word summary that makes up chapter 2 may be perfectly understood upon first reading. They certainly weren't for me. That's precisely why I've expanded on them on the pages that follow.

After fifteen years of working to apply these messages in my life and, during that same decade and a half, searching to find the clearest, simplest way of explaining—in answer to thousands of questions from audiences around the world—what the messages say and how they can be applied, I assess that I am now ready to contribute this book.

So here we go. Oh, but now, hold on to your seat. Some of these ideas may be considered by many to be heretical, so this could be quite a ride. Yet I believe it is as George Bernard Shaw famously noted: "All great truths begin as blasphemies."

2

Here, in one thousand words, is all that the human race needs to know in order to live the life for which it has yearned and which, despite trying for thousands of years, it has yet to produce. Carry these messages to your world:

1. We are all One. All things are One Thing. There is only One Thing, and all things are part of the One Thing there is. This means that you are Divine. You are not your body, you are not your mind, and you are not your soul. You are the unique combination of all three, which comprises the Totality Of You. You are an individuation of Divinity; an expression of God on Earth.

2. There's enough. It is not necessary to compete for, much less fight over, your resources. All you have to do is share.

3. There's nothing you have to do. There is much you *will* do, but nothing you are *required* to do. God wants nothing, needs nothing, demands nothing, commands nothing.

4. God talks to everyone, all the time. The question is not: To whom does God talk? The question is: Who listens?

5. There are Three Basic Principles of Life: *Functionality*, *Adaptability*, and *Sustainability*.

6. There is no such thing as Right and Wrong, there is only What Works and What Does Not Work, given what it is you are trying to do.

7. In the spiritual sense, there are no victims and no villains in the world, although in the human sense it appears that there surely are. Yet because you are Divine, everything that happens ultimately benefits you.

8. No one does anything inappropriate, given their model of the world.

9. There is no such place as hell, and eternal damnation does not exist.

10. Death does not exist. What you call "death" is merely a process of Re-Identification.

11. There is no such thing as Space and Time, there is only Here and Now.

12. Love is all there is.

13. You are the creator of your own reality, using the Three Tools of Creation: *Thought*, *Word*, and *Action*.

14. Your life has nothing to do with you. It is about everyone whose life you touch and how you touch it.

15. The purpose of your life is to re-create yourself anew in the next grandest version of the greatest vision ever you held about Who You Are.

16. The moment you declare anything, everything unlike it will come into the space. This is the Law of Opposites,

producing a contextual field within which that which you wish to express may be experienced.

17. There is no such thing as Absolute Truth. All truth is subjective. Within this framework there are five levels of truth telling: *Tell your truth to yourself about yourself; Tell your truth to yourself about another; Tell your truth about yourself to another; Tell your truth about another to another; Tell your truth to everyone about everything.*

18. The human race lives within a precise set of illusions. The Ten Illusions of Humans are *Need Exists, Failure Exists, Disunity Exists, Insufficiency Exists, Requirement Exists, Judgment Exists, Condemnation Exists, Conditionality Exists, Superiority Exists,* and *Ignorance Exists.* These illusions are meant to serve humanity, but it must learn how to use them.

19. The Three Core Concepts of Holistic Living are *Honesty, Awareness,* and *Responsibility.* Live according to these precepts and self-anger will disappear from your life.

20. Life functions within a Be-Do-Have paradigm. Most people have this backward, imagining that first one must "have" things in order to "do" things, thus to "be" what they wish to be. Reversing this process is the fastest way to experience mastery in living.

21. There are Three Levels of Awareness: *Hope, Faith,* and *Knowing.* Spiritual mastery is about living from the third level.

22. There are Five Fallacies about God that create crisis, violence, killing, and war. First, the idea that God *needs* something. Second, the idea that God *can fail to get* what

He needs. Third, the idea that God *has separated* you from Him because you have not given Him what He needs. Fourth, the idea that God still needs what He needs so badly that God now *requires* you, *from your separated position*, to give it to Him. Fifth, the idea that God *will destroy you* if you do not meet His requirements.

23. There are also Five Fallacies about Life that likewise create crisis, violence, killing, and war. First, the idea that human beings are separate from each other. Second, the idea that there is not enough of what human beings need to be happy. Third, the idea that in order to get the stuff of which there is not enough, human beings must compete with each other. Fourth, the idea that some human beings are better than other human beings. Fifth, the idea that it is appropriate for human beings to resolve severe differences created by all the other fallacies by killing each other.

24. You think you are being terrorized by other people, but in truth you are being terrorized by your beliefs. Your experience of yourself and your world will shift dramatically if you adopt, collectively, the Five Steps to Peace:

- Permit yourself to acknowledge that some of your old beliefs about God and about Life are no longer working.

- Explore the possibility that there is something you do not fully understand about God and about Life, the understanding of which would change everything.

- Announce that you are willing for new understandings of God and Life to now be brought forth, understandings that could produce a new way of life on this planet.

- Courageously examine these new understandings and, if they align with your personal inner truth and knowing, enlarge your belief system to include them.

- Express your life as a demonstration of your highest beliefs, rather than as a denial of them.

25. Let there be a New Gospel for all the people of Earth: "We are all one. Ours is not a better way, ours is merely another way."

The one thousand words here, embraced and acted on, could change your world in a single generation.

3

Some of those messages are crystal clear and some beg for clarification. Most of us can probably agree, for instance, that "it is not necessary to compete for, much less fight over," our resources. On the other had, we might have a difficult time with the idea that "there are no victims or villains in the world," even if the statement is qualified by "in a spiritual sense."

Especially in a spiritual sense, we have believed that "right and wrong" are intrinsic parts of the universal scheme of things—of "the Law of God," if you will—and most people cannot conceive of a world with no moral absolutes. If fact, what many people think is *wrong* with the world today is that there seem to be fewer and fewer moral absolutes.

This creates a major problem. Many human beings don't appear to know how to exist with no one outside of them telling them what to do and what not to do. It's hard enough to find happiness in a world where someone *does*. What would we do without any rules at all? And what would restrain us if there were no judgment, condemnation, and punishment, *especially* in the "spiritual sense"?

So we see that the first difficulty with, and the biggest challenge of, the *Conversations with God* material is that it pulls the underpinning from humanity's moral constructions and ideas about God. Never mind that those constructions and religious dogmas have done little to produce a world free of hatred, violence, and fear. Never mind that those moral values and teachings about God have failed to eliminate suffering, reduce abject poverty, or even do something as simple as end hunger on our planet.

Did you know that six million children die every year on Earth from *starvation*? That's fact, not polemic.

We get terribly upset—and we should—when a man with a gun kills 20 children in a school, but we sit by and watch 684 children die *every hour* of hunger and allow it to go on. There's nothing, we say, that we can do about it.

It is sadly true that when it comes to our global values and the religions from which they emerge, the majority of the world's people have refused to do what they have allowed themselves to do in every other area of human endeavor.

In science, they have encouraged it. In medicine, they have encouraged it. In technology, they have encouraged it. But when it comes to religion—presumably the most important area of all—they have actively discouraged it.

And what is it that people in science, medicine, and technology routinely do that, when it comes to religion, they stubbornly refuse to do?

Question the prior assumption.

Leave the Apples Where They Are

Apple-cart-upsetting is not something that people on this planet like to do. They don't want anyone tampering with their most sacred beliefs. Even if those beliefs are clearly and demonstrably wrong, or obviously and totally ineffective in producing the outcomes they espouse or predict, human beings will cling to their beliefs with a stubborn rigidity that is both shocking and appalling.

For instance, did you know that—paleontological and archaeological discoveries of the past quarter century notwithstanding—surveys show that over 40 percent of this planet's population continue to believe that the world is no more than ten thousand years old?

People believe what they want or need to believe in order to support their previously held point of view. In a startling number of instances, it truly is a case of "don't bother me with the facts."

Nowhere is this in greater evidence than in the area of religion.

We know what we know about God and we don't want to hear anything else. And there's a powerful reason for this. Our thoughts about God form the bedrock of our entire understanding of Life. This is true even for those who have no belief in God at all.

So whether people are "believers" or "nonbelievers," their thoughts about God create a foundation upon which many build their entire moral code. Understandably, then, *new* thoughts, *new* ideas, *new* concepts about God are not easily welcomed or enthusiastically embraced by most folks.

A New Truth about God would be—for agnostics, atheists, and adherents alike—the Great Apple Cart Upsetter of all time.

Flying into the Window Pane

Since most people want to leave their religious beliefs alone, we find ourselves insisting on building a life in the first quarter of the 21st century with 1st-century spiritual tools.

In medicine, this would be like trying to perform surgery with a very sharp stick. In technology, it would be like trying to send a rocket to the moon with the spark of a flint stone. In science, it would be like trying to conduct an experiment in a cave by the light of a small fire.

Still, leaving our religious beliefs untouched could make sense *if* those tools were working. Yet we are not allowed to even *question* if they are working. The problem is not with the tools, we tell ourselves, the problem is that we are not using them.

Yet the keen observer would realize that the problem is exactly the opposite. The problem is that we *are* using them. And we are using them *against each other.*

Thus, the tools of our ancient religions have proven ineffective (to put it mildly) in creating a world of peace, harmony, sufficiency, and dignity for all.

What is wrong here?

That is a question we are not supposed to ask. We are supposed to keep on doing the same thing we have always done, expecting to get a different result. (And that, of course, is the definition of insanity.)

Like flies against a windowpane, we keep banging our heads against that which we do not see—or, in our case, which we *refuse* to see: that there must be something fundamentally flawed in our beliefs about God and about Life, or we would be way past where we are now in terms of our social and spiritual development.

We would not live on a planet where people still kill each other in order to resolve their differences.

We would not live on a planet where people still die of starvation by the millions while enough food is thrown into the garbage every day to feed half the population.

We would not live on a planet where 5 percent of the population holds or controls 95 percent of the wealth and resources—and considers this perfectly okay.

We would not live on a planet where "every man for himself" is actually considered preferable to "all for one and one for all."

What Are We Willing to Do?

Yet we do live on such a planet. And so the question is, are we willing to continue all of this?

Are we willing to just go on as we have been, bequeathing to our children and to theirs a world that can unlock the mysteries of the human genome but cannot unlock the love within the human heart?

We say we are not. We say we want a better life, and to produce a better life for our offspring, but what are we willing to do about it?

Are we willing to do *the bravest thing of all*? Are we willing to challenge our most sacred beliefs? Are we willing to consider the possibility that there may be something we do not fully understand about God and about Life—the understanding of which would change everything?

Are we willing to consider—to at least explore—new ideas, new thoughts, new constructions within the human story? Even if, on the surface, they seem to contradict what we think we already know about God and Life, can we at least explore their possibilities? Must we dismiss every new concept, every new hypothesis, out of hand simply because it does not agree with the story we have been telling ourselves for centuries and millennia?

No. We do not have to. And a civilization that hopes to advance cannot afford to. Thus, the messages here become extraordinarily important, for only when we are open to all ideas are all possibilities open to us.

4

There is good news here. Today, as the world faces economic crises, political upheaval, civil unrest, societal breakdown, environmental degradation, spiritual confusion, ongoing conflict, and war, people everywhere are finding the courage to *not* leave their religious beliefs alone. They are searching for new guideposts, new insights, new answers, new ways of being human.

Most important of all, a small but growing number of people are now yearning for new ways of understanding and relating to God, because they have come to a new awareness that humanity's ideas about God greatly impact, and in some cases even create, its ideas about humanity itself, about who we are in relationship to each other, and about how Life works.

And it is clear now—today more than ever, because of our ability to see ourselves, to communicate with our entire world, in an instant—that some of our old ideas are no longer functional.

It is doubtful that they were ever functional, but it didn't matter in the past. Not on a global scale. Because things kept going. Life went on. But now, things can't keep going anymore. Not as they have been. Too much is known by too many too fast. Our old ways of doing things, our old ways of *being*, are no longer even considered partially functional by part of the world. And this is what people everywhere are beginning at last to acknowledge. In the past, one place on the Earth could hide its dysfunction from another place. Now, we all know everything about what's going on everywhere. This makes dysfunction harder to hide—and harder for the world at large to tolerate.

Too many of us are seeing our self-inflicted wounds. And we're also seeing that we're running out of Band-Aids. We can't just keep patching everything together.

We're running out of fertile soil in which to plant our crops. We're running out of cooler, damper climate to stop our Earth from parching. We're running out of pure water. We're running out of clean air. And we're running out of ways to ignore all of this.

We're running out of money to make things better. We're running out of time in which to do it. Worst of all, some people are running out of the *will* to do it, as they sink deeper and deeper into fear and frustration, thinking that the only solution is to turn *on* each other rather than *to* each other.

This Group Does Not Include You

You're not among those who believe this, or you would never have picked up this book. You're among those who are clear that it's not too late to change this—even if you don't exactly know what part you can play in doing it. (More on that later.) What you *do* know is that what must be accomplished now is the complete overhaul of our way of being.

Not a small task, but not impossible. Our species has experienced such a complete re-creation of itself before—a renaissance, a rebirth, if you will. And this renaissance need not take three hundred years. It can be accomplished in one-tenth the time, precisely because of the instantaneous and transparent nature of our modern-day communication—a condition that I call *instaparency*.

I want to suggest that our turnaround might best begin with a new writing, an expansion, of our cultural story, of the words that we tell ourselves about ourselves, of the lessons we teach our children about the reason and purpose for Life itself, and—most important of all—of the narratives we share with everyone about what we call "God."

This is where the power lies. This is where the leverage is. This is where we find the fuel that drives the engine of the human experience.

Yet what new Divinely inspired addition to our hallowed human story could capture our attention and cause us to even consider changing our age-old behaviors? That is the question. What new ideas from God could be as powerful and as inspiring, as exciting and as motivating as those of Lao Tzu or of Buddha; of Moses or of Jesus; of Muhammad or of Krishna? What expansion of our story could be as moving, as life-impacting, and as experience-changing as the messages of the belief systems and religions to which the followers of those teachers gave birth?

That has been the key question for a very long time. What new ideas could expand our ancient story sufficiently to offer brand-new possibilities for an entire species?

It's Not About Rejection or Abandonment

I come here to respectfully suggest that the contemporary ideas of what I have come to call the New Spirituality might offer one outline for those additions. They could at least offer a basis for opening discussions, for beginning explorations.

This will not happen, however, if people see such explorations as a rejection or abandonment of humanity's Ancient Story, for we hold that story dear to our hearts—as well we should. It has, after all, gotten us this far.

So it should be made clear at the outset that *Conversations with God* never suggests such a thing. Indeed, it makes the opposite point: Much of what has been given to us by our world's religions is valuable and good. That is why religion itself has lasted so long. If religions have produced conflict between people, it is not because their teachings are "wrong" but because they may be incomplete.

It is my observation that many human beings are as children who have learned to add and subtract but have not yet heard about multiplication and long division (to say nothing of geometry, trigonometry, and calculus), yet *they think they know all there is to know about mathematics.*

There may be much more to be revealed about God and about Life than we now assume, and I believe it is a mistake to imagine that we have in hand everything there is to know on these subjects.

The intention of *Conversations with God* is not, therefore, to reject wholesale or completely abandon humanity's old ideas about the Divine and about Life, but to add to, build on, extend, widen, broaden, deepen, clarify, and enrich our Ancient Story.

Ending the Blockade

There is no need for this expansion of our original understanding to generate rage, much less block us forever as we seek to move forward on our spiritual voyage, any more than expanded scientific, medical, or technical understandings have blocked us forever from advancing in our evolutionary journey.

Yes, there have been some stumbling blocks, there have been some delays, on the evolutionary journey of science, medicine, and technology, but nothing that we allowed to stop us completely. It took us awhile to admit that the sun did not revolve around the Earth; it took us awhile to acknowledge that washing our hands before delivering babies would decrease infant mortality; it took us awhile to "get" that computers need not pose a threat to human beings; but ultimately we embraced these and other advancements and stepped forward.

We didn't throw out the whole of our scientific knowledge to accept a new discovery, we didn't throw out the whole of our medical knowledge to adopt a new procedure, we didn't throw out the whole of our technical knowledge to apply a new development. We simply enfolded the new within the old, allowing ourselves to modify and expand our understandings, and then we marched on, all the better for it.

It is time now for us to do the same with religion.

5

What is needed now on Earth is a Civil Rights Movement for the Soul, freeing humanity at last from the oppression of its belief in a violent, angry, and vindictive God, and releasing our species from a spiritual doctrine that has created nothing but separation, fear, and dysfunction around the world.

We need to replace this dogma, finally, with what my friend Rabbi Michael Lerner would describe as an ethos of unity and cooperation, understanding and compassion, generosity and love.

The first step in this movement is to initiate a global conversation that begins with a rarely asked blunt question: "Honestly, and without bias, would you say that our world's belief systems, including its religions, have produced the outcomes for which humanity has yearned?"

If the answer to this question is no, the next question must be: "Why do you think our belief systems have failed to do this?" And finally, any beneficial discussion would lead to this inquiry: "What beliefs or understandings do you feel *would* produce the outcomes humanity says it desires?"

These questions could form the basis of what I call the Conversation of the Century—and this is something in which all of us can take part. You could engage in the Conversation of the Century right now in the worldwide virtual community that gathers daily at www.TheGlobalConversation.com. This is an Internet newspaper I created that relates the expanded spiritual concepts of the New Spirituality to the news of the day, making spirituality itself *vital* again, *meaningful* again in our daily lives.

You could also launch an Evolution Revolution Group in your community right now, meeting in your home once or twice a month.

Talking about important topics generates energy around them. Every major change that has ever occurred in our social, political, economic, and spiritual systems began when one person talked to another person about it. This may seem almost absurdly obvious, yet I observe many people who want to see changes in their world and in their lives nevertheless saying: "What can I do? What impact can I possibly make?"

So make no mistake, people talking together about the same thing at the same moment become very powerful. So powerful that, as Victor Hugo said, "All the armies of the world cannot stop an idea whose time has come."

Rewriting humanity's cultural story to include expanded beliefs and deeper understandings about God and Life, enlarging upon the primitive and simplistic beliefs of our past, is just such an idea.

It takes time, but large clusters of people—whole societies—*can* have a change of mind about things. Martin Luther King Jr. helped create a change of mind about blacks. Betty Friedan and Gloria Steinem helped create a change of mind about women. Harvey Milk helped create a change of mind about gays. We can all now help create a change of mind about God.

A New Gospel

To "change the world's mind about God!" Ah! What a goal!

And *that* is the goal of the New Spirituality. That is the goal of *Conversations with God*. That is the goal of every soul who knows and loves God, and who can no longer sit by idly and watch people grapple with teachings of a fearful, vengeful, violent God, and ignore all the damaging outcomes that such beliefs have inflicted upon the human race.

Those of us in that group know that the first thing we must help people change their mind about is God's relationship to us. Then, our relationship to God. And finally, the relationship of all people to each other, and to Life itself.

These three topics form the through line of the most important messages of *Conversations with God*, summarized in chapter 2. I believe with all my heart that these messages provide a pathway to the kind of life experience for which Earth's people have yearned, both individually and collectively, for thousands of years.

Please note that I said "a" pathway, not "the" pathway. My choice of words was specific and deliberate. Conversations with God offered humanity a New Gospel in the book *Friendship with God*. That New Gospel concludes the summary in chapter 2.

So let's start there. Let's *begin* our exploration of this thousand-word summary where it *ends*. Let's start at the bottom and work our way up.

6

As we look at the 25 Core Messages emerging from *Conversations with God*, last to first, I'm going to devote one chapter to each, and divide every chapter into two sections: Meaning and Application. Thus, we'll expand in two ways on the messages themselves, taking many people who have not had a chance to go there before into new territories.

Here, then, is our look at the most daring message of all . . .

CWG CORE MESSAGE #25

Let there be a New Gospel for all the people of Earth: "We are all one. Ours is not a better way, ours is merely another way."

This was for me one of the most wonderful messages in the dialogue with Divinity that I had the wonderful fortune to experience. In that sweet exchange, God softly told me that we could bring an end to much of the anger, hatred, division, and violence in our world by simply adopting and spreading a new teaching, a simple fifteen-word new doctrine: *We are all One. Ours is not a better way, ours is merely another way.*

God called this the New Gospel, and I have to admit that I was at first very reluctant to use those words because, after all, the word "gospel" holds such a special significance for so many people. But I have never edited a single thing that I have been given in these dialogue experiences, and I couldn't justify suddenly starting . . . so I left the phrase exactly as I received it.

I do believe that what we could all use right now is a new gospel. Not one to replace the old, but to add to it, to enlarge upon it, giving it deeper, richer meaning. So, in my talks and workshops around the world I have invited our economic leaders, our political leaders, and our spiritual leaders to speak this New Gospel to their audiences.

So far, no one has done so. I do understand. I know why not one major world leader, not one global spiritual figure, not one titan of business and industry has dared to utter those words from their podiums and pulpits and boardroom tables. They simply don't believe it would work, that it would ever be accepted by those who listen to them, who look up to them.

In fact, because of the very positions these leaders hold, they may feel that they have to declare exactly the opposite. Why would anyone follow them if they did not announce that their way was the better way?

Yet nothing blocks the creation and sustaining of peace in our world more than thoughts of superiority—especially if they are accompanied by righteousness.

And this, sadly, is what we are seeing more and more of in our increasingly polarized society. "Not only," our leaders say, "do we have a good idea . . . it is the *only* good idea there is. Our way is the *right* way. Everyone else is not only wrong, but *bad* for even suggesting something else."

This is what our exchange of views is sounding like more and more each day—and it is so sad that we don't even notice that we are creating the polarity ourselves, with our righteousness.

As pointed out here earlier, when humans believe they are "right" about something, some of them—perhaps most—hold on to their views tenaciously, even when facts reveal their viewpoint to be inaccurate or render it obsolete.

It is true that people can change their mind about things. Harvey Milk, Gloria Steinem, Martin Luther King Jr., and others, God bless them, proved that. But it is not an easy task to help them to do so. For it is as we have been told in *Communion with God*: The idea of superiority is seductive.

It is, that book tells us, one of the Ten Illusions of Humans. It cannot be real . . . and I will explain why in just a moment . . . but it can sure seem real. And it feels so *good*.

Nowhere is the idea of superiority more pervasive than in religion, another point made earlier. That is what makes the New Gospel so dramatic and so striking—and so challenging for many people to embrace.

Yet precisely because it *is* challenging, it invites our closer examination. So let's take a more-than-surface look at it.

Is God Not "Everything"?

The New Gospel begins with the words "we are all One." Thus, this final revelation in the 25 Core Messages of what God said brings us right back to its first revelation, closing a circle.

That first message is: "We are all One. All things are One Thing. There is only One Thing, and all things are part of the One Thing There Is."

If that opening statement is true, it carries with it an important implication—a *remarkably* important implication—that would amount to a major expansion of humanity's previous understanding of the relationship between God and Man.

The implication, of course, is that if *everything* is One Thing, and if we are *part* of everything (which we obviously are), then *we are part of God*, unless God is *not* part of "everything," but stands outside of "everything"—in which case "everything" is not everything at all.

This is, in fact, what many, many people believe. They believe that there are, essentially, *two things* that exist in ultimate reality: (1) Everything That Is, and (2) that which *created* Everything That Is.

In this cosmology, God stands outside of Everything That Is. In order to conceive of this, many people define "everything" as only that which is *physical*, and define God as that which is *spiritual*. Yet this is an unfair delineation, because it gives an altered meaning to the word "everything."

It also forces us to assume that *we* are not spiritual . . . or that if we *are* spiritual *and* physical, the part of us that is spiritual is not part of "everything." Because, by simple logic, if the part of *us* that is spiritual is *included* in what we call "everything," then a God who is spiritual must be part of "everything" as well.

This leads some of us to take all sorts of twisted pathways and to use every kind of tortured logic to explain how a God who is spiritual is not part of "everything," even though the part of us that is spiritual *is*.

Presumably, God's spirit is a different kind of spirit, a different *type*. Not simply grander or bigger or more powerful, but a different *type* altogether—a type that does not fall within the category of "everything that is."

It is the first big challenge of the New Spirituality to coax us away from this fractured reasoning and gently guide us into considering that there may be a pattern to life's Essential Energy (that some people, including myself, call "God") that allows it to express as both physical and spiritual *at the same time*, even as we clearly observe that we, as humans, are doing.

In other words, we may wish to consider the possibility that what we can do, God can do, and that even as we are both spiritual and physical, so, too, is That Which Is Divine.

This would make Humanity and Divinity one and the same, except as to proportion. God is All Of It, whereas we are part of that which *comprises* All Of It.

Does this not make much more sense?

And have not major religions declared that we are "made in the image and likeness of God"?

Our Stories Tell Us Otherwise

Previously, we have been told by most of humanity's cultures, through myths and tales, that God separated us from the Godhead. Not that God *divided* us (in which case we would all be simply divisions of the Same Thing), but that He *separated* us. Consider the difference.

A company that has divisions in several cities is still one and the same company. Yet a company that has *split off* and sold one or two of those divisions has created *separate entities* that are no longer a part of the original firm.

Is this what God has done? Yes, say most religions. Thus, they tell us that God is one thing and we are another. This separation occurred, so the teaching goes, because God was displeased with us. His displeasure, we have been further informed, is the result of our having disobeyed Him. (Or, at least, of our earliest ancestors having done so.)

And so, the Story of Separation was seeded in the human

psyche. This story is foundational and crucial to the world's religions, for if we believe in God at all, and if we hunger in any way for God's safety, for God's love, for God's magnificence, then getting *back* to God becomes our number one priority—and that is where religions come in. They promise us the way to do that.

To make sure that we understand the urgency of this undertaking, religions have added a caveat: If we *don't* get back to God, we'll wind up going to that other place . . .

The Unhappy Alternative

If we have not found the way to return to God, who will forgive us for every unkindness and misbehavior during our life on Earth, we will not be absolved of our sins, and, as punishment for our misdeeds, we will be sent to a place of interminable and indescribable suffering, called, variously, Hell, Hades, Ğahannam, Nār, Perdition, Infernum, the Netherworld, Sheol, Acheron, Gehenna, Tophet, the Abyss, or the Pit (among other things).

Complicating this process is the fact that, according to at least one religion, there is *only one way* to get back to God and be forgiven, and that is through Jesus Christ. No one else has the power to forgive us, including, presumably, God Himself, and so we need to take this one path to salvation.

Indeed, according to this doctrine, one can live a virtually perfect life, demonstrating kindness, caring, compassion, generosity, and every other divine virtue in every moment of one's life, and still not "get to heaven" (as the return journey is called). In other words, one cannot "earn" one's way to heaven, but can only get there if one "accepts Christ" as one's Lord and Savior. And the reason that it is only Christ who can offer salvation, and not God Himself, is that it was Christ who "paid for our sins" through his willingly accepted torture and death, thus appeasing a "just" God (who others may see as a wrathful, vengeful God) who otherwise would have made us pay for them ourselves.

Even if one were to die moments after birth, an utterly innocent baby having been unable to commit a single offense against God, there is Original Sin to deal with, this particular religion asserts. That is the sin committed by the first souls—the ones who got thrown out of heaven to begin with—the burden of which has been passed down to us to carry, by virtue of our heritage.

This is the Doctrine of Inherited Imperfection. Unless a soul is spotless, this doctrine declares, it may not return to God. And no soul—not even that of a baby—is spotless.

We are *born* imperfect. We can find forgiveness, however, and return to spotlessness, by claiming Christ as our Savior. In the case of an infant, this is done through the sacrament of Baptism, in which Christ is accepted *on behalf* of the baby, by an adult.

(The child can accept Christ again later, through the sacrament of Confirmation, in which she or he, having reached the age of reason, confirms and renews the baptismal promise, and is thus said to be able to receive the Holy Spirit. This occurs usually between the age of seven and fourteen, depending upon local custom.)

None of this is a small matter, we are told, because if we don't accept Christ's gift of redemption, our own payment for our sins will go on forever. That is, for Eternity. So great has been our offense against God . . . including the greatest offense, which would be to not accept God's gift of the tortured and sacrificed Christ.

By this measure Jews, Hindus, Muslims, Buddhists, and members of every other faith (as well as those of no faith at all) are going to hell.

Expanding Our Concept of Deity and Reality

Is this how it really is?

The New Spirituality invites us to look closely at this teaching and decide for ourselves if it matches our concept of an all-loving God who is the source of everything and therefore needs nothing.

The first and last of the 25 most important messages in *Conversations with God* expands our entire concept of Deity—and of Ultimate Reality itself. It describes a reality in which nothing is separated from anything else, and a God who is expressed in, as, and through all things that exist.

I will explore the inferences of this in greater detail when Core Message #1 is addressed separately, toward the end of this book. For now, let's stay with Core Message #25, and take a look at the second half of this fifteen-word statement. It says: *Ours is not a better way, ours is merely another way.*

As with the first half of the New Gospel, this sentence carries larger theological implications than might at first be apparent. More than a simple magnanimous or humble declaration, it expands our current thought that one way to God, and only one way, is the "better" way, and that one and only one religious doctrine forms the basis of the One True Faith.

What God seeks to tell all of us is that every faith is the One True Faith to those who hold it as True. This is because "as you believe, so will it be done unto you." That is, pure faith empowers itself, producing the results that it calls for. And *this* is because of the nature of who you are and how life works (which, again, we will explore in later portions of this book).

So if you believe that your following the teachings of the Prophet Muhammad, bless His holy name, will lead the way to Paradise, it will. If you believe that accepting Christ as your Savior will guarantee you a place in heaven, it will. If you believe that modeling the behavior of Buddha will bring you peace, it will. Whatsoever you believe, so shall your experience be.

What this means is that there is more than one way to the mountaintop. It also means that no one way is "better" than another. All roads lead to the same destination. Indeed, says *Conversations with God*, there is no way *not* to get what we call the Kingdom of God, because there is *nowhere else to go*. (This idea will be explored in chapter 23.)

This place, too, has many names. Some call it paradise, Jannah, nirvana, Zion, the hereafter, the next world, the next life, the Kingdom of God, Elysium, the Elysian Fields, Valhalla, the empyrean, or, simply, heaven.

Spiritual Surgery Removing a Fatal Flaw

What the second sentence in the New Gospel does is extract righteousness from religion, thus removing something that is not very good from something that is otherwise very good in many ways.

The idea that there is only One Right Way to return to God has caused more death and destruction, and therefore caused more people to run *from* God, than any other single notion.

The New Gospel is like spiritual surgery, reaching in and cutting out the poison from the otherwise glorious and healthy thoughts that most humans hold about their religion and their Deity.

I believe that somewhere deep inside, most people know that if there is a God at all, it cannot be a Lord Of The Brand Name, who thinks that all facial tissue must be Kleenex, all transparent adhesive strips must be Scotch Tape, and all people going to heaven must be Christian (or Muslim, or Hindu, or Mormon, or whatever logo your God has on His name tag).

What the New Gospel from *Friendship with God* offers is a chance to allow our theology to catch up with our twenty-first-century awareness. It is an opportunity to discuss a central question: "Is it possible that our previous information about the Kingdom of God, and who is 'eligible' to be there, was incomplete?"

For the billions of people who hold that souls can return to God only along a particular pathway, the belief that all roads lead to heaven is an invitation to expand their concept of God, making the Divine Being large enough to reach by any route. Or, as I heard someone put it delightfully a few years ago: "If God is your target, you can't miss!"

Had this idea of an "Only For Us" paradise been eliminated from the spiritual constructions of our species centuries ago, thousands upon thousands of lives would have been saved, as countless people have been martyred for not accepting and practicing the "right faith."

Even today, people around the world are shamed and marginalized, rebuked and admonished, and in some cases still persecuted, for not embracing the "one true religion."

APPLYING THIS MESSAGE TO EVERYDAY LIFE

This remarkable message offers all of us an opportunity to join in the healing of humanity.

Fear of damnation is no longer considered a loving way to gain converts to any religion, even if people say that they are doing it out of "concern" for someone they love. And being made "bad" or "wrong" is no longer a healing way to get any-one to agree with your point of view on *any* subject.

The New Gospel has applications far beyond the sphere of religion. Practiced in the political arena, it could return civility to civil discourse. Embraced in the economic arena, it could replace ruthless competition with collaboration and co-operation. Accepted in the educational arena, it could bring an end to the teaching of only those things with which we agree.

The idea that ours is not a better way, ours is merely an-other way, applied across the board in our lives, would alter the entire social landscape in ways that we can only begin to imagine, and that would only improve human life for all.

Here are some suggestions for application of this insight into your daily experience:

- If you are a religious person, determine as of this day (if you have not already done so) to never again suggest to another person that your religion is the only way to get to heaven, or that every single person on the face of the Earth who does not practice your religion is going to hell. Use love of God, not fear of God, as your motiva-tor to encourage others to take a closer look at your faith as their possible spiritual home.

- If you are deeply involved in politics, resolve to honor the political point of view and the ideas of others. Wel-come them into your discussions. Do not confuse emo-tion for passion. It is one thing to be passionate about your point of view, it is another to become all emo-tional (as in "angry") about it. If you feel anger rising within you, if you find yourself starting to use abusive or disparaging language in advancing your point of view, take a step back from the discourse and turn down the temperature of the exchange. Own responsibility for allowing the conversation to get out of hand, apologize for ratcheting up the negative energy, and simply start to speak slower and a bit more quietly. It can do wonders.

• When you start to feel that your way is not only a "better" way but the "only" way to see things or to do things, think of a time in your life when you have felt that you had the only good answer to something and life proved that you were not entirely accurate in that assessment. Ask yourself if this could be the case now.

• Look at the other person's point of view and intentionally search for something—*anything*—of worth or value in what they believe. See if you can find common ground, even a postage-stamp size of common ground, with that other, and restart the discussion there.

• Think of the desired outcomes you and others have in common. Focus on these outcomes that you both seek, rather than pathways or methods to achieve certain results. Often when we see the commonality of outcomes, we find a mutual respect that allows us to begin sharing and creating collaborative approaches to resolving disagreements and solving problems.

• Here is a miracle statement that I have found to be marvelously helpful in moving what could have been a discordant conversation forward: "I can understand how you could feel that way." This does not say that I agree with how you feel, but it does say that I do not think you are totally absurd or crazy for thinking the way you do. It honors your background, or life experience, and the path that brought you here today. Sometimes all that people need to break the ice is to feel that they have been heard. Not even agreed with, just fairly heard.

• Regarding the first part of the New Gospel, begin practicing the movement into unity with another by remembering a time when you felt the same way as the person before you right now. See things not just from their point of view, but from a time when you may have had the same or nearly the same feelings. Remember, feelings are not a point of view. They are what *sponsor* a point of view. Feelings of betrayal, for instance, or of anger. Feelings of loneliness, or of being misunderstood. These are all feelings that we have all had at one time or another. Seek to relate to another person's *feelings*, not their viewpoint or their specific words, and you will begin the practice of "oneness" as a lifetime experience.

• Allow yourself to feel your own natural feelings of oneness with others—and, for that matter, with other forms of life—and practice doing this every day. Choose two other people with whom you interact daily or frequently, and see if you can identify any feelings you have observed them to have, that you have also experienced in your own life at one time or another.

These simple steps can work magic in your relationships—and in the way that you relate to the entire world around you. The New Gospel, these 15 words, are all that you will ever need to change your life for the better. And, excitingly, there are *985 more* words for us to explore.

7

On September 12, 2001, I was besieged with emails from readers all over the world wanting to know how the messages of *Conversations with God* could help the world prevent a repeat of the horrific and terrifying events of the day before. I wanted to know the same thing. Unable to sleep on the night of 9/11, I went to my keyboard and began an urgent exchange with God. Here is the beginning of that exchange, verbatim . . .

God, please be here. We need help.

I am here.

We need help.

I know.

Right now.

I understand.

The world is on the brink of disaster. And I'm not talking about natural disaster; I'm talking about man-made calamity.

I know. And you're right.

I mean, humans have had disagreements before, and serious ones, but now our divisions and disagreements can lead not simply to wars—which are bad enough—but to the end of civilization as we know it.

That is correct. You have assessed the situation correctly.

You understand the severity of the problem, you simply do not understand the nature of the problem. You do not know what is causing it. So you keep trying to solve it at every level except the level at which it exists.

Which is?

The level of belief.

The problem facing the world today is a spiritual problem.

Your ideas about spirituality are killing you.

You keep trying to solve the world's problem as if it was a political problem, or an economic problem, or even a military problem, and it is none of these. It is a spiritual problem. And that is the one problem human beings don't seem to know how to solve.

Of course I begged God, "Then *tell* us how to solve it!" An entire book emerged as a result of that plea, titled *The New Revelations*, and I consider the most important passage of that book to be . . .

CWG CORE MESSAGE #24

You think you are being terrorized by other people, but in truth you are being terrorized by your beliefs. Your experience of yourself and your world will shift dramatically if you adopt, collectively, the Five Steps to Peace:

- Permit yourself to acknowledge that some of your old beliefs about God and about Life are no longer working.

- Explore the possibility that there is something you do not fully understand about God and about Life, the understanding of which would change everything.

- Announce that you are willing for new understandings of God and Life to now be brought forth, understandings that could produce a new way of life on this planet.

- Courageously examine these new understandings and, if they align with your personal inner truth and knowing, enlarge your belief system to include them.

- Express your life as a demonstration of your highest beliefs, rather than as a denial of them.

It's hard to beat this message for clarity. It means exactly what it says, and there's no room for ambiguity. Yet it is more than a prescription for preventing future 9/11s. It is a stirring call to action. A challenge and an invitation to the entire human race: Find a new way of being. Explore the possibility of changing your fundamental beliefs.

Yet is this necessary? Why must changing, or even challenging, our beliefs be part of the so-called "steps to peace"? Why can't we just leave our beliefs alone? It isn't as if they are what causes all the turmoil in the world.

Or is it . . . ?

I used the words "fundamental beliefs" in the paragraph above advisedly. It is the fundamentalist movement in religions and in politics—the refusal to budge off of a belief, or even consider for a moment any new idea about it—that is exposing humanity to the danger of ongoing and endless self-inflicted wounds.

This is true in religion *and* politics. It is especially true when you put them both together.

Need some examples?

A gentleman named Richard Mourdock, campaigning for the U.S. Senate in Indiana in the 2012 general election, famously declared that if a woman became pregnant as a result of a rape, "it is something that God intended to happen," and for that reason abortion should be opposed and outlawed, even in cases of rape or incest.

When he lost the election (only a week before he made his remarks he was widely predicted to win), Mr. Mourdock in his concession speech did not say, "Well, I may have gone a bit too far." Instead, he remarked: "I will look back knowing that I was attacked for standing for my principles."

He simply could not admit that some of his old beliefs about God and about Life are no longer working.

He is not alone.

This example is brought up here only to show how incredibly rigid, how unyielding, many people can be regarding their beliefs, even in the face of common sense, particularly when it comes to the most sacred of those beliefs—many of which come from what are said to be humanity's holy books.

The Bible says, in the Book of Deuteronomy: "If a man has a stubborn and rebellious son who does not obey his father and mother and will not listen to them when they discipline him, his father and mother shall take hold of him and bring him to the elders at the gate of his town.

"They shall say to the elders, 'This son of ours is stubborn and rebellious. He will not obey us. He is a profligate and a drunkard.' Then all the men of his town shall stone him to death. You must purge the evil from among you."

Of course, no one today would seriously consider such a "purging" for a son who, in youthful disobedience of his parents, occasionally over-imbibes, right?

Wrong.

> *The maintenance of civil order in society rests on the foundation of family discipline. Therefore, a child who disrespects his parents must be permanently removed from society in a way that gives an example to all other children of the importance of respect for parents. The death penalty for rebellious children is not something to be taken lightly. The guidelines for administering the death penalty to rebellious children are given in Deut. 21:18–21.*
>
> —Charlie Fuqua, 2012 candidate for Arkansas State House of Representatives, in his 2012 book, *God's Law: The Only Political Solution*

Mr. Fuqua was also not elected.

Apparently some people *are* able to permit themselves to acknowledge that some of our old beliefs about God and about Life are no longer working. Syed Ghaisuddin, a minister of education for the Taliban in the Middle East, may not, however, be one of

them. Asked why the Taliban declares that women need to be con-
fined to home, he told the press: "It's like having a flower, or a rose.
You water it and keep it at home for yourself, to look at it and smell
it. It is not supposed to be taken out of the house to be smelled." In
other words, a woman is a *possession*. A man's possession.

These are the kind of ancient views that may come from politi-
cians, you might say, but surely members of today's contemporary
clergy—people who we hope will lead us and guide us as we seek
to create a better life—are able to see when old views are no longer
working, yes?

Well, not exactly . . .

> *Women cannot handle power. It is not within them to han-*
> *dle power . . . The real and true power comes from God, and*
> *God is the one that gave man the power and the authority*
> *over the wife.*
>
> —Rev. Jesse Lee Peterson, a popular Christian fundamentalist
>   pastor, in his Sunday service webcast, "How Liberal Women
>   Are Building a Shameless Society"

All he left out was that women need to stay at home, do the
dishes, take care of the children, put supper on the table, handle
the housework, and keep the laundry basket empty. Oh, and of
course, perform her wifely "duties" for her husband.

And so we see that even in our supposedly modern society, in
this supposedly enlightened period, we continue to be confronted
with the need to make determinations: *Are* some of our old ideas
about God and about Life no longer working? Or are these 2012
voices offering solutions that truly do and can work today just as
they did in 1412, or 1012, or the *year* 12?

What the Five Steps to Peace offer us is a way to answer these
questions.

Step One

The first of those steps—noticing that some of our old beliefs about God and about Life are no longer working—is without a doubt the biggest. So difficult is it for humanity as a whole to take this step that even a modest number of people doing so would create a revolution.

Why is it so difficult? Because of where humanity's old beliefs came from in the first place.

One of my life's most wonderful spiritual teachers, Dr. Terry Cole-Whittaker, startled me one day years ago when she put a brilliantly insightful question to her congregation (of which I was fortunate to be a member) at a Sunday morning service: "Who would you have to 'make wrong' in order to get Life 'right'?"

Terry offered the observation that in order to avoid making our mother wrong, or our father wrong, or our favorite teacher wrong, or our most hallowed spiritual messenger wrong, we will cling to what they told us, even if it is clearly no longer working (presuming it *ever* worked!).

She then invited us all to muster the courage to step out of our comfort zone and consider the possibility that what we assumed to be true, given its apparently authoritative source, may not be true at all—or may be, at least, *incomplete*. That is, there may be more to know on the subject.

It was Dr. Terry who ignited me to wonder: Has evolution stopped? Did humanity cease to grow and to advance in its understandings of life during the time of my mother and my father? Or the time of theirs? Or during the time of our earliest teachers and messengers? And if so, exactly how far back need we go to find the stopping point?

When, precisely, did spiritual evolution cease?

Or is it possible—just *possible*—that within each new generation is born the capacity for the acquisition of new and even larger
understanding? Put simply, *is wisdom static or organic?*

People such as Dr. Terry take us by the hand and lead us to the
edge of our comfort zone, promising us that they will be there for
us in our moments of fear. It is these *new* teachers, as well as the
old, who we do well to revere, for they lead the way to places yet
untraveled by the largest number of us, taking steps into the unknown *for* us and coming back to report *to* us what they have
found.

These are the Finders of Tomorrow . . . and always, always you
can tell the true ones from the false, for the true ones, without fail,
invite us to *join* them, not to *follow* them, on life's most spectacular
expedition, The Journey of the Soul.

(The work of Dr. Terry Cole-Whittaker, for your information,
may be accessed at www.TerryColeWhittaker.com. The program
she offers is perfectly titled Adventures in Enlightenment.)

Step Two

Once we get to a place where we can at least admit and acknowledge that some of humanity's old beliefs about God and about
Life—even some of the most sacred ones—are no longer working,
the second of the Five Steps to Peace invites us to explore the possibility that there is something you do not fully understand
about God and about Life, the understanding of which would
change everything. That is, that our knowledge in this area may be
Incomplete.

I capitalized that last word in order to signify its importance. I
want to make the point here again that the problem is not that the
Old Teachings are "false" or "wrong." I believe the problem is that

in some cases they do not go far enough. Or perhaps *we* have not gone far enough in our search for a deeper understanding of them.

Or perhaps both.

Acknowledging that some of the teachings or our searching may be *incomplete* is for many also an enormous step. It is one thing to observe and concede that our Ancient Story may no longer be functional, but it is another thing altogether to embrace the notion that this may be because we never had, from the *beginning*, the whole story. That kind of admission takes spiritual humility. We have to grant that we *do not know it all* when it comes to the topics of God and Life—and that *we never did*.

And by the way, before we move forward into a territory that may feel injurious to our collective spiritual ego, I'd like to point out that the word "some" as found in the first of the Five Steps to Peace is a very important qualifier, and is best not passed over lightly in the reading.

Clearly, the intention of the Divine in this revelation is to make it known that it is not the whole of humanity's Ancient Story about God and Life that is incomplete and could benefit from expansion, but rather, portions of it. This point has already been made repeatedly in the present text, *on purpose*, so that no one could mistakenly assert that *Conversations with God* is being held up as a replacement for what it declares to be Utterly Errant Scripture.

I wish to note again that, quite to the contrary, *CWG* declares that the vast majority of the messages in the Holy Scriptures of most of the world's religions are of enormous value, and can be trusted *to the letter* to provide wise, caring, insightful, and beneficial observations. They thus offer us wonderful guidance.

Are there some cases, nonetheless, where the advancement of human understanding may add useful expansion to the time-honored words of our Ancient Story?

Of course.

And this *expansion into new territory* is what the second of the Five Steps to Peace invites us to undertake.

It also lures us with its wording, inferring that, should we be daring enough to look beyond the parameters of our present perceptions, we might chance upon deeper spiritual truths, *the understanding of which would change everything.*

This is not a small enticement.

A Brief Notice

May I please take a break right now from this narrative to offer a brief explanation as to style?

You have no doubt already noticed that the track of this text is annular, circling back on itself in clearly observable repetitions. That is by intention, and should not be considered a fault of redundancy, but rather, a deliberately employed literary convention. It is used because the narrative of *Conversations with God* itself, upon which this book is based, is also circular, making its points over and over again in contextual roundabouts, until they become familiar enough to reveal themselves as straight-line logic.

Now, to return to the narrative . . .

Step Three

Even the acknowledgment that there may be something still to learn about God and Life is not the end of our task. We must *announce that we are willing for new understandings of God and Life to now be brought forth, understandings that could produce a new way of life on this planet.*

What good does it do to know that your car keys are missing if you're not willing to go looking for them?

Observing Earth's societies today, it is clear that we're stalled, and we can't get the engine going again without some key elements in place. Yet if we're unwilling to look for the keys, we'll never get anywhere.

That's where we are now. We're at a major intersection here—a three-way intersection between Yesterday, Today, and Tomorrow—and the engine has conked out at just the wrong time, inviting a huge crash. We've got to get out of this intersection and on our way.

We've got to find those keys! And we won't find them if we're not willing to look anywhere but the same old places they used to be, but are no more.

Recently I bought an old reference book that I was excited to read. But when I got to the end, I found that there were pages missing. It was a much-sought-after book that I'd found in a used bookstore, one that must have been treasured and read by many. I was frustrated by the lack of a concluding narrative, but I didn't simply sit back and say with a sigh, "Well, I hope that what was on the missing pages isn't important and that all there is to know on this subject was contained on the pages that I did read." I went to a bookstore that sold *new* books, found an updated text on the topic, and got it!

Humanity has "bought" a lot of ideas about itself, about Life, and about God, but now we're discovering that there are some pages missing in these wonderful old books we've been reading. We need to get a new book, one with no missing pages!

This doesn't mean that we're *throwing out* the old books, it merely means that we're willing to *not stop there* when it's obvious to us there's something missing, and that we're choosing to add to what we've learned by reading something more, expanding what is already known with additional information.

Forever Stuck, or at Last Made Free?

So, the "key" issue now is: Are we willing for new understandings about God and about Life to be brought forth? Are we open to finding our keys, even if they are not where we thought they would be? If our answer continues to be no, we may be forever stuck in an old story with missing pages.

Of course, this brings up other concerns that have caused humanity to stumble and stop at this third step in the past. Top among them: What new ideas, from what new sources, should we seriously consider? It's a fair question. Do we listen to just anybody standing on a soapbox under a sandwich board declaring the End Is Near?

That's not something I would do. I wouldn't read just any book, buy just any recording, attend just any lecture, go to just any workshop or retreat. I'd want to know something about the source of the material I was considering, and I'd want to know if anyone else felt good enough about that material to recommend it.

If I found new messages in a book that was read by millions in thirty-seven languages, I would probably be encouraged to consider it. I might not automatically agree with it, but I might want to know, if nothing else, why so many millions found it of value and made it a bestseller.

It has been my experience that material that reaches such a level of popularity does so not so much because it brings people something new, but because it causes them to *recognize and remember* something they *already know*.

This feeling of instant recognition is experienced when the Soul tells the Mind: "Here is pure and deep truth of which you have always been aware, but which you may have forgotten."

Having felt that impulse, I would nevertheless—after investigating where it took me—listen to myself. *I would never take anyone else's word for anything.* Rather, I would tune into my own inner guidance, to see what it told me about what I was exploring. That is why Step Four of the Five Steps to Peace invites you to embrace new ideas about God and about Life only "if they align with your personal inner truth and knowing."

But I certainly would not fail to explore a new idea simply because it seemed radical. I would give everything a chance. For it is as I have said earlier . . .

Only when we are open to all *ideas* are all *possibilities* open to us.

Step Four

Okay, now it's time to put up a sign: Bravery Needed.

Once you have entered into a state of willingness to allow new understandings about God and Life to be seriously considered, the next step will require spiritual stouteartedness—for now you will be invited to courageously examine these new understandings and, if they align with your personal inner truth and knowing, to *enlarge your belief system to include them.*

This is not a small step by any means. Some of your own most sacredly held ancient spiritual stories, and the sources from which they came, will no doubt be put to question, and it will take bravery—intellectual and spiritual bravery—to withstand the mental buffeting that such inner questioning often produces.

And this says nothing of the public ridicule and marginalizing that will take place (you can count on it) should you confront your questions out loud, much less *dare to offer answers* that violate orthodoxy.

Yet today, if we truly want peace in our lives and peace in our world, we would do well to look at the outcomes that our ancient story has produced in our lives, and ask whether there might be another way to achieve what we say we seek to accomplish as a species.

It will take the spiritual version of Ignaz Semmelweis in this the twenty-first century to do that. Who shall be the spiritual version of Ignaz Semmelweis? And, will there be more than one? Might there be thousands? Maybe even millions?

That is what the Civil Rights Movement for the Soul invites: Millions of Semmelweises.

Idea Heroism

It was in 1847 that Dr. Ignaz Semmelweis, working at the Vienna General Hospital's maternity clinic, made a remarkable and, no doubt, scary observation: At least one way that medicine was being practiced was actually killing people.

In Vienna, as elsewhere in European and North American hospitals, puerperal fever (or childbed fever)—which caused a fatal infection in women during childbirth—was becoming an epidemic, sometimes affecting up to 40 percent of admitted patients. Dr. Semmelweis theorized that doctors who had recently conducted autopsies were then giving internal exams to pregnant women, thereby transferring decaying matter from the corpses to the genitals of the women. He proposed a new hand-washing procedure using chlorinated lime, which has since become a known disinfectant.

Having the courage to explore his idea—which was radical in that moment—Dr. Semmelweis found that its application *reduced the incidence of fatal childbed fever tenfold* in maternity institutions.

It didn't matter.

That's right. That's what I said. All the evidence didn't matter.

Dr. Semmelweis's thoughts were contrary to the medical beliefs and practices of the time, and so his ideas were ridiculed and rejected and he basically became an outcast in the medical community in Vienna, dying in 1865 in a mental institution.

It was not until the twentieth century that his ideas were accepted, with untold numbers of babies' lives having been saved since.

I dea Heroism is what I call this, and there is no doubt that had there been hundreds of Ignaz Semmelweises displaying such heroism and supporting such obviously beneficial changes, the outcome would have come about faster, and his own life would not have ended as it did.

Yet how long will it take for others—not just a stray individual here and there, but hundreds or thousands of others—to come along to challenge the *biggest* beliefs of our species, our *spiritual* beliefs, and to propose obviously beneficial changes? And who will begin?

Put more directly: If not now, when? If not you, who?

Step Five

The last of the Five Steps to Peace is where the rubber meets the road. Having accepted that some of our old beliefs about God and Life are no longer working, having seen that this may be because there is more to know on these subjects, having moved into willingness for new understandings to now be brought forth, and having enlarged our belief system to include those new understandings that align with our inner truth and knowing, we now are called upon in Step Five to *express our life as a demonstration of our highest beliefs, rather than as a denial of them.*

It is not easy to "walk your talk." I learned that very quickly. After producing twenty-seven books about what I have experienced and declared to be conversations with God, I have been expected (rightly so) to live up to my own writings. Of course, they were not my own writings at all, and that is all I can offer as a weak defense when others point (rightly so) to my failings. "You aren't a very good example of the messages you proclaim in those books," they tell me when they get to know me, and they're absolutely correct.

"You probably didn't even get the ideas in your books from God," others say. "How dare you claim such a thing? God does not talk directly to people, and He certainly doesn't give them entire books!"

Well, let me address that last comment first.

I know of a man who once said that God spoke directly to him—and five books arose out of those inspirations. That assertion seems perfectly acceptable to people. The books are called Genesis, Exodus, Leviticus, Numbers, and Deuteronomy. The man's name was Moses. An entire religion sprung up around those books.

I know of a man who claimed that an angel directed him to buried golden plates inscribed with revelations that he published in what he said was an English translation of the plates, calling it the Book of Mormon. His name was Joseph Smith. An entire religion sprung up around that book.

The list of people in this category could go on. And I am not suggesting for one minute that a religion should spring up around the books in the *Conversations with God* series. But I am suggesting that we may wish to explore what came through in those books, and not simply dismiss them out of hand because the human scribe who wrote them down is still living, or because the incident happened less than twenty years ago, rather than twenty centuries ago.

As for being a not very good example of the messages in those books, at the very least this could help to establish the veracity of their source. If the books were filled with ideas and notions, proclamations and declarations that I simply made up, you would think I would at least make up stuff that I could live up to! (Nobody likes to be called a hypocrite or a faker—and those are two of the milder invectives that have been used on me.)

So no one is more aware than I am that the last of the Five Steps to Peace is very challenging. Yet it is for me the most inspiring step of all. It calls me every day to a new level of commitment, invites me every day to a deeper determination, beckons me every day to re-create myself anew in the next grandest version of the greatest vision ever I held about who I am and who I choose to be in this world.

That's the opportunity here. For me and for you and for the whole human race. And actually, it has nothing at all to do, in the specific sense, with *Conversations with God* or the New Spirituality. Step Five, and *all* of the Five Steps to Peace, can be taken by every member of every one of the world's organized religions—and by people who belong to no religion at all.

What the Five Steps to Peace are all about is simply looking at what's going on in our world and in our individual lives and, if we would like to see some things change for the better, undertaking a fair exploration to determine if there might be something that we don't fully understand about Life and, yes, about God, the understanding of which could alter the entire experience. Then, it's about incorporating into our daily lives what our exploration has brought us.

It's as simple—and as daring—as that.

Applying This Message to Everyday Life

If I were asked what actions the average person could take to bring peace to their lives and to our world faster than any other, I would choose these invitations in Message #24 from the thousand-word summary of *Conversations with God*.

Here are some suggestions for application of this insight into your daily experience:

- Print out a copy of the Five Steps to Peace and post them somewhere in your home—on the refrigerator, or the mirror in your bathroom, etc.—where you will see them every day. Then, read them every day as if you have never seen them before. Even if you've read them so often that you can recite them, read them again. Keep bringing them to the forefront of your mind. This is where you make decisions about how to react to daily life.

- Post the Five Steps to Peace in the guest room in your house, the guest bath, or elsewhere visitors to your home might be expected to see them. This may generate spontaneous conversations about them with friends who read them and ask you what all of that is about and where you got them.

- Have a number of extra copies of the Steps printed in advance and located in a place where you can easily find them, so that if someone says, "I wish I had a copy of those," you can say, "You do now," and hand one to them.

- Start a Steps-to-Peace Journal and make an entry when you find yourself challenged by the Five Steps—especially Step Five. Ask yourself, in writing, "What aspect of what I truly believe about God and about Life am I having a difficult time embracing right now? What, if anything, could I do tomorrow to embrace and live this belief?" Then, answer your own questions with a short essay in the journal.

- Start an Evolution Revolution Group in your community and invite its members to meet once a week or twice a month and discuss the entries in their Steps-to-Peace Journal. Design ways to support each other within the group in embracing the highest beliefs you hold about God and about Life, and in demonstrating them daily.

- Post the Five Steps to Peace on the church house doors in your community, as Martin Luther posted his *Ninety-Five Theses* on the doors of All Saints' Church in Wittenberg, Germany, in 1517. His action ignited the Reformation. Your action could ignite the Civil Rights Movement for the Soul. Ask the pastor for permission to do so. If permission is not given, ask why not? What about the Five Steps to Peace is not acceptable? Start an Evolution Revolution Group at your church to discuss these steps, whether or not you've been allowed to post them on the church doors.

- Hand the Five Steps to Peace to friends, put them under windshields in cars at shopping centers, publish them in Letters to the Editor in your newspaper, purchase small ads in the paper, in your church bulletin, etc., listing the Steps.

* Call radio talk shows and discuss the Five Steps to Peace.

* Truly begin, truly be the instigator of, a Civil Rights Movement for the Soul in your community, state, or nation based on the Five Steps to Peace. Place a petition on the Internet. Get the energy around this idea moving.

8

In the book *The Storm Before the Calm*, I made it very clear that in the final years of the twentieth century and the initial quarter of the twenty-first, our species has been and will continue to be undergoing what could be called the Overhaul of Humanity.

This process is not about the destruction of our global community and its way of life, but about the purposeful disassembling of it, piece by piece, leading to the reassembling of it *with new parts*—much as an engine is overhauled so that it works better. It is not a process in which we are uninvolved, even if all we do is simply observe it. On the contrary, it is a process in which all humans are collaboratively engaged. Most of us simply do not know it, because our participation is unconscious rather than conscious.

There is nothing to be afraid of here if the people of our world engage in this process with knowledge of what is happening and with clarity about the outcome they wish to produce.

The process is going to occur, however (indeed, it is occurring right now), whether we participate in it in this way or not. With or without us, life is going to change. The question is not whether the experience of our species is going to be different, the question is, in what ways will it be different—and who will make those decisions?

Conversations with God and other books and movies, programs, and social projects have come along during this time to assist us in taking a look at the disassembled parts of our society's engine, allowing us to decide which parts have not been working and need retooling. In *Conversations with God* much of this is explored in . . .

CWG CORE MESSAGE #23

There are Five Fallacies about Life that create crisis, violence, killing, and war. First, the idea that human beings *are separate* from each other. Second, the idea that *there is not enough* of what human beings need to be happy. Third, the idea that in order to get the stuff of which there is not enough, human beings *must compete* with each other. Fourth, the idea that some human beings *are better* than other human beings. Fifth, the idea that it is appropriate for human beings to resolve severe differences created by all the other fallacies *by killing* each other.

The intent of Core Message #23 is to lay out in very specific terms—without generalizations or gauzy language, without ambiguity or dancing around the subject—the root cause of the behaviors that have triggered (in this case, an unhappily appropriate word) humanity's continually angry and violent interactions.

Remember, Core Message #23 was given in direct response to my urgent question the day after 9/11. I, like the rest of the world, desperately wanted to know: *How could human beings do this to each other?*

The problem, God tells us here succinctly, is that we have em-

braced as "truth" a small but amazingly d
regarding life on Earth.

Five of those glaring errors will be dis
I'll expand on five more—which are
next.

Why bother looking at such dismal stuff? For the same
one looks at an engine that is no longer working as it should. You
can't fix the problem if you don't know what the problem is. Of
course, if one has no interest in fixing the problem, or if one is perfectly satisfied with the way things are and does not even agree that
a problem exists, then one would have no interest in looking more
deeply at our present circumstance.

You know where you are on that scale, and that will determine
whether you hear what is ahead as important diagnostic news, helping you and your world become healthier and happier, or as information in which you have no interest.

Our First Fallacy About Life

The first mistake humanity has made is imagining that its members
are separate from each other.

This thought derives from the idea that humanity is separate
from God.

Not everyone believes that there is a God, of course. But of
those who do believe in God, by far the highest number believe that
God separated us from Her, for reasons about which He has not
been entirely clear.

Hence, we may not know exactly why, but we do know that
God removed us from Paradise, sent us down to Earth, and here we
all are now, trying to get back.

s may be a simplistic way to lay it out, but this is the way most
ur belief systems about God have put it, in basic terms. Some
lief systems even try to clarify why this has happened. They say
that God kicked us out of the Garden of Eden because our spiritual
"parents" (presumably Adam and Eve) sinned. Their sin was that
they dared to acquire the knowledge of Good and Evil—and thus,
to become like gods.

God would have none of this hubris, this story goes, and so the
first humans (and all of their progeny thereafter forevermore) were
punished by being made to live in an environment of both Good
and Evil until we mended our ways, sought forgiveness for any evil
in which we found ourselves engaged, and were allowed to return
to the realm, or Ultimate Reality, where only that which is Good
existed.

What Really Happened

Okay, so now let's look at what is actually true about all this. The
following discussion is not a detour or a diversion from the main
topic here. Getting our story straight about our relationship with
God is extremely important, because that story forms our ideas
about ourselves and each other.

Because we think we are separate from God, we imagine that
we live in a *universe* of Separation; that this is, in fact, the fundamental construction of things, the essential configuration, the basic
organization and nature of the Universe.

This is at once the most pervasive and the most damaging idea
our species has ever conceived. And that is why God took so much
time with me in explaining what I have come to call the Actuality
of Reality.

It was made clear to me that there are three realms in the Kingdom of God. Most humans who believe in God and in the existence of such a "kingdom" at all, imagine that it contains two realms. Namely, "heaven" and "hell." Most believers do not include the Earth, nor any of the known universe, as part of God's Kingdom. They classify all of this as the "physical" realm, which God *created*, and they think of God's Kingdom as the "spiritual realm," or the "other world," or the "other side," etc.

This is the configuration of Separation that I just spoke about. It is this dramatic misunderstanding of the nature of things that produced our "story" that God cast us out of the spiritual realm, in which we lived as spiritual beings, and that we are now forced to live in the physical realm, as physical beings, until our death, when we return to the spiritual realm—and hopefully that *part* of the spiritual realm called "heaven," not the part called "hell"!—where we spend the rest of eternity.

As I alluded to earlier, exactly why our species has been "thrown out" of the paradise of heaven, exactly why the spiritual realm also includes the place we call hell or Hades, and exactly what it takes to make sure we find ourselves in the first place rather than the second after our death, is the subject and the focus of most of the world's religions.

My understandings of all of this changed dramatically after my conversations with God. I was told that God did not "kick us out" of Paradise, although it is true that each of us *have* left the Realm of the Spiritual and entered the Realm of the Physical. Our souls have done this quite voluntarily—and, in fact, happily—as part of the Process of Life Itself.

Here is the setup and here is the process, explained as God explained it to me, in metaphor, so that the human mind can understand. Let's move through this narrative point by point.

A New Understanding

1. There are three realms in the Kingdom of God, not two, and the place we call "hell" is not one of them. Such a place does not, in fact, exist.

2. The Kingdom of God is not separate from the physical universe and from our world, but includes it.

3. The three realms of God's Kingdom are the Realm of the Spiritual, the Realm of the Physical, and the Realm of Pure Being. This third realm might loosely be described as the first two, combined.

4. The purpose of the three realms is to offer Life Itself (read that: God) three ways in which It may manifest and experience Itself, by which triad process It may know and express Itself completely.

The biggest secret of Life is that it is a triad. Most of us have thought of it as a dyad, or duality. Even in our physical realm we tend to think of things as black and white, when, in fact, there is gray—the part that is both. Maturity is achieved when we stop seeing everything as absolutes—black and white, right and wrong, yes and no, stop and go, here and there, now and then, etc. (We'll look at this more closely in just a bit.)

A Way to Visualize This

It may help to understand Ultimate Reality if we think of it as a triangle. Perhaps you might picture a triangle in your mind right now, even as we are talking about this.

Allow yourself to imagine the top of the triangle as the place where the Realm of Pure Being exists. Then make the bottom right angle the Realm of the Spiritual, and label the bottom left of the triangle the Realm of the Physical.

Good. Now see yourself as a soul (perhaps imagine this as a speck of light), moving on an eternal journey around this triangle.

You start at the top of the triangle, then journey to the bottom right, where you stay and glow for a while, then move across to the bottom left, where you stay and glow for a while, then shoot up to the top again, where you burst with magnificence in a fireworks display—and then one of the specks of light from that fireworks display drops like an ember down to the bottom right corner of the triangle again, beginning the soul's journey all over.

As I said, this is a metaphor, of course. See if you can just allow yourself to imagine it in your mind. Imagine this as the soul's Sacred Journey, with the triangular relationship being what some religions call the Holy Trinity.

Now, to return to our point-by-point narrative:

5. In the Realm of the Spiritual, all things exist in their absolute form. Thus, this realm might also be called the Realm of the Absolute. In this realm there is nothing but Absolute Love, and it is always Here and Now. This is the nature of God's Eternal Essence and of Divinity's Existence.

6. Divinity wished to do more than simply exist, however. It wished to *experience* Itself. In order to do this, Divinity needed to experience something that was *not* Itself— because there needs to be a *contrasting* element for *any* element to be experienced.

"Fast" is not "fast" in the absence of "slow."
"Big" is not "big" in the absence of "small."

"The light" is not "the light" in the absence of "the darkness."

You get the picture. For a thing to be experienced, its opposite must exist. This is called the Law of Opposites. It is an illusion within the Realm of the Physical.

The part that is illusory is the idea that anything that is *not* God can exist. Such a thing is impossible, of course, since nothing exists outside of That Which Is—and That Which Is is but another name for God. Yet Divinity *can* create and produce the experience of *forgetfulness* in any and each of Its Divine manifestations. It has done this through the creation of levels of Consciousness.

The degree of Consciousness of each living thing is what brings it an Awareness of Ultimate Reality at individual levels.

In this way God can come to know Itself again—and to *experience Itself* as it knows Itself to be. This is the purpose and the function of all of Life in all of its manifestations.

Once More, If You Please

Now I realize that all I have just said may be a bit challenging or difficult to track. It certainly was for me when I was first told this in my conversations with God. So, with your gentle indulgence, allow me to go over it again, in just a little bit different way—because Things Said Twice sometimes make things more clear.

In the Realm of the Spiritual, All That Is is all there was, and there was nothing else. If God wanted to *experience* what it was *like* to be God, it would have to find Something Else with which to compare Itself. Yet this was impossible, because there *was* nothing else. God is all there is.

Since God could not find anything that was separate from Itself, God did the next best thing. God *divided* Itself into Its own constituent parts, then instilled in these parts varying levels of Its Essential Energy (we shall call this Consciousness), so that each element of Itself could look back upon the Whole and know of Its magnificence through *experiencing* the relationship of all of Its parts as they are expressing *degrees* of the Whole. Put another way, Consciousness is the ability to look at the World of Illusion and see within it the Ultimate and Only Reality.

Opposites, in Fact, Do Not Exist

The truth is, there are no "opposites" in Ultimate Reality. There are only what *appear* to be opposites. What we *call* that which appears to be the "opposite" of something is merely One Thing, in *degrees of expression.*

To use a perfect example, what we call "hot" and what we call "cold" are not the "opposite" of each other—that is, they are not two different things—but merely *degrees* of the Same Thing, which is something we call temperature.

In exactly the same way, God—the One Thing That Is— expresses Itself in varying degrees by dividing Itself into parts that are smaller than the Whole.

This is accomplished through the process of physicalization, or what could be described as a movement of the Whole from Spirituality to Physicality. This movement through the passageway from one realm to another (remember, this is a metaphor) causes the Whole to be divided, much as white light passing through a prism is divided into its constituent parts, which we call *colors.*

What we describe as the various and multitudinous elements of the physical universe are nothing more than colors on the palette of God. The Realm of Physicality is *where God goes to experience Itself.*

So we see that Separation is not the Essential Configuration of things, but rather, Division. And Division and Separation are not at all the same thing.

For an immediate experience of this, simply glance at your hand. You'll see that while your fingers are Divided from each other, each with individual characteristics and purpose, they are in no way Separated from your hand—nor is your hand Separated from your Body.

Neither are you separated from the Body of God.

You cannot *see* the connection between you and God with your eyes any more than you can see, for instance, infrared light, but you are energetically connected, and you can *feel* that connection, just as you can feel infrared light as heat. No physical contact or medium between you and an infrared heater is needed for the energy transfer. And infrared heaters can be operated in a vacuum or an atmosphere. We see here, then, a perfect metaphor for God. God's energy, likewise, can be transferred without physical contact—and throughout the vacuum known as the Universe. So if you think infrared *light* is a miracle, wait until you more fully understand (to say nothing of when you more fully feel) *God!*

As promised earlier, the Oneness of Everything will be explored further near the end of this book, when we examine *CWG* Core Message #1. There, we will look at exactly how and why early humans came up with the idea of Separation (and of "God") to begin with. It's fascinating, and it helps us understand why and how we ever embraced our Original Story, based on the information available to us at the time, and our limited early ability to analyze and comprehend the world around us. The tragedy is that we have continued to *retell* that story without *revising* it.

We are finally seeing now, in the twenty-first century, that our first mistake was that we thought God *separated us* from *God*—whereas what God actually did was simply *divide Itself.*

Our Second Fallacy About Life

Having totally (and mistakenly) accepted that we are separate from God, and thus, live in a Cosmology of Separation in which we are separate from each other, we have created for ourselves the experience that there is "not enough" of that which each of us feels we need to be happy.

The idea of insufficiency would not even have occurred to us as long as we thought there was only One of us. If you don't have to interact with anyone else for the next twenty years (as a man in solitary confinement, for instance), there is always enough time. And if you don't have to share with anyone else, there is always enough of whatever "stuff" you need to exist. If there were not enough of what you need to exist, you would not exist. Therefore, the fact of your existence is the evidence of your sufficiency.

Yet if you think there is more than one of you, you may feel that your existence is threatened to the degree that you imagine that That Which Is Not You will take or use that which You need in order to exist.

Life then becomes a struggle with the Other for existence.

This is a precise description of Life on Earth as we have created it. This is exactly what we have been experiencing—and continue to experience, no matter what our technological achievements, no matter what our medical miracles, no matter what our scientific discoveries.

It does not matter how brilliantly we advance; we will forever be in competition with each other—sometimes ruthless, to-the-*death* competition—so long as we imagine there is *not enough* of what we need to be happy or to survive. And we will *always* imagine that there is not enough so long as we hold on to, with teeth-gritting determination, our Story of Separation.

The Celebration Meal Parable

Consider the meal of celebration that you may place on your table at special times. In the United States and Canada it might be Thanksgiving. In Italy it might be the Feast of the Seven Fishes (*Festa dei sette pesci*) in celebration of Christmas Eve. In Korea, it might be New Year's Day. Virtually every culture has its meals of celebration.

Now imagine that at one of these meals, with everyone gathered, a knock comes at the door. It is a long-lost relative, a beloved uncle, with his wife and six lovely children. They have not attended such gatherings for years. This year he heard about it again, and he decided at the very last minute that he wanted to close the gap. He humbly asks if they may join in.

As the host, you realize that you have prepared for only so many. Will there be enough food to go around? You think about this for only a moment. Of course there will. You need only to share. You welcome them with open arms. Everyone is happy to see them. The table's bounty is divided into somewhat smaller portions. Nobody notices, really, and in truth, no one cares. After all, *this is family*.

Now rearrange the imagining. It is the same celebration meal. The same knock at the door. But outside is a total stranger, in rags, with his wife and six children, equally bedraggled. He says he saw the warm glow of light in the window, and humbly asks if they may join in the festive meal.

And your response?

Of course, you invite all of them in. And they are welcomed with open arms. After all, *this is family* . . .

. . . unless it's not. Unless you consider them interlopers, intruders, encroachers, invaders, outsiders, strangers, aliens, gate-crashers. In this case it may very well feel that there is not enough to go around to perfect strangers. You may, out of charity, give them a little food and send them on their way, but you will not be seating people at your table who have no "place" there because you don't even know them and they are not "family."

We have done worse to each other on this planet. All out of a thought that there is *not enough*, because we are Separate from Each Other and not "family" unless we are blood related.

Our Third Fallacy About Life

Because we are convinced there is *not enough* of what we need to survive and be happy on this planet, we have had to devise a way to approach, as fairly as possible, the parceling out of the Stuff Of Which There Is Not Enough.

The way that we have devised is called Competition. We will set up, we've decided, a process by which it can be fairly decided and determined who *deserves* to have the Stuff Of Which There Is Not Enough. It is a matter of *earning it*, we have declared. The Stuff should not simply be parceled out to everyone, merely because they exist.

One's existence is not sufficient credential to establish one's worthiness to *continue* to exist. One must justify one's worthiness.

Children are the exception. Children are worthy simply because they are children, and cannot be expected to have to render themselves worthy by contributing something of value and thus *creating* some of the Stuff Of Which There Is Not Enough. They get some of it automatically.

(Or do they? As we have already noted, nearly seven hundred children are allowed to die every hour on Earth for lack of food.)

Yet at what chronological point in their lives does Automatic Worthiness end and Earned Worthiness begin? Chimney sweeps in days gone by were typically seven-year-old orphaned waifs who either climbed the sooted shafts of brick and scraped them clean or didn't eat. Child labor is even today more widespread than you would think an advanced civilization would allow.

And so, from early on we have learned that we must contribute in some way to the creating of the Stuff Of Which There Is Not Enough—and then we must *compete* for the very thing we have created. Thus, the laborers in many factories earn one-one-hundredth of the income of those who boss them.

And our competition does not stop with material goods and gains. We've actually told ourselves that we must compete for *God.* We call those particular competitions "religions."

As in all other competitions, the understanding is: *To the victor go the spoils.*

Those who can't seem to match up to whatever the latest standard is that society has set for worthiness are labeled "losers." And so, humanity has bisected itself. There are Winners and Losers.

Today, something like 5 percent of the world's population hold or control something like 95 percent of the world's wealth and resources. *And most of those in that 5 percent think this is perfectly all right.* After all, they *earned* it.

How the Dominoes Fall

Of course, the fallacy that we must compete with each other to earn our worthiness to share in the world's abundance is based on the preceding fallacy that there simply is not enough of that abundance to go around; that it is not abundance at all, but paucity, insufficiency, sparseness. And *that* notion emerges from the fallacy that we are Separate from each other, not One Family at all, not One Essence at all, not One Being at all.

If we simply rejected the notion of Separation, the fallacy of

Insufficiency would fall. If we simply dropped the notion of Insufficiency, the fallacy that Competition is required would fall.

I call these fallacies Humanity's Dominoes. They tumble on top of each other, creating total collapse.

Our Fourth Fallacy About Life

When society split itself into Winners and Losers, it created the idea that the first group was "better" than the second. Then, by the marvelous device of circular logic, it concluded that being "better" was the reason that those in the first group were the Winners in the first place. They *deserved* to be.

Whites *deserved* to be Winners over people of color, because they are Better. Males *deserved* to be Winners over females, because they are Better. Straights *deserved* to be Winners over gays, because they are Better. And these groups were not Better for human reasons, but *better in the eyes of God*.

This is how we have *justified* our obviously outrageous judgments regarding qualifications and worthiness in our society.

It was *God* who said that whites are superior to blacks. Ask the Mormons, whose leaders from the founding of the Church of Jesus Christ of Latter-day Saints in the mid-1800s declared that blacks were not qualified to become lay priests, because theirs was an inferior race.

(To their credit, Mormons repudiated and reversed that dogma in 1978.)

It was *God* who said that men are superior to women. Ask thousands of religious clerics in the world, who still believe and preach this doctrine today.

(To their credit, thousands more have repudiated and rejected such notions.)

It was *God* who said that straights are superior to gays because same-gender sexuality is, God declared, an abomination. Ask any fundamentalist within virtually every religion on the Earth.

(To their credit, many of the world's religious people have since repudiated and rejected those ideas.)

At one point—and not thousands of years ago, either, but *when I was a child*—it was thought that left-handedness was a sign of the Devil; that interracial and interdenominational marriage should be forbidden; and Catholics thought that only Catholics were going to heaven.

Jehovah's Witnesses, on the other hand, said that only 144,000 of their adherents will join God in heaven, while the rest of those who believe in Jesus and live good lives and preach the faith will enjoy paradise on Earth. Many Jews, meanwhile, declared themselves to be God's chosen people.

So we can see that lots of folks have bought into the idea that with regard to the superiority of people it is "on Earth, as it is in Heaven"—some people are just Better in the eyes of God.

Few ideas have caused more damage to our species. Indeed, this idea has given moral authority to the biggest fallacy about life of all . . .

Our Fifth Fallacy About Life

More people than you might believe feel very certain that it is okay to resolve differences between people that have been created by all the other fallacies . . . by killing each other.

Wherever did we gather such a notion? Read the Bible with a calculator nearby. This particular Holy Scripture tells us that over a million people have been killed at the hand or the command of

God. Or look closely at the Muslim tradition of violent empire building in the name of Allah.

We know that Pope Urban II launched two hundred years of war, known as the Crusades, in 1095 that killed hundreds of thousands—mostly Muslims.

Likewise, many died as a result of what are known as the Islamic Conquests, which sought to create the largest spiritual/political empire the world has ever seen, and which went on in various places across the globe from 634 to the early 1800s.

Expanding the Moral Code

In more modern times, killing by groups or countries for the purpose of simply getting one's way or building an empire has been repudiated by most of the human race. The result: These days all such attack is called self-defense. This allows the species to justify atrocities under a moral code that most people accept: it is not ethically or spiritually inappropriate to defend oneself and to kill another in the process of doing that.

And now, segments of humanity have taken this idea one step further. They have declared that *preemptive strike* is an acceptable *means* of self-defense. That is, it is totally permissible to attack and kill people in other nations *before* they have attacked and killed people in your nation, on the grounds that it *looks as if* they want to do so in the future and are only waiting for the perfect time.

This is an expansion of humanity's more recent moral codes that pushes the acceptability of killing beyond previous boundaries.

The concept of self-defense apart and aside, massive swaths of human culture have been increasingly inundated with messages in everything from motion pictures to television programs to video games that depict violence and killing not just as a tool of self-defense but as a tool of anger and revenge, intimidation and threat, assertiveness and rebellion.

Killing as a means of resolution of one's problems or grievances has become more widespread now than ever before. It is increasingly seen not as a horrible last resort, but as the first action of the powerful.

First Cause

Yet again we do well to step back and observe the domino effect. It is our idea that we are separate from one another that allows us to entertain for even a moment the thought of perpetrating violence upon one another. This is First Cause, and we are either not recognizing it or refusing to acknowledge it.

If we thought that We Are All One and that what we do to others we do to ourselves, it would never occur to us to resolve our differences through violence and killing. What we have not wanted to see is the circular effect of our perspective—and the actions it produces. We have been blind to the fact that what goes around comes around. Or worse yet, we see this and we don't care about that.

It was Einstein who observed that a problem cannot be solved using the same energy that created it. Yet we continue to try to end violence with violence, killing with killing, injustice with injustice. We meet hatred with hatred, anger with anger, contempt with contempt.

Somewhere the cycle must end. It is not about "an eye for an eye and a tooth for a tooth," it is about another scripture altogether: "Love your enemies, and pray for those who persecute you."

Or, perhaps, an even newer Gospel: "We are all One. Ours is not a better way, ours is merely another way."

Applying This Message to Everyday Life

The Five Fallacies About Life can be overcome by anyone—but it requires patience, courage, and real determination, because these false ideas about "how it is" on the planet Earth are deeply engrained in humanity's culture. In short, *we think these things are true.*

Furthermore, the observed experience of our species absolutely supports that notion. So what you are now being invited to do is hold as our truth an entirely different set of ideas with which very few other people currently agree.

And that brings us to the first thing you can do to apply Message #23 in your life:

- Find other people immediately who understand your view of life and who agree with it—or who, even if they do not agree with it, will nevertheless support you in the choices you are making regarding the truths you wish to embrace.

I think it's very important to understand that it's okay for your truth to be what you say it is, rather than what others say it is. This is a key to changing your life. A *major* key. I cannot stress it often enough when I am working with small groups and individuals who seek to fundamentally alter their daily experience in a way that brings huge improvement to their lives.

We have been living far too long on this planet by someone else's set of rules. *Everyone* else's rules. And it wouldn't be so bad if the rules worked. But they don't.

As I have said here now more than once, *none of the rules*

are working. Not the political rules, not the economic rules, not the ecological rules, not the educational rules, not the social rules, and not the spiritual rules. Not one of them is producing the outcome that the Rulemakers *said* it would produce. It's worse. As noted earlier, each is, sadly, producing exactly the opposite outcomes. Still—and this is even sadder—*we keep playing by the rules.*

What is clear now is that someone needs to change the rules. That looks like you. And me. And us.

We'll explore this more deeply when we discuss *CWG* Core Message #17, which says that there is no such thing as absolute truth. (Which brings us a circular question: Is that absolutely true?) For now, simply know that it's important to immerse yourself with energy that vibrates in harmony with your own.

Notice that it doesn't have to match your own, but it does have to blend, it does have to be able to exist simultaneously in the same space without violent disruption or major, blocking opposition.

Life—*all* of it—is comprised of energy. Energy creates everything, produces everything, comprises everything, expresses everything, is everything. And energy impacts upon itself. That is, energy *affects* energy and changes it.

How energy changes energy depends upon the energies that are interacting. It is all about *which* energies are mixing. This is the best news you could ever receive, because this is something you can control. You cannot totally control the energies outside of you, but you can totally control the energy within you—and that is where the power is.

And . . . you can control the energies outside of you to some degree. I want to talk more about all of this a bit later, so hang in there with me. We're going to cover a lot of ground here. For now, exert what control you can on the energy around you.

If you are not surrounded by harmonious energies in your present daily environment, there are three choices you have. You can (a) adapt or "remodel" the environment in which you now spend much of your time, (b) create a new or alternative environment and consistently spend quality time there, or (c) leave your present environment altogether and move to another.

Here are some suggestions surrounding those ideas:

- Invite the person (or people) you are living with to explore and discuss your thoughts about life on a regular basis, not just once or twice a year when they express their disagreement with you.

- Ask those around you to support you on your journey and in living your truth, and to make it easy for them, suggest specific ways in which they can do that.

- Find or form a Discussion and Exploration Group of people from outside your daily environment who agree with your point of view about life and who are living it, and create or attend gatherings with them on a regular basis to give and garner emotional and spiritual support. (This could be a New Thought church in your community or simply a small circle of acquaintances who regularly get together in their homes—or both.)

- Use the Internet to connect with like-minded persons and to share your ideas about how our mutual experience could be if we dropped the Five Fallacies About

Life and embraced new truths regarding separation, insufficiency, competition, superiority, and conflict resolution. Remember this motto: "Sharing helps sharpen." Sharpen your clarity about your point of view by expressing it and exchanging ideas about it with others on websites designed for such interaction, like www.The GlobalConversation.com, which was created for exactly this purpose.

• Keep an Insufficiency List, and every time you think you do not have "enough" of something, jot down what that is on your list. Then, take a really good and fair look at *why you think you need more of that*—and at what having "enough" of that would look like. Ask yourself how you've managed to survive so far without "enough" of that, and then ask: "What does having 'enough' of this have to do with my true reason for being on the Earth?"

• Be sure that you are crystal clear about your true reason for being on the Earth. You may wish to read *The Only Thing That Matters* and other texts in the *Conversations with God* cosmology to help you move into a deeper understanding of this.

• Create a Superiority History Notebook and in it begin a recollection narrative of all the people to whom you have felt superior at one point or another in your life. Write a paragraph about each person or group (i.e., "fundamentalists," "Republicans," "Jim Brown," "today's youth," "my husband's family," who*ever*) and explain why you felt superior, and what caused you to change your mind about that. Or, if you haven't altered your opinion, ask yourself what, if anything, *might* change if you dropped your idea of being "better," in some way, than that other person or group. Be honest with yourself around this. Nobody is looking and nobody is going to read your notebook.

- Make a list of all the things you see in a person of whom you disapprove that you also see in yourself. Do this person by person as you run through the names of people you don't like (or at least, don't choose to spend a great deal of time around—which, if you are honest with yourself, may be the same thing).

- As an exercise with your Discussion and Exploration Group, invite the group to devise at least five ways that it believes violence or war could be circumvented in instances of major disagreement between nations or between people within nations. See how many of these approaches could be applied in your own life.

- Ask your Discussion and Exploration Group to write passages of a New Cultural Story for Humanity in the following areas: Politics, Economics, Ecology, Education, Society, Spirituality. Share these passages in discussions with the group, and see if it can reach consensus on their content. Notice how the group itself approaches and resolves differences. Submit your final wording as suggested content for Humanity's New Cultural Story at www.TheGlobalConversation.com.

9

It is very clear that the point of view of *Conversations with God* is that a major factor in the creation of many of humanity's biggest problems is humanity's concept of Divinity.

We simply have no idea who and what God is, what God wants, what happens if we don't supply it, what happens if we do, and what any of this has to do with life on Earth.

We have been trying to figure all this out for thousands of years and seem no closer to the answer today than we were in the time of Lao Tzu, Mahāvīra or Buddha, Moses, Christ, or Muhammad, Bahá'u'lláh or Joseph Smith. Nor have we been able to come to any agreement or consensus on these questions in the years since they each brought us their answers.

This is the reason that the world is in the situation it finds itself in today: unable to govern itself politically, unable to support itself economically, unable to sustain itself ecologically, unable to improve itself educationally, unable to unite itself socially, and unable to evolve itself spiritually.

We live on a planet filled with lack and suffering, anger and violence, murder and war, and we shake our heads sadly, proclaiming that we don't know why. We don't know what it would take to change things. We can't find the formula, we don't have the answers, we aren't able to produce solutions to our oldest and biggest problems, we simply do not, after all is said and done, have the capacity to create what we all say we want: peace, prosperity, opportunity, security, dignity, health, joy, happiness, and love for all.

It is not because we have not been offered solutions or given suggestions. We have been. Over and over again. And now we are here being offered answers once more. Yet these answers are dissimilar to the ones we have heard most often before. Indeed, they are in some cases a direct contradiction of those earlier teachings. Yet they are not new answers, not new ideas, but simply thoughts about all of this that have been rejected in the past.

Perhaps it is time to reconsider our rejection of them—and to reject that rejection. Perhaps it is time to explore these ideas anew, given that the teachings we have been firmly embracing and adamantly refusing to adjust, adapt, or amend, have failed utterly and absolutely to produce what they have promised.

Perhaps it is time to ponder whether expansion of our earlier concepts and the forming of a far more sophisticated story about God might be in order.

Yet why are our concepts about Divinity so important? Why does any of this matter? We have said it before and we will say it again. It is because our ideas and concepts about God form our ideas and concepts about ourselves, and about Life. One emerges from the other, and this is true (as we have also already noted) even in the lives of people who do not believe in God at all.

Simply look at the laws and mores, the social dictates and customs of any land, and see how many of them are rooted and based in what their citizens believe to be true about *what God wants*.

CWG CORE MESSAGE #22

There are Five Fallacies about God that create crisis, violence, killing, and war. First, the idea that God *needs* something. Second, the idea that God *can fail to get* what He needs. Third, the idea that God *has separated* you from Him because you have not given Him what He needs. Fourth, the idea that God still needs what He needs so badly that God now *requires* you, *from your separated position*, to give it to Him. Fifth, the idea that God *will destroy you* if you do not meet His requirements.

That is why I earnestly and urgently invite all of humanity to consider . . .

The fallacies about God are even more damaging to us than humanity's fallacies about Life, because we are at least willing to consider that some of our ideas about Life may not be accurate, yet such considerations regarding our ideas about God are absolutely not acceptable. Thus, a movement away from these fallacies is extremely difficult to produce.

Unless it's not. Unless we decide that the time has come, finally, for our species to consider the possibility that our current body of knowledge does not contain *all there is to know about Divinity*.

Can we admit that there may be data missing, or something about which we may have been *mistaken*, regarding God?

That's a Really Big Question. Is there something, *anything*, about which we may have been mistaken regarding God?

That's a question that believers in God have, in the main, been extremely reluctant to ask. It's virtually taboo. Because the majority of believers in God believe that they have the Right Answers about

God, and they will tell you that you must believe in God *a certain way*. If you do not believe in God *this* way (that is, *their* way), you do not believe in God at all, but in some heathen *idea* of God that God will *punish you for*.

There are, of course, millions of people who do not accept the God of such doctrines and dogmas and nevertheless hold in their reality an awareness and an experience of Divinity. However, the largest number of people (by *far* the largest number) cling to the first understanding and proclaim that God must be understood and embraced in a certain way, or you have *lost* your way—and have lost, as well, any chance of being reunited with God in heaven. Coming to God in a Certain and Particular Way is, this group declares, God's *requirement*. This brings us to . . .

The First Fallacy About God

We begin our litany of errors with the idea that God *needs* something.

This runs counter to the expanded idea of Divinity in the New Spirituality that includes the notion that God is Everything, and there is nothing that is *not* God. In this view, God is not a being who created elements or expressions of Life that are not Divine, but rather, God is both the Creator and the Created.

Thus, God needs nothing, since God is everything that God could possibly need. Or, as *Conversations with God* put it: All Things are One Thing, and that One Thing is sufficient unto Itself.

Take away the idea that God *needs* something and you take away virtually the entire basis of all the world's major religions. If God needs nothing, then why would God require anything, demand anything, command anything? What would be the purpose? What would be the motivation? What lack would God be fulfilling? What would be the basis of God's desires or directives?

When we get to our discussion of the Third Fallacy about God, below, we will uncover an additional and important implication of the idea that God needs nothing.

The Second Fallacy About God

As remarkable as it is that humanity would conceive of a God who needs something, it is even more remarkable that we would then decide that this God can somehow *fail to get what He needs*—the second fallacy that humanity holds about Divinity. This second error is the basis of most of humanity's theology.

We are told in those theologies that it is God's failure to get what He needs (obedience, honor, subservience, and exclusivity, among other things) that creates God's reactions to us. If God needed nothing, God would require nothing, and hence, have nothing for which to be angry. And that would pull the underpinnings out of every theology on the planet. And *that*, in turn, would remove the Moral Authority from half of the earthly choices, actions, and decisions of human beings. Much of our justice system uses God's supposed reactions to not getting what God needs as its moral authority. Our political decisions likewise. (Note the controversy surrounding gay marriage in the United States, the political strife around abortion even in the case of incest or rape as earlier noted, etc.) As well, our social choices. (Too many to be listed are based on what religions tell us about what makes God angry.)

The Third Fallacy About God

This fallacy holds that God *has separated* you from Him because you have not given Him what He needs. Separation from God is proclaimed to be a *punishment* for, or the consequence of, our not having met God's needs.

According to the myth, God *needed* us to obey Him, and our failure to meet this need is what caused God to seek retribution. (Because God also, apparently, has a need for revenge—although some religions, again, would frame it as a need for "perfect justice.")

This third fallacy arose out of *humanity's* need to explain to *itself* why, if there *is* a God, we would be separate from Him. We couldn't figure out why, but we certainly knew why we separated ourselves from each *other!* It is because we displeased each other. So we figured that God must have tossed us out of His Kingdom for the same reason. We thus constructed our God in the image and likeness of Man.

Yet it is a fallacy that God separated us from God because we failed to give God what God needs—for the reason that God *cannot fail* to get what God needs, for the reason that God *has* no needs.

If God and we are not separate, then God and we are One. If God and we are One, and if God needs nothing, then *we* need nothing—and the implication of this is enormous.

That is the True State of Things, and that is one of the biggest secrets of Life.

Right now most of us think that we *need* things. (We will look at this more expansively in our exploration of *CWG* Core Message #18.) This idea rules. It has created the basis of virtually every choice and decision we make. And we can begin to see now how that domino effect I spoke of earlier has played its effect on the whole of humanity's experience.

The Fourth Fallacy About God

From all of the above fallacies flow the next: the idea that God still needs what He needs so badly that God now *requires* you, *from your separated position*, to give it to Him.

This leap from Separation as a *punishment* to the idea that we are required to *now* meet God's needs, even though we've already been punished for not doing so, is an example of Continued Mistake Making.

Our whole construct around God has been fascinating, and nothing is more fascinating than this idea that, while God threw us out of Paradise for not fulfilling Her needs, God still wants us to meet His needs right now, from *outside* of Paradise.

It is not unlike some sort of celestial divorce, in which God demands that we supply God with what God needs, even though God has separated from us because we failed to do so when we were *with* God. It is as if we are now required to provide Spiritual Spousal Support.

We are to do on Earth what we (or our "spiritual parents") did not do in Paradise: We are to obey God, we are to honor God, we are to please God and in no way to displease God, we are to find the One and Only Right Path back to God, using it exclusively. If we do these things, God will accept us back to the place from which He cast us out.

If, on the other hand, we do not do as God now commands . . .

The Fifth Fallacy About God

We are told that God will not simply punish you, but completely annihilate you. This is the fifth and final fallacy about God: God will *destroy* you if you do not meet His requirements.

Many religions and billions of their followers believe this. They will tell you that failure to meet God's requirements will result in your being burned and left suffering immeasurably and unrelentingly in the everlasting fires of hell.

This is what I have come to call the Second Punishment of God. The First Punishment was ejection from the Garden of Eden. The Second Punishment is rejection of *eligibility to return* and sentencing to everlasting torture.

The First Punishment was, presumably, a warning. Sort of like the warning ticket you get from a traffic cop. The Second Punishment is your penalty after being judged guilty of breaking the law yet again. Now you're going to the Mother of All Jails, a prison of anguish and pain.

According to certain doctrines, here you will be destroyed—but never quite completely. That is, the punishment will never quite be over. You will be punished forever and ever, and even forevermore for your relatively few moments of disobedience. Your life on Earth has been a blip, really—less than the blink of an eye—in the life of the universe, but your torturous punishment must be eternal. Thus, the punishment will not fit the crime, but far exceed it. This is, some religions say, God's idea of Fairness and Justice.

So now, let's see if you understand . . .

You have a God who needs things, who can't get what He needs, who sent you away because He couldn't get what He needed from your forebears a hundred billion years ago, who now demands that you give Him what He needs in this moment, and who will punish you eternally if you do not.

Got it?

It May Be Now or Never

Could it be time, do you think, for us to relinquish these notions of our Deity? Would it be a good moment for us to announce that we find these concepts simplistic and limited?

Might this be a fine stretch of eternity during which to declare that there is clearly something we don't fully understand about God, the understanding of which would change everything?

To put it more dramatically, is it possible that unless we enlarge and expand our primitive ideas about God and about Life in the decades just ahead, we may find that we have backed ourselves into a corner, from which there is no escape?

Conversations with God told us that humanity nearly rendered itself extinct once before. Barely enough of us survived to regenerate the species and start over. Are we at this same turning point again? Have we arrived once more at the intersection where theology meets cosmology meets sociology meets pathology?

Right now we are still embracing a Separation Theology. That is, a way of looking at God that insists that we are "over here" and God is "over there."

The problem with a Separation Theology is that it produces a Separation Cosmology. That is, a way of looking at all of life that says that everything is separate from everything else.

And a Separation Cosmology produces a Separation Psychology. That is, a psychological viewpoint that says that I am over here and you are over there.

And a Separation Psychology produces a Separation Sociology. That is, a way of socializing with each other that encourages the entire human society to act as separate entities serving their own separate interests.

And a Separation Sociology produces a Separation Pathology.

That is, *pathological behaviors of self-destruction*, engaged in individually and collectively, and producing suffering, conflict, violence, and death by our own hands—as evidenced everywhere on our planet throughout human history.

Only when our Separation Theology is replaced by a Oneness Theology will our pathology be healed. We have been *differentiated* from God, but not *separated* from God, even as your fingers are differentiated but not separated from your hand (to reuse an earlier illustration). We must come to understand that all of life is One. This is the first step. It is the jumping-off point. It is the beginning of the end of how things now are. It is the start of a new creation, of a new tomorrow. It is the New Cultural Story of Humanity.

Oneness is not a characteristic of life. Life is a characteristic of Oneness. Life is the *expression* of Oneness Itself. *God* is the expression of Life Itself. God and Life are One. You are a part of Life. You do not and cannot stand outside of it. Therefore you are a part of God. It is a circle. It cannot be broken.

APPLYING THIS MESSAGE TO EVERYDAY LIFE

Nothing has damaged humanity more than the Five Fallacies About God. Once we understand this, we can begin to live and create our lives in ways that *demonstrate* that these are fallacies and that exemplify the truth.

Once again we come across that big word: Truth. In fact, there is no such thing as Truth. And yes, we will talk more about this in chapter 14 when we explore *CWG* Core Message #17. For now, let's use the term "our truth."

As I experience it, the word TRUE is an acronym. When we say that something is "true," what we are saying is that it is The Reality Understood Existentially.

And so in my world, in my own internal experience (in which I get to freely decide for myself what is "so"), the ideas about God that most of humanity holds are mostly fallacies, and what is "true" is that God needs nothing, God could not fail to get what God needs if God *did* need something, God has not separated humanity from Herself, God does not require us to give God anything, and God will never destroy us for not meeting God's nonexistent requirements.

By my living this truth, my life becomes a reflection of it. The dictionary defines "reflection" as that which indicates, shows, displays, demonstrates, offers evidence of, registers, reveals, discloses, expresses, communicates, and evinces. So when my life becomes a reflection of my freely chosen internal experience, my outer world becomes a mirror image of my inner world, which then becomes a mirror of my outer world, which then becomes a bigger mirror of my inner world, as each continues to reflect the other *upon* the other, producing an entire life of deep reflection.

I have found that such ongoing moments of deep reflection generate outgoing moments of great joy, as the illusions of Life are at last broken. Or, more correctly, as *other people's illusions* are at last discarded, in favor of my own.

All of Life is an illusion. This is something we do well to recognize and acknowledge. Physical life as we are experiencing it is not real. Our life experience is what we *think* it is. Each moment is what we *experience* it to be, based on a whole series of internal decisions (described in wonderful detail in the sections on the Mechanics of the Mind found in *When Everything Changes, Change Everything*).

As Shakespeare wrote: "Nothing is evil lest thinking make it so." Descartes put it another way: "I think, therefore I am."

How to make all of this practical in your daily life? That's the question. And here are a few suggestions:

- Create a "Beliefs About God" Notebook. (I'm a big one for notebooks, as you can tell. Taking note, in a book that you can look at, of what you feel, what you believe, how you move through life, and how you would choose to if you thought you could have your way, is a valuable exercise. I often suggest making separate notebooks covering separate aspects of life, as opposed to a single running diary. This allows you to access quickly a record of your thoughts and experiences on any given subject of major impact upon your life—and to *track* those thoughts and experiences throughout your life, so that you can see Where You've Been, Where You Are, and Where You're Going.) In your "Beliefs About God" Notebook make a list of all of your current thoughts about God. If your thoughts about God as they relate to a particular aspect of Divinity are unclear or unknown, just report that.

- Indicate in your Notebook what you believe that God needs, what you believe that God requires, what you believe that God commands, and what you believe that God condemns.

- In the same Notebook, indicate which of those things that you believe that God condemns (if any) you have done (if any).

• Answer the following questions in your Notebook:
Who do you believe to be the Ultimate Authority in
your life? What is Right and what is Wrong? (Just
name some things.) What is Good and what is Evil?
(Just name some things.) What is Appropriate and
what is Inappropriate? (Just name some things.) What
is authentically You and what is not authentically You?
(One more time, just name some things.) These last
questions open huge topics, of course, so don't try to
write a Thesis for All Mankind, just jot down a few
things that come to your mind. Then, close your Notebook and come back to it later.

• Now, after some time has passed, return to this Notebook and look at the questions again, reviewing the
short lists that you created as answers. Ask yourself:
Who said this is "right" and that is "wrong"? Who said
this is "good" and that is "evil"? Who said this is "appropriate" and that is "inappropriate"? Who said this is
"authentically You" and that is not "authentically You"?
And, in each category . . . *why*? What is the reason you
have applied these labels? Look to see what this tells
you about your current beliefs.

• Toward the center of this Notebook, create a section
called My Daily Report, and there, make a note each
night for thirty days of any judgments or assessments
you remember yourself having made that day about the
topics above (or similar aspects of your experience). Do
this at the end of every day without fail for one month.
Watch the changes in yourself as you watch yourself.

- Go to an online encyclopedia and look up the beliefs of all the world's major religions (and a few of the minor ones). This is a long-term project, so do a little of it each week. Spend an hour here and an hour there, and just give yourself permission to discover what people of various religions and faith traditions believe. As you make yourself aware of these things, ask yourself (and record your answers in your "Beliefs About God" Notebook) what in that particular religion or tradition *you* hold as part of *your* belief system.

This last project is a wonderful activity for your body, mind, and soul. It will give you a chance to feel fully integrated regarding what you really think and declare is "true" in your own reality about the most important topic of your life: God.

Let's do three together, just to get you started.

SEVENTH-DAY ADVENTISTS

Seventh-Day Adventists believe in the unerring truth of Scripture and teach that salvation comes only through faith in Jesus Christ. Adventists believe in conditional immortality. They believe that human beings do not have an immortal soul that lives forever on its own, but rather, that life can only continue eternally through the power of God. If one does not believe in God, one ceases to exist, because one has willfully denied God's existence and power. There is no such place as hell, however. A human is not tortured but simply ceases to be.

Adventists also believe in "thought inspiration": that God inspired the thoughts of the authors of the Bible, and that they then expressed these thoughts in their own words.

How do these ideas line up with your own beliefs? Have you even thought about these things? If so, what are your thoughts and conclusions? Enter these in your Notebook. If you have other questions about the religion, look up Seventh-Day Adventists in the encyclopedia or any spiritual reference book. Or just do an Internet search on your computer.

Jehovah's Witnesses

Jehovah's Witnesses believe that God will soon end this present age of human existence. A heavenly government over Earth, established by Jesus Christ, will replace existing human governments and all non-Witnesses will be destroyed, creating a society of true worshippers.

Jehovah's Witnesses interpret much of the Bible literally and base all of their beliefs on the Bible, as interpreted by the Governing Body. Jehovah's Witnesses believe God is the Creator and Supreme Being. They believe God, whose name is Jehovah, is "infinite, but approachable"; He resides in heaven and is not omnipresent; it is possible to have a personal relationship with God; He is kind and merciful, and would not eternally torture wicked people in a place called hell. He does not force His sovereignty on people, but saves only those who want to serve Him.

Jehovah's Witnesses believe that Satan was originally an angel who developed feelings of self-importance and wanted to be worshipped as God. Satan persuaded Adam and Eve to obey him rather than God. Instead of destroying Satan, God decided to test the loyalty of the rest of humankind, to see if having been granted free will, people would obey God under both temptation and persecution. Jehovah's Witnesses believe that Satan is God's enemy and the invisible ruler of the world.

They believe that demons were originally angels who rebelled against God and took Satan's side in the controversy.

Jehovah's Witnesses teach that God's kingdom is a literal government in heaven, established in 1914, ruled by Jesus Christ and 144,000 humans raised to heaven. God will use this kingdom to make Earth a world free of crime, sickness, death, and poverty, and ultimately transforming the Earth into a paradise. Witnesses believe that the soul does not continue to exist after one dies and consider death a state of nonexistence. Witnesses believe that the only hope for life after death is in the resurrection, in which God will re-create the same individual with a new body. They believe that 144,000 people will be resurrected into heaven to be priestly rulers under Christ, but the rest of humanity that "believes" will be relegated to physical life in a paradise on Earth.

Jehovah's Witnesses have consistently claimed to be the only true religion, and believe all other religions are under the control of Satan.

How do these ideas line up with your own beliefs? Have you even thought about these things? If so, what are your thoughts and conclusions? Enter these in your Notebook. If you have other questions about the religion, look up Jehovah's Witnesses in the encyclopedia or any spiritual reference book. Or just do an Internet search on your computer.

BAHÁ'Í FAITH

The Bahá'í Faith, founded by Bahá'u'lláh in nineteenth-century Persia, emphasizes the spiritual unity of all humankind. The Bahá'í Faith recognizes "divine messengers" throughout history—including Moses, Buddha, Jesus, and Muhammad—who established religions that suited the needs of the time.

For Bahá'ís, the most recent messengers are the Báb and Bahá'u'lláh, and they believe Bahá'u'lláh's life and teachings fulfilled the end-time promises of previous scriptures.

Bahá'ís believe that we, today, are called to establish peace, justice, and unity on a global scale.

Bahá'í doctrine is based on three core principles: the unity of God, the unity of religion, and the unity of humankind. They believe God periodically reveals His will through divine messengers, whose purpose is to transform humankind. Religion is thus seen as orderly, unified, and progressive from age to age.

Per Bahá'í writings, human beings have a "rational soul," and thus we can recognize God's station and humanity's relationship with its creator. Every human has a duty to recognize God through His messengers, and to conform to their teachings. Through recognition and obedience, service to humanity and regular prayer and spiritual practice, the soul becomes closer to God, which they believe is the spiritual ideal.

Bahá'ís believe that when one dies, the soul passes into the next world, where it is judged based on its spiritual development in the physical world and advances accordingly in the spiritual world. Heaven and hell are spiritual states of nearness or distance from God, not physical places of reward and punishment achieved after death.

Shoghi Effendi, the appointed head of the religion from 1921 to 1957, wrote the following summary of what he considered to be the main principles of Bahá'u'lláh's teachings and foundation of the Bahá'í Faith:

> *The independent search after truth, unfettered by superstition or tradition; the oneness of the entire human race, the pivotal principle and fundamental doctrine of the Faith;*

*the basic unity of all religions; the condemnation of all
forms of prejudice, whether religious, racial, class or national; the harmony which must exist between religion
and science; the equality of men and women, the two
wings on which the bird of humankind is able to soar; the
introduction of compulsory education; the adoption of a
universal auxiliary language; the abolition of the extremes
of wealth and poverty; the institution of a world tribunal
for the adjudication of disputes between nations; the exal-
tation of work, performed in the spirit of service, to the
rank of worship; the glorification of justice as the ruling
principle in human society, and of religion as a bulwark
for the protection of all peoples and nations; and the estab-
lishment of a permanent and universal peace as the supreme goal of all mankind—these stand out as the essential
elements which Bahá'u'lláh proclaimed.*

How do these ideas line up with your own beliefs? Have
you even thought about these things? If so, what are your
thoughts and conclusions? Enter these in your Notebook. If
you have other questions about the religion, look up the
Bahá'í Faith in the encyclopedia or any spiritual reference
book. Or just do an Internet search on your computer.

COMPARING THEOLOGIES

It might be interesting here to compare some of the teachings
of these three faiths with the Core Messages in *Conversations
with God* as found in chapter 2 here.

Is *Conversations with God* a religion? No. Emphatically and
unequivocally . . . *No.* Is it a theology? Yes. Emphatically
and unequivocally . . . *Yes.*

The dictionary defines theology as "the study and analysis of
God, and of God's attributes and relationship to the universe."

More broadly, and closer to its origin and earliest use, we are told at the website www.eHow.com that the word "theology" can be traced back through Old French and Latin to the Greek *theologos*, meaning "one who discourses on the gods," from "theos" (God) and "logos" (words).

Given these parameters, *Conversations with God* is absolutely a theology, or a study of God.

Among other things, *CWG* posits that there is no inerrant or infallible Scripture from or about God. Books such as the Bible, the Bhagavad Gita, the Qur'an, the Upanishads, the Talmud, the Book of Mormon, the Vedas and others are just that: books, written by human beings in moments of great inspiration, but by human beings nonetheless. Thus, they can contain great wisdom and they also can contain error. It is most beneficial to take no such book absolutely literally, word for word.

CWG quite clearly advises on its pages that people should not and never take its words as "God's Truth," but rather, place them in the For What It's Worth Department, considering them along with other sources of insight and wisdom that they have found in their life, but always referring ultimately to their own response to them, to their own deep knowing, their own inner guidance, their own personal experience, as the Only and Ultimate Authority in all things spiritual.

Like the words of Ellen G. White, like the writings of Mary Baker Eddy, like the ideas of Charles and Myrtle Fillmore, like the thoughts of Ernest Holmes, like the pronouncements of William Miller or Charles Taze Russell or Joseph Smith Jr. or Bahá'u'lláh, or any other human messenger, the messages received in *Conversations with God* should be considered only the sharing of words by one human among many who have experienced themselves to have been inspired by the

Divine to bring through, illuminate, and clarify spiritual wisdom and insight that is *not theirs* but was received by them through their imperfect human filter, to record and transmit as purely as they could.

Unlike the others on the list above, however, I do not hope or wish, expect or request, suggest or recommend that a religion be created around the messages that have come through me. I hope only that they will be examined and explored deeply, that they will be accorded fair consideration and serious contemplation, toward the end that if the *CWG* Core Messages are deemed workable and beneficial in people's lives, they may be embraced and usefully applied in a person's day-to-day encounters, and will be helpful as tools in the fashioning of a more wonderful, more joyful, more peaceful, more glorious group experience upon the Earth—all as part of the Soul's eternal journey and of God's never-ending expression.

10

It is all very nice to talk about the Journey of the Soul, but it is the Passage Through Life that concerns most human beings. And rightly it should. The purpose of our life on Earth is not to *ignore* our life on Earth, but to live it fully, making the passage from birth to death with joy, with wondrous creative expression, with our goal the reaching of self-realization, without suffering, and without causing suffering in others. I believe we would be best served if this was our prime focus.

In *Happier Than God: Turn Ordinary Life into an Extraordinary Experience*, the text begins with this remarkable observation . . .

Life was meant to be happy.

Do you believe that?

It's true. I know it doesn't seem like it when you look around, but it's true. Life was meant to be happy.

You were meant to be happy. And if you *are* happy, you were meant to be happier. Even if you're *very* happy, you can be even happier.

How happy? Just *how* happy can you be? Well . . . you can be *happier than God.*

I once heard a lady describing a gentleman who was very

wealthy. She said, "He's got more money than God!" That's how I mean this. I mean to use the ultimate superlative . . .

. . . As it happens there is a *formula* by which you can be happier than God. All mystics have known it, most teachers of mystical wisdom have known it, some contemporary spiritual messengers know it, but it's become, through the centuries, sort of a "mystery formula" . . . because it's not talked about very much. Not very much at all.

Why? Simple. Very few of the folks to whom spiritual teachers and messengers might be talking have been able to believe what the "mystery formula" is said to be able to produce. And when you talk about things that no one believes, you can become very unpopular.

So even today, in what is supposed to be a time of intellectual and spiritual enlightenment, not many teachers and spiritual messengers reveal this formula, even if they know it. Or if they are talking about it, they are talking about only half of it. Most of them are keeping the other half, the most breathtaking part of this formula, under wraps. So what we have here is an amazing truth, but *you don't know the half of it.*

The book goes on to describe in wonderful detail an approach to life that virtually guarantees that you will be happy, no matter what is going on around you. I wrote this text as an expansion of the message in the movie *The Secret*, which told of the enormous influence that affirmative thought can have in our lives, much in the tradition of *The Power of Positive Thinking* by Dr. Norman Vincent Peale. Yet *The Secret* all but ignored the role of God in the process of personal creation. The book *Happier Than God* fills that huge gap, changing "the secret" dramatically.

I have not found it beneficial to leave God out of any process in Life, since God *is* Life and Life *is* God. The words are interchangeable. So living my life without God would be like trying to breathe without using my lungs, or see without opening my eyes, or think without engaging my mind. How can I live without involving God?

I cannot, of course. Such a thing would be impossible. Yet it would not be impossible to *imagine* that I am doing so. And this is what many people are doing today. They are imagining that they are *living Life without God*.

There's nothing wrong with that, incidentally. I mean, it's not an act of moral turpitude; it's not an offense against the Most High. (It is not possible to "offend" God.) But it is a bit like trying to drive a car without turning on the engine.

Now you can *do* that, actually . . . as long as you're coasting downhill. But some of Life is an uphill climb, and that's when you might find that using the power makes the journey a lot easier.

In Life you're *always* "using the power," of course, because Life *is* "the power"—but doing so *consciously* makes a big difference. Not doing so consciously would be like carrying a lit flashlight in the dark, but keeping it in your pocket because you forgot—or didn't even know—it was there.

The trick regarding the Power of God is to *be aware it is there.* And that brings us to . . .

CWG CORE MESSAGE #21

There are Three Levels of Awareness: *Hope*, *Faith*, and *Knowing*.

Spiritual mastery is about living from the third level.

What *Conversations with God* is about is not just laying out a new theology, one that could provide a new spiritual template for humanity, but also offering all of us practical tools with which to rebuild our lives—this time the way we've always wanted them to be. The nine books in the *CWG* series provide a veritable road map, helping us traverse the sometimes treacherous terrain of our Earthly encounters.

In short, knowing with great clarity what God said can help us to ease our day-in/day-out experience, and even move us to mastery in living. That is why I have taken the time to search through the three thousand pages of the *CWG* dialogue and pull out the 25 most important messages from that nine-book exchange. Those messages show us how to get to where we wish to go in our Journey of the Soul. They also tell us why making this trip is momentous—and how not to trip *up* on the trip *there*.

One place that most sentient beings seek to go to is the place of Awareness, so let's look at that now.

Some teachers talk in terms of "expanding" your Awareness. You can't do that. In strictest terms a "growth" in your Awareness is not possible. Minneapolis doesn't get bigger just because you've arrived there, and Awareness doesn't expand just because you reached it.

Your Awareness is what it is; it does not "grow" larger and larger. That's because your Awareness rests within your Soul, and your Soul does not get bigger, or in some way "more," than it always was and is now.

It is your *Mind* that expands. For easy understanding, it could be said that Awareness rests in the Soul and Attention resides in the Mind.

So to put what may be occurring in your life right now another way, you are now paying *greater Attention* to your Awareness. It's one thing to be "aware," but it is another thing altogether to pay attention to what your Soul is aware of (instead of ignoring it, which most people do most of the time).

This mixture of the two is what might be called Consciousness.

When your Mind pays attention to your Soul, and your Mind and Soul thus carry the same data, hold the same idea, and possess the same perspective, you might be said to be *fully conscious.*

So in real terms, it is your Consciousness that is expanding as the Awareness of your Soul comes to the Attention of your Mind.

There are three stops on the pathway by which your mind may experience a higher state of Awareness, and *Conversations with God* discusses each of them.

The Place of Hope

Hope is the first place at which one seeking to reach Awareness arrives. I have heard hope delightfully described as the energy that runs between the eyes and the tail of a dog. Hope is a wonderful energy and it is my wish that you never abandon it, for it produces, initiates, and sponsors all sorts of positive actions, choices, and decisions, and generates enthusiasm and excitement along the way.

Having said that, we note that it is only the first stop on the path to Awareness. And why is it not the last stop? Because Hope is a place where we seem to be acknowledging a high possibility that a something may *or may not* happen. If we were *sure* it was going to happen, we would have no need to "hope" that it will. If we were *sure* that something is "so," we would not have to "hope" that it is "so."

So, Hope is an admission that a particular condition, situation, or circumstance may or may not eventuate. A person who hopes is a person who wonders whether what she or he is hoping for will come about. There is not a sense of assurance, but there is a sense of wishfulness, a sense of optimism that it *could* happen. And that's good. That means that one hasn't said to oneself, "There's no chance." Yet Hope is the weakest energy in the Process of Personal Creation.

Again, this does not mean that it is an ineffective or useless energy, but simply that there are even stronger energies that God has given us to work with as we move toward Awareness, and the mastery that it produces.

It is Awareness that is the energy that ultimately produces inner experiences and outer manifestations in one's life. This is because Awareness allows us to know that the outcome *has already occurred*; that it is *already so*, and that it is simply waiting for us to become aware of it. (More on this later.)

So, Hope allows us to reach the outskirts of the State of Awareness. It is not like being totally within that sacred state, but it is better than being far, far removed from it.

The Place of Faith

Faith is the second stop on the pathway to Awareness. One is much closer to the center of that sacred state when one has reached a place of Faith.

Faith is not about wondering whether something will occur, or thinking that it could happen, it is about *feeling* sure that it will happen. This is a quantum leap from wishing. It is a much higher energy, a much more powerful one.

If we think of energy as a magnet, a tool that draws certain outcomes and experiences to us, then Faith has more pulling power than Hope by a factor of ten. It strongly pulls outcomes to us from the Contextual Field in which all outcomes exist—what my friend Deepak Chopra calls "the field of infinite possibilities." (More on this later, too.)

Faith lies inside the State of Awareness—but not at the center of it. Yet we have crossed the border of doubt, and that's very good. We have come a long way, and we long ago left the place of wondering or conjecturing or speculating about outcomes. We have *faith* that particular outcomes will ensue, meaning that we *trust* that they will, we hold a *conviction* that they will, we have *confidence* that they will, and this generates a high level of *optimism* about it.

Still, Faith is an announcement that there still remains the possibility that a particular outcome may *not* materialize. It is important to see that "trust" (which is Faith by a different name) *is not necessary* in the space of certainty.

The definition of "faith" is "complete trust" in someone or something, and the definition of "trust" is "a firm belief" in something or someone. Yet a "belief" is still a *belief*, and not Absolute Awareness. Believing something is one thing, knowing it is another.

A person should not have to "trust" or "believe" that the outcome of a particular event will turn out "right." They should be so certain of it that "trust" is not even part of the equation, and "belief" has long ago been left behind, having given way to simply knowing that every outcome, whatever it might be, is the perfect next step in their personal evolution.

The Place of Knowing

This last stop on the pathway to Awareness is the most powerful place that a person could ever be. It is the place of Absolute Knowing. Here is found peace. Here is found a gentle joy. Here is found the kind of deep assurance that births total tranquility and sacred serenity.

This is not about "feeling sure," it's about being "positive." There's a difference.

The Initiate has Hope, the Student has Faith, the Master has Knowing. And what the Master knows is that any outcomes that occur in Life will produce the highest and best for all concerned. It can be no other way in the Master's world. Therefore, the Master does not hope for particular outcomes, nor have faith that specific results will manifest. The Master *knows* with a *certainty* that all outcomes are perfect—just as they are; exactly as they arise; precisely as they present themselves.

And the Master knows this because the Master understands that all outcomes in the physical world are co-created, collaboratively manifested, and jointly produced to exactly serve the agenda of every soul in every situation in every moment in every place in "All the When/Where's of Existence" (to borrow a marvelous phrase from author Robert Heinlein).

Getting to Awareness

The sincere seeker traveling the Pathway to Awareness may now be expected to say, "Okay, I understand. I now have these questions: How do I get to these three places? And, can I hopscotch across one or two of them, or must I go through them step by step?"

The answer to the first question is that to get to them, one may find a map useful. And that, as I have said, is what *Conversations with God* offers. It is an Instruction Book. (Or in this case, a series of them; nine books in all.) It is a Guide for the unendingly inquisitive mind. It offers a blueprint, a pattern, a touchstone, a template for the heart. A *way to get there.*

Yet it is not the only way to Awareness. It makes this point clear time and again—just as we are doing here. Yet it is one way, and for millions across the globe it has been a very effective way.

And yes, one can go straight to Knowing. It is not necessary to stop at Hope or Faith, any more than it is necessary to step on every rung of the ladder to get to the top. But this can sometimes make the climb easier. So let it be okay with you if you're not at the place of Absolute Awareness yet—or if you've found yourself there, and then found yourself *not* there; and then there again, and then *not* there again.

In my own life I've moved in and out of the place of Total Knowing, and I have not so far been able to remain there for a vastly extended period (much less the rest of my life). But some people have. And not just ancient masters, saints, or sages, either. There are people living on the planet right now who have. Some of the people whom I know personally have. So I can promise you it is possible.

I'm working on going there and staying there permanently. If you want to work on that with me, you're invited to join the community at CWG Connect. Thanks to today's marvelous technologies, people from all over the world can now connect with each other, share with each other, encourage each other, support each other, remind each other, and walk with each other on the Journey of the Soul. This global community is a loving group of people who have found *Conversations with God* to be a wonderful pathway to awareness. If you would feel supported by joining me there, simply get on any computer and go to www.CWGConnect.com.

Applying This Message to Everyday Life

The tools for Life, or stepping-stones to Awareness, that I have described as Hope, Faith, and Knowing are all (I want to make it clear again) powerful. The first is powerful, the second is even more powerful, and the third is the most powerful.

May I suggest one or two ways to use these tools in your day-to-day encounters with Life?

- Begin to observe your own language around situations and circumstances as you go through life. While it is not necessary (or even recommended) that you watch every word that comes out of your mouth in order to make sure that you "speak appropriately" ("spiritual correctness" is a first cousin to "political correctness," and both can sometimes be a blight upon the land), it is useful to know that words do carry energy (indeed, they are *made up of* energy)—and words that are repeated over and over again tend to create a mind-set that can have a long-term effect on one's thinking, and thus one's Process of Personal Creation.

- Decide to change the words "I hope" to the words "I feel very sure" or even "I have faith" that all will occur in perfect order. Later, as you slowly eliminate "I hope" from your vocabulary, switch from "I feel sure" or "I have faith" to "I know."

- When engaging specifically in the Process of Personal Creation (as opposed to simply talking around the house or chatting with friends), try to consciously invoke the energy of "I know," giving yourself permission to become less and less requiring of particular outcomes and more and more relaxed around whatever outcomes may occur. Let "I know that everything will turn out perfectly" begin to replace "I hope" or "I feel sure" that this or that particular outcome will occur. If you want to know more about the Process of Personal Creation, obtain and read *Happier Than God.*

- Add *feeling* to your words when you say (or even think) them—especially if you are using your words and thoughts in seeking to deliberately experience something. *Conversations with God* says that "feelings are the language of the Soul." Use this language of feelings to communicate to the Universe what it is you wish to experience. If there really is a particular and specific outcome that you have a deep desire to see made manifest in your life, use feelings with your verbalizations. Allow yourself to picture a particular outcome in your mind, then let yourself feel *exactly how you would feel if what you're picturing was happening.* This golden trio of Thought/Visualization/Feeling is the most powerful combination I have ever found to call forth, to magnetize from the Contextual Field of infinite possibilities, specific results and experiences.

- Let go of expectations or requirements when engaging the Process of Personal Creation. Once you set your intention and state your desire, drop any idea that it *has* to happen this way and this way only. Say, "Thank you, God, for this or something better"—and mean it!

- Do an Awareness Exercise at least once every day for the next thirty days. Change the time of day that you do this. Make it, say, ten a.m. on Monday, noon on Tuesday, three p.m. on Wednesday, six in the evening on Thursday, late night on Friday, and so on. Actually *schedule it* on your smartphone. When the alarm goes off, stop whatever you're doing and take an Awareness inventory. Ask yourself, "What am I aware of right here, right now? What was I acutely aware of an hour or two ago? If I wasn't aware of anything specifically then, is there something that I am aware of now as I look back on it?" Stop and breathe deeply. Look around you. See what you see when you look deeply into every single thing offering itself for your attention in the Present. Hear what you hear. Feel into what you feel in the moment. Know what you know about it—and *know* that you know.

Awareness can be cultivated. Give yourself permission to move into your State of Awareness—and then to go beyond it, to a place where you become *aware* that you are Aware.

This is like seeing your reflection in a mirror in a mirror in a mirror. All of us have had that experience. You can do this with your Mind as well. Let yourself—call upon yourself, invite yourself—to be aware of what you are aware of, and *aware* that you are aware of what you are aware of.

This can be a mighty tool in the expanding of your Consciousness. Remember, Awareness cannot be expanded, but Consciousness can. Give yourself permission to be *fully* Conscious as much of the time as possible. The day's events, the to-do lists, the distractions of the moment, the pressures and details and requirements of your life, can be compelling and diverting. It's okay. Just notice it. Soon, you will learn how to *use* the events and pressures and requirements to lead you *to*, rather than away from, your Innermost Awareness, and to feel in fullness, rather than only in part, your Higher Consciousness.

- And speaking of that, obtain and immediately read what I suspect will become one of the most important books of your life: *A Handbook to Higher Consciousness*, by Ken Keyes Jr., who celebrated his Continuation Day a number of years ago, but who left for all of us a gift of unspeakable proportion. This book altered the course of my life. I will be grateful for it forever. It is available from most online bookstores.

11

From the earliest moments of my childhood until I was past fifty I tried to figure out how life worked. That's over a half century of looking at the same question. I did it in ways both casual and concentrated, simple and sophisticated. You would think that all of that effort would have brought me some wisdom, perhaps, or some insight, but no, I wasn't experiencing that. At the age of fifty I felt that I knew little more than I did at fifteen.

I'm not exaggerating.

I had no experience of God, I felt I knew nothing about love, I didn't understand how relationships worked, and all the mysteries of life *remained* mysteries. I had no idea why I was here or what this was all about. I just knew that here I was, plunked down in the middle of all this stuff we call Life on Earth, and I was trying to make the best of it.

But surely there must be some *reason* for all this, or at least some *method* to this madness (as my mother used to say). Yet if there was, I had zero knowledge of either; no conception whatsoever. So, I got up each morning just trying to hook myself on some sort of goal or hope or desire, some sort of activity or experience or project, some sort of purpose or function or objective for the day, anyway, or maybe even the week or the month, if not for my life.

If none of this sounds familiar to you, you're one of the lucky ones. You've known for a while Who You Are and Why You Are and What You Are and Where You Are Going and How Come You're Going There and The Way to Get There.

These are not small questions, and if you've had answers that have satisfied you, good for you, and God bless you. I'd turned the corner toward sixty and had none of them.

Then, suddenly, I had all of them.

As you can imagine, this shook me to the core. Could I believe what I was all at once given? Was it even functional or applicable in daily life? Did it have any on-the-ground value at all?

I have found that the answer to all three questions is yes. Emphatically, *yes!* But I had to really "get" and really embrace and really *use* something I'd heard in my conversations with God first, or none of the other pieces of the puzzle would fall into place, none of life's mysteries would be resolved.

This is surely one of the most important things I've ever heard in my life. It's one of the most critical bits of data about life I've ever encountered. It knocked down—*finally* it knocked down—the door. It didn't answer all my questions, but it resolved all my problems. It made life much easier. I am talking here about . . .

CWG CORE MESSAGE #20

Life functions within a Be-Do-Have paradigm. Most people have this backward, imagining that first one must "have" things in order to "do" things, thus to "be" what they wish to be. Reversing this process is the fastest way to experience mastery in living.

When I say that most people have this formula for life backward, I am not kidding. I observed this in myself for the first fifty-three years of my life.

Book 1 in the *Conversations with God* dialogue, and then later, *Book 3*, brought me to a place of great clarity about this very quickly. I was reminded in *Book 3* that most people believe Life works along these general lines, or through this general progression: Have-Do-Be.

Folks believe that if they "have" a thing (more time, money, love—whatever), then they can finally "do" a thing (write a book, take up a hobby, go on vacation, buy a home, enter a relationship), thus allowing them to "be" a thing (happy, peaceful, content, or in love).

In actuality, they are reversing the Be-Do-Have paradigm. As I said, I did this, too. It's the way I was told that life worked.

Getting Things in the Right Order

In the universe as it really is (as opposed to how we think it is), "havingness" does not produce "beingness," but the other way around. First you must "be" the thing called "happy" (or "peaceful," or "content," or "in love," or whatever), then you start "doing" things from this place of beingness—and soon you discover that what you are doing winds up bringing you the things you've always wanted to "have."

So the formula is Be-Do-Have, not Have-Do-Be.

The way to set this creative process (and that's what this is . . . the Process of Personal Creation) into motion is to look at what it is you want to "have," ask yourself what you think you would "be" if you "had" that, then go right straight to *being*. Start there, rather than trying to get there.

In this way you reverse the way you've been using the Be-Do-Have paradigm—in actuality, set it right—and work *with*, rather than *against*, the creative power of the Universe.

Here is a short way of stating this principle: How life works for you is very much a matter of what and how you are *being*.

Book 3 illustrates this by inviting us to think of a person who just knows that if he could only have a little more time, a little more money, or a little more love, he'd be truly happy. He thinks there is a direct connection between his "not being very happy" right now and his not having the time, money, or love he wants.

Now, think of a person who is "being" happy in every moment. Isn't it interesting to observe that she seems to have time to do everything that's really important, all the money that's needed, and enough love to last a lifetime? She finds she has everything that she needs to "be happy" . . . by "being happy" to begin with!

Something for the Refrigerator

It turns out that deciding *ahead of time* what you choose to be *can often produce that in your experience*. "To be, or not to be. That is the question," as Shakespeare put it. Happiness is a state of mind. And like all states of mind, it reproduces itself in physical form.

Like much of what's here, that's a statement from *CWG* Book 3 that's fit for a refrigerator magnet: "All states of mind reproduce themselves."

But you might ask, how can you "be" happy to begin with, or "be" *anything* you are seeking to be—more prosperous, for instance, or more loved—if you do not have what you think you need in order to "be" that?

The answer is to act as if you do, because you *do, and simply don't know it.* This is the most important part of the "secret formula." You already have happiness, you already have contentment, you already have love, you already have prosperity, peace, joy, wisdom, and every other aspect of Divinity, all stored within you. It is Who You Are. These things are Who You Are. You do not have to find them elsewhere; you merely have to *draw them out from your Self.* You merely have to *be* Who You Really Are.

This is what is meant by "starting" where you've been wishing you could "end up." It is a case of *knowing* that you are the *source* of these things, not the *seeker* of them. It is about Awareness.

What it is *not* about is trying to "trick" yourself with an approach to Life that some have called "Fake it until you make it." You can't really be "faking" when you are "being" something. Your actions must arise sincerely. *Everything you do, do out of sincerity, or the benefit of the action is lost.* Natural Law requires the Body, Mind, and Spirit to be united and aligned in thought, word, and deed for the Process of Personal Creation to work.

Sincerely Experiencing Sincerity

So how can you "be" happy if you are not sincerely feeling happy? How can you "be" prosperous if you are not sincerely feeling prosperous? How can you "be" loved if you are not sincerely feeling loved?

You must sincerely *experience that you are.* You must experience that you are all the things that you are not sincerely feeling. And the fastest way to experience something you are not sincerely feeling is to *cause another to experience it because of you.*

This is a great secret. It may be the greatest secret of Life. Causing *another* to experience what *you* wish to experience makes you

Aware that you are the source, and not the seeker, of that experience. This shifts the whole paradigm of your life. Instead of trying to find what you want, you try to find ways to give away what you want.

Yet how can you give away what you do not have?

By knowing that you *do* have it.

And how can you come to know that?

Ah, circular logic: By giving it away!

Therefore, if you choose to be happy, cause another to be happy. If you choose to be prosperous, cause another to prosper. If you choose to be loved, cause another to be loved.

It is as simple as that. And as *powerful* as that.

Do this sincerely—not because you seek personal gain, but because you really want the other person to have a particular experience—and all the things you give away will be experienced by you.

Again, one last time: How? Why? Because the very act of giving something away causes you to experience that you have it to give away. This principle has been put into three words in the *Conversations with God* books: Be the Source.

Which Comes First?

Since you cannot give to another something you do not now have, when you are being the Source in the life of another of everything you want, your Mind comes to a new conclusion, a New Thought, about you—namely, that you must have this, *or you could not be giving it away.*

Yet, you might say, if you can be the Source of something in the life of another, why can't you call it forth in your *own* life?

You can, and I am giving you the process right there.

Yes, you might respond, but why do I first have to give it to another? Why can't I give it to myself first?

The answer, *CWG* says, has to do with human psychology, and the story we have been taught about ourselves. In brief, we've been taught that we are unworthy. Therefore it is very hard to allow ourselves to give to ourselves. We can easily see and acknowledge, on the other hand, that others are worthy and deserve whatever help we can give them. The trick, then, is to give to others frequently and intentionally.

Yet you can't do this as a means or a method of getting the same thing for yourself, of obtaining something you lack, because the very motivation behind the process creates a sponsoring thought that will continue to generate your reality.

No, when you give to others you must do so from a place of knowing and demonstrating that you already have that. If you can't do that, then just don't think about it. Don't analyze it or calculate things. Just give away what you want if you see others needing it. Do it spontaneously. Surprise yourself. Reach into your wallet and just give that twenty-dollar bill. You'll realize next month that it didn't hurt you at all. It fact, it made you feel great. And fascinatingly enough, it was just a week later that you got a sales bonus. Or that tax refund check you forgot about. Or that call from the lawyer back East about an inheritance.

And then you'll wonder: Which came first, the chicken or the egg?

It's All About Training the Mind

You can train your Mind in exactly the same way you train your hair. As you show your Mind a New Thought about you over and over again through your demonstration of it, it becomes your experience. You start "being" that more and more. And once you start "being" a thing, you've engaged the gears of the most powerful creation machine in the universe—your Awareness. You've come to *know* what is really so, what is really true about you, by *demonstrating* what is true (appearances to the contrary notwithstanding).

When you think about it, the simplicity of this process is remarkable—and obvious. You know very well that you never feel happier than when you are making someone else happy. Your life has taught you that you never experience prosperity more than when you share with others. And you are very clear that the most profound and blessed feeling of being loved is yours when you have been the direct cause of another person feeling loved.

The messengers of all the world's great religions have taught this principle precisely, each in their own way. The message with which I am personally most familiar: "Do unto others as you would have it done unto you."

This is not simply a sweet saying or a nice aphorism; it is an explicit instruction about *how Life works.* This is not about morals, this is about mechanics.

When you know this, you are ready to achieve mastery in living.

APPLYING THIS MESSAGE TO EVERYDAY LIFE

Never have I found any more powerful, practical, or easy-to-use tool for spiritual and joyful living than the Be-Do-Have paradigm.

It is a spiritual tool because it calls upon the spiritual Awareness that resides within each of us, and allows us to demonstrate that we are clear about our spiritual identity. There is nothing in Life more spiritual than experiencing Divinity flowing through you.

It is a practical tool because it works "on the ground" in real life, and immediately. Not in a week or two or a month or so, but in the very moment the tool is employed.

Here are some suggestions on how you might use the Be-Do-Have paradigm in your own day-to-day experience:

- Choose ahead of time how you want to "be" in every given circumstance that you know with certainty will repeatedly arise in your life. For instance, if you are a regular traveler, you can know for a certainty that eventually, on some trip your flight is going to be delayed. If you're married and your spouse has a tendency to be late for appointments, you know for a certainty that there's going to be another time when your spouse is going to be late for something you really needed him to be on time for. How do you decide to be in those situations?

- If something occurs in your life that is unexpected, stop for just a moment and ask yourself, "How do I want to 'be' with regard to this?" Then, step into that State of Being. This is a creative process rather than a reactive process. Remember, Life was *designed* as a process of creation, not a process of reaction. And what you are being invited by Life to do in every golden moment of Now is to recreate yourself anew in the next grandest version of the greatest vision ever you held about Who You Are. So, if you unexpectedly find yourself in a stressful situation—a minor car accident, the loss of your house keys, a friend who you never thought would do so lets you down—you can use this as an opportunity to ask yourself in that moment how you want to "be" with regard to what is going on, and then step into that.

• Make a list of five things you wish you had more of in your life right now. These could be physical things or experiences. Then be "on the lookout" for people who clearly have even less of these things than you seem to. Give these things to them. Do it at once, without thinking or calculating or analyzing. Just *give it away*. When their face lights up, observe how incredible it feels to notice that *you had that to give them*. Let that feeling inform your sense of Self.

Now you might say, "Okay, I can see how this might be able to work with abundance or love, but how would it work with physical things, like a better place to live? Say that what I really want is a better place to live. How do I manifest *that* by giving another person a better place to live?"

I remember that I had a lady in one of my weekly classes in Practical Metaphysics that I taught years ago who asked this exact question. We'll call her Sue.

Sue and her husband had been living in the same small apartment for years, working hard, both of them, saving their money so that they could one day afford the home of their dreams.

"How can your theory work for me?" she wanted to know, and she wasn't too friendly about it. It was her frustration speaking, I knew.

"Are you willing for it to?" I asked. "Are you willing for the theory to work?"

"Look," she said, "there's no way in the world that I can 'be the Source' of a better home for someone else. We can't even do it for ourselves. Your little 'process' will not work."

"Are you willing for it to?" I asked again.

She looked me straight in the eye.

"Okay," she said. "I'm willing. But it can't work on something like this."

"If you say so," I said.

"What's that supposed to mean?" she asked.

"It means that as you speak it, so will it be done unto you."

"I love it. More platitudes. You gotta love this guy."

"Sweetheart, I know that you're frustrated with your life. I understand that. But the Universe cannot give you what you say it cannot. That's the rule. That's the . . . what do they say on that TV show? . . . that's the Prime Directive. So if you say this process won't work, guess what? It won't work. You're putting too many obstacles in the way. Your energy either creates obstacles or opportunities. You get to choose."

Sue became silent for a moment, then:

"Okay, fair enough. My husband says I'm a continual pessimist, too. So I'll try to give that up."

"Terrific. Now, are you willing for this process that I've been talking about to work?"

"Yes, I really am. I really want it to."

"Do you think it can?"

"When I think positively, I suppose it can."

"Good. The trick is, don't ask how. Just move into willingness."

"Okay. I got it."

ONE WEEK LATER . . .

Now, are you holding on to your hat? Sue came back to the very next class—I'm talking one week later—brimming with excitement. She couldn't wait to share with the group.

"It was Thursday night, I think," she began. "I was reading the paper and it said that volunteers were wanted for a project that was going to be launched last weekend to put a family that had been burned out of their house into a new home in three days! There's a group called Habitat for Humanity that does this. And they were putting out a call for volunteers. They said that anyone and everyone was welcome.

"You go to a building site and they tell you exactly what to do. If you can use a hammer or carry a piece of wood or shine a just-installed faucet you can be of help. And I thought, 'My gosh, this is a way *that I would give someone else what I want*— namely, a nice place to live!' So my hubby and I went down there on Saturday.

"There must have been a hundred people there. We put up an entire house in three days. And then they came around with a pledge sheet on a clipboard and asked us if we would be willing to donate a small amount each month to pay for materials for Habitat for Humanity projects like this elsewhere. And we said 'Sure,' and so we found a way to be the Source of better housing for another, right then and there."

The group was amazed at the synchronicity, but Sue was nowhere near finished.

"Wait! There's more," she exclaimed. "On Monday night we got a call from my uncle George. He said that he had been offered a big promotion by his company—an important upper management position had suddenly opened up—and the job was across the country, but it was too good to pass up, so he had to move with his family and wondered what he would do with his four-bedroom house.

"He wanted to know if we would 'house-sit' for him for a few months while he figured it all out, or better yet, if we would be interested in renting it from him. I told him we could never afford to rent a place like that and still put money aside for a home of our own.

"He said, 'What if you rented with an option to buy? I'll give you a good rental rate, and every penny will go toward the purchase price if you decide you like the house and want to buy it. Plus, I'll carry the paper for you. You don't have to go to the bank to qualify for a mortgage. You're family, and I know you're good for it. Besides, we'd rather have the house go to someone we know and love, not to strangers."

Sue was now breathless when she said, "We move in *next month!*"

The class cheered wildly.

And the angels sang.

And God?

Well . . . God just smiled a lot.

12

It seems to me that life continues to be an unfolding mystery for nearly everyone. There have been, and are now, true Masters living in ongoing peace and harmony (no matter what was or is happening). So we know that reaching such a level of personal and spiritual development is possible. Still, I have seen very few people achieve it "in a flash."

My observation is that for most of us life continues to reveal itself one layer at a time. That certainly has been the case with me. Even my Conversations with God took place over a period of years.

What I notice is that the world is still full of seekers. Despite all the wisdom that's out there, despite all the data in all the encyclopedias, despite all the spiritual messages in all the sacred books of all the world's religions, despite all the deep insights offered to us by the world's philosophies—despite all of it, we still have no idea about many things regarding the life that we're living. So we search for guideposts. We search for insights. We look to each other for suggestions on how to get through all of this, on how to get by, on how to get on. And if we're lucky, we have a relationship—a *personal* relationship—with God.

If we're lucky, we have the ability to relate with this Source of

Wisdom that exists in the universe. If we're very fortunate, we are able to interact with this source, to experience it as a friend, to use it as a resource.

I have been lucky enough to do that, and so I have been given spiritual roadmaps and many guideposts that have helped me along the way, and that have made me more comfortable with myself and with the whole life experience as I move into my seventh decade than I have ever been before.

I've had a chance to observe and to remember a great many things, and I've dared myself to put it all together over these most recent fifteen years of my life and to create a holistic approach to my day-to-day experience.

Putting Together the "Fractured Self"

We've heard a lot in the past few decades about "holistic living." Twenty-five years ago, I was even the managing editor of a weekly newspaper in San Diego called *Holistic Living News*. The dictionary defines holistic as "characterized by comprehension of the parts of something as intimately interconnected and explicable only by reference to the whole."

What?

I wonder who wrote *that* definition! If I were defining the word, I would simply say that it means "a whole systems approach to anything."

Living holistically means, to me, living in a way that the whole of who I am is expressed and experienced as I interact with the whole of everyone and everything else, rather than part of me interacting with *part* of someone or something else—which is how I notice that I and most people most often live.

Many of us have had fleeting moments when we had a *felt sense of oneness* with another person, or with every other person for that matter—and even with every other *thing*.

If you have had such a moment once or twice, you may recall it as a rapid passage through sheer bliss. The *experience* of Oneness, as opposed to the conceptualization of Oneness, is often an astonishment. The Mind doesn't know exactly what to make of it, or where to go with it. (Which is no doubt why it pulls us back into Separateness as fast as it can. You have to understand, the ego thinks our very *existence* is threatened when we experience Oneness.)

All my life I've wanted to know how to live as a whole person—which is the first step to experiencing Oneness in all of Life. I experienced myself in the past as being, in a sense, "fractured." That is, a part of me was going in one direction, a part of me was going in another, and a third part of me was trying to go both ways at once! I've felt "torn" many times in my life.

This fractured sense of who I am is, I have no doubt, what caused me to live a life that until most recent years was anything but smooth, anything but easy, anything but peaceful. Not that I was having a particularly terrible time of it, mind you, but my life certainly had more challenges, more disappointments, and more deeply unhappy moments than it needed to have. And, I am sorry to say, more moments in which I made other people deeply unhappy than I ever imagined it would.

Yet, as I mentioned before, life is meant to be happy, and most of the time there really should be no reason for it to be otherwise. Certainly, there is no reason for life to be an experience of *ongoing* unhappiness. But when we are living as fractured people, trying to serve two masters and three agendas and four different thoughts that four different people have about who they think we are supposed to be, life can become very stressful and unhappy indeed.

So the invitation of Life is to "unfracture" ourselves, to become whole once again.

Terrific Guidelines

We came into this physical experience as a whole and perfect being, but we have allowed Life to pull us apart, and in some cases *rip* us apart.

So now it's about returning to that place of Original Wholeness, and then coming from there in all of our interactions. And I don't know about you, but I have needed guidelines, as I said a moment ago, to help me get to that place, and to assist me in living from that place. So I was delighted when *Conversations with God* presented me with . . .

> *CWG* CORE MESSAGE #19
>
> The Three Core Concepts of Holistic Living are *Honesty, Awareness,* and *Responsibility.* Live according to these precepts and self-anger will disappear from your life.

I didn't even realize that self-anger was part of my life until I was about halfway through it. Somewhere between my 35th and 40th birthday it became apparent to me that I was really not very happy with myself—and that, yes, I was actually *angry* with myself about many things.

Mostly, I was angry with myself for being the person I was showing up as in the world. Not that I was such a terrible, awful, rotten human being, but I sure wasn't experienced by other people in the ways that I thought of myself. In fact, I held an idea about who I am that was *wholly different* from the experience that people around me reported that they were having of me.

"Nobody understands me," I would tell myself and occasionally complain to a few friends. "In fact, I may be the most misunderstood person I know."

Now, none of this may sound familiar to you, or a lot of it may. But I can promise you that what I'm describing about my own experience is not unique. So I began searching for guideposts, for suggestions, for insights into how I could literally pull myself together. And I have to be honest with you, I rejected most of what religions and philosophies and psychology was telling me, because it all felt so simplistic.

Then I encountered the *Conversations with God* experience. And what *it* said, too, felt simplistic. Even, in some cases, unsophisticated and naive. But in this case, I decided to listen, because the experience itself was so remarkable, so spiritually opening. So I allowed myself to take its messages in, to consider the possibility that there was more here than meets the eye, that what might appear on the surface to be very simple was, in fact, offering me an opportunity to look at life and to experience myself more deeply, more richly, and with more appreciation of the true complexity of what, on the surface, appeared to be simplistic.

That's particularly true of the 19th Core Message of the *CWG* dialogues. On the surface of it, it seems to be so obvious and so simple, almost embarrassingly naive. Of *course* honesty, awareness, and responsibility are important attributes in anyone's life. That's pretty easy to understand.

But when I looked beneath the apparent simplicity of the message, I saw and found more than I originally imagined was there. Let's look at these three core concepts, one by one.

Honesty

One thing I've discovered in my life is that it's not easy to be honest. I thought it was, but I was wrong. I've also observed that other people have apparently discovered the same thing.

We have become fractured selves because we have learned to break ourselves apart into little bits and pieces. Some of those pieces are the truth about us in the many areas of our lives, and some of those pieces are the shields that we put up to stop people from knowing the truth. Sometimes, to stop *ourselves* from knowing the truth. (Or having to admit it to ourselves.)

The irony of the human experience is that many parents teach their children to tell the truth, explaining to them that honesty is a very important character trait, all the while modeling lack of honesty—not only in their direct dealings with their children, but in other areas of their life that their children witness. Children hear their mother lie about having a previous social obligation to avoid going to a party she knows will be boring; they hear their father call in sick to work when in fact he's going to a baseball game. Thus, parents teach their children that they should be dishonest in order to avoid disapproval or punishment or having to do something they don't want to do. It doesn't take children very long to get the picture.

So honesty has become a real challenge for many people, because we've learned that—contrary to what we've been told—honesty doesn't always pay. Too *often* it doesn't pay. Too often it produces exactly the opposite result of that for which we had hoped. So we learn to be dishonest. Hopefully, not about terribly important or really big things. But sometimes, yes, once in a while, even about those.

The plan is not to be honest or dishonest but to get through the moment. It's our survival instinct that kicks in, and it is that instinct that drives the engine of the human experience. We learn to be honest if and when it helps us to survive, and to be dishonest for precisely the same reason.

So there is more here than meets the eye with regard to this "honesty thing." There is courage involved, and not a little of it. There is determination involved, and not a small amount. There is willingness involved, and not in minute measure. We have to be willing to take the flak that we most assuredly will receive if we decide to be honest about everything with everyone all the time.

We have to be resolved to tell the truth, no matter what. This requires jaw-setting resolve. We have to have the strength to endure whatever consequences may ensue from our determination and our willingness to be honest at all costs.

In a couple of chapters we'll be exploring this business of honesty in more depth as we look at the Five Levels of Truth Telling. But for now, just know that if you think that this is a simplistic idea, a simple, almost naive instruction, about how to live a holistic life, you are mistaken. It is anything but.

So let's just be honest about it: *Honesty ain't for sissies.* It takes a very high level of commitment to one's own growth.

Must We Be Honest . . . Always?

And let's explore *that* for a moment. Is "honesty" really about growth? What does it matter if we are totally honest about everything all the time? Who cares? And if it hurts at least as often as it helps, how can it even be justified in every case? Maybe sometimes dishonesty is the best policy. Could that be true?

If you have questions about all this, as most people do, I want to recommend the wonderful writings of Brad Blanton. He's a brilliant if unconventional psychologist who wrote a book called *Radical Honesty.* I co-authored a book with him a number of years ago titled *Honest to God.* In it we discuss—"argue back and forth" might be a better description—whether honesty in every single case with every single person was, in fact, the best policy. You might find that dialogue interesting.

I'm not going to get into all that here, because there's a whole book's worth there. But I will let you know that I agree with Dr. Blanton that there are very, very few instances in this life when anything less than total honesty is beneficial. (Actually, I believe Brad says there are *none*.)

This doesn't mean that I practice total honesty in every single minute with every single person; it means that there are very rare instances when it is not beneficial to do so. Even having said that, I find myself often "protecting myself" by saying less than "the truth, the whole truth, and nothing but the truth, so help me God." I find other people doing it, too. A lot.

So I realize now that to live as whole human beings, to bring an end to the ongoing expression of our fractured selves, we would benefit as a species from working more diligently on what might seem to be a relatively simple task: Just. Tell. The. Truth.

Let me say one more thing about this, if I may. It seems to me that the only way that I could find it easy to tell the truth *always* would be if I imagined that I could not possibly be hurt by any of the consequences of doing so. And it seems to me that the idea that I could not possibly be hurt rests within the larger concept that I have of myself with regard to who I am. If I see myself as an aspect and an individuation of the Divine, I will move through life with a deep *awareness* of both my identity and the implications of that identity. And that brings us to our next exploration.

Awareness

We've already talked about awareness in an earlier portion of this text. Awareness is a state of being that can become, ultimately, a state of mind. The pathway to awareness contains, as we have previously explored, three stopping points: Hope, Faith, and Knowing. With regard to the discussion at hand, my present state of awareness will cause me to either "hope" that my telling the truth will not hurt me, "have faith" that it will not, or "know" that I can't be hurt or damaged in any way.

If I rest in the state of full awareness of who I really am—and for that matter, of who everyone else really is—I will never shrink from being honest. There would be no reason to. So awareness is surely a bigger key to holistic living than I might have originally thought. Awareness is also used in the context of this discussion as being sensitive to the experience of others, and especially to the experience that I may be stimulating others to create.

It seems to me that if we are living holistically we are "taking in" the whole of the present moment, and of every moment in which we find ourselves. We listen not only to what people are saying but to what they are feeling. We watch not only what *we* are saying but what *we* are feeling. And we become attuned to the fact that if we think we can hide our feelings from others, we are most often wrong about that.

So awareness is about tuning in to the Whole Moment and all that it contains for you and for everyone else experiencing it. This also takes courage, determination, and willingness, because there are many elements and aspects of each of our life's moments that we would rather ignore. They make us uncomfortable, or they reveal too much about us—or they reveal too much about others. "TMI," as we are fond of saying. We don't want Too Much Information about others or about the moment we are presently encountering.

So how do we experience full awareness if full awareness brings us too much information? That becomes a fascinating inquiry. And it lays out in clear terms the challenge faced by most of us as we move through life.

In my own case, I have decided that allowing myself to be open to all the data, all the experience, all the emotion, all the feeling, all of the information that all of the moments of my life hold is the only way to live. Yet, as with honesty, I don't claim to live that way all of the time. But I know that it is the way to go.

And as with honesty, there is much more to "awareness" than meets the eye. Because the more that I know and the more that I am aware of, the more I am responsible for what is going on right here, right now, for how it is occurring, for the role that I am playing in causing it to occur in a particular way, and for the outcomes that proceed from that. All of which brings us to the last of these three little words that seemed so simple just a while ago.

Responsibility

Unless we are willing to take full and complete, absolute and total responsibility for everything in our lives and for the experiences that we may have stimulated others to create in their lives, we cannot live a holistic life. We can pretend to, we can act as if we are, but we cannot actually do it. We must accept the fact that we are at cause in the matter of our lives.

I observe that when people learn to take full and complete responsibility for their lives, those lives change. The decisions and choices that people make change. The actions and undertakings they embrace change. Even their thinking changes.

Conversations with God tells us that there are no victims and no villains. The implication of that statement is that we are all responsible for everything that is happening to us, and that has happened *through* us, in our lives.

People's first reaction to this statement when I share it at lectures is to run from it. Folks want to bring up immediately all the instances in their lives when things happened to them for which they were *not* responsible. Yet we are talking here not physically, but metaphysically.

At a metaphysical level, which is the only level from which we can proceed in our lives if we choose to live holistically, we are responsible—and must be, given our true identity—for every event, situation, circumstance, and outcome in our life. We are co-creating in a giant collaboration with all other souls, but that partnership does not relieve us of responsibility for the role that *we* have played in every event and condition. Including, at a metaphysical level, the drawing to ourselves of exactly the right people, places, and circumstances that allow us to re-create ourselves anew in the next grandest version of the greatest vision ever we held about who we are.

The most vivid example of this that I can think of would be a person such as Jesus Christ. When we explore his life and his death, we have to ask ourselves, *At what level was he responsible for what he was experiencing?* Was he the victim of his own crucifixion, or at some very high spiritual and metaphysical level was he at cause in the matter?

If we accept that he was at cause in the matter—that nothing happened *to* him, but everything happened *through* him—then we must ask ourselves: *Have we been at cause in the matter, at a very high spiritual or metaphysical level, regarding every "crucifixion" in our own lives, however big or small?*

If we say that Jesus was responsible for his crucifixion but that we are not responsible for ours, then we are declaring a metaphysical untruth: That we are not all one, that some of us are superior to others of us—and that some of us are, perhaps, Divine, while others of us are "only human."

These statements amount to a denial of Ultimate Reality with regard to your personal identity and mine. And so we are left with no place to go but to be responsible for everything our life has brought us and has sent *from* us to others.

So we see that honesty, awareness, and responsibility may sound simplistic as ingredients for holistic living, yet they are anything but that. Still, they do not have to be experienced as a burden.

The master does not experience these three elements of a holistic life as millstones but rather as gemstones—wonderful opportunities to move fully into the richness of that expression of life for which all of us came to the Earth.

Indeed, it has been my experience that in the moments when I am honest, when I am just as fully aware as I can be, and when I am willing to experience my own high level of responsibility for everything that ever went on, is now happening, and ever will happen, I feel more free, more joyful, more powerful, and more excited to be alive than I ever have before. So burdens these are not. Gifts and marvelous tools they are. And that's what's true about that.

Applying This Message to Everyday Life

Here are some suggestions on how you can apply Core Message #19 in your everyday life:

- Make a list of the last four things that you can remember being dishonest about with anybody. Look to see what it would take for you to go to that person or those people and clean it up. Ask yourself why you would not do this. Then call or contact those people and tell them that you are engaging in a personal process of spiritual expansion and you would like to clear something up about a statement you have made in the past that was not totally forthcoming. Give yourself permission to do this. Do not worry about the consequences. You will feel so much better for it in the end that you will get in touch with the Miracle of Honesty.

- Remember a time when you were involved with other people and were aware of the impact of something negative or hurtful that was said or done, either by you or by others, and ignored it. Look to see how it felt in your stomach to have watched that moment pass without responding to your awareness of what it contained. Make a decision in your life to never create such an experience again.

- Think of three things in your life that have occurred in your relationship with others for which you denied responsibility because you truly felt that you were not responsible. Upon re-examination of those memories, explore with yourself if there is any way at all that you *could* have been, at a high spiritual or metaphysical level, responsible for the event or circumstance. Write a three- to five-paragraph description of what that exploration has brought to your consciousness.

- As you move through the next three days of your life, place before your mind a single question: What if I was responsible for everything that's happening in my life and in the life of those with whom I am now interacting, without reservation and without limitation? Is

there any way in which I would change or alter how I
am moving through this moment?

• Ask yourself: At what level, if any, am I responsible for
the feelings and responses of others? Write down your
response to this question in a little notebook that you
can look at weeks from now when you finish reading
this book.

• Finally, ask a remarkable metaphysical question: Who
is responsible for the content of this book that you are
now reading? Have I put it here? Or did *you* cause it, at
a very high spiritual and metaphysical level, to be put
here *by* me, and then to be brought to your attention?
Who is doing what here? Who is the magician and
what is this trick all about?

13

The interesting outcome of asking God to explain to you exactly how life works is that God *will* explain it to you.

The interesting outcome of *that* is that you'll never again be able to see life as you saw it before.

And the interesting outcome of *that* is that the whole of your experience from morning to night will change.

The wonder and the excitement of the *Conversations with God* material is precisely this: Read from cover to cover, from book to book, it presents us with an entirely new cosmology. A brand-new construction. A wholly different structure supporting the larger experience that we call life itself.

This structure is not only different, it is far more suited to who we are as emerging intelligent entities in the cosmic community of sentient beings. We are far more than our Old Story about ourselves reveals to us about us.

I think that last sentence is important enough to deserve repeating. I *said* . . . We are far more than our Old Story about ourselves reveals to us about us.

What the *Conversations with God* material does is offer us a New Story. It gives us another way of looking at life, a way that supports us, rather than defeats us, in experiencing and expressing exactly Who We Are, and that serves the agenda that we came to Earth to complete.

And of all the books in the *CWG* series, none was more impacting on me than *Communion with God*. This book was delivered in the first-person voice of God, with no questions or interactions from me at all. It constitutes, in essence, God's message to the world as we approach our future in the twenty-first century.

An Extraordinary Claim

I know it is very brazen of me to suggest that God has spoken to the world by this means, but I have no other choice. I can only share with the global audience that has found its way to the *Conversations with God* material exactly what my experience has been and what I have been given to bring to humanity.

Even that statement—"what I have been given to bring to humanity"—sounds presumptuous. When I see the words on the computer screen before me, I have to force myself to leave them there. I have to force myself not to hit Delete and change everything that I have come to this book to say. Or even to publish a book at all. Every time I do, I fight the same internal battle with myself. *What if I imagined this entire thing?*

As you may know if you have read the material, I asked God this very question. God's answer?

"*What would be the difference?* Do you not see that I could just as easily work through your imagination as anything else? I will bring you the *exact* right thoughts, words or feelings, at any given moment, suited precisely to the purpose at hand, using one device, or several.

"You will know these words are from Me because you, of your

own accord, have never spoken so clearly. Had you already spoken so clearly on these questions, you would not be asking them."

"Well, then," I asked, "to whom does God communicate? Are there special people? Are there special times?"

The reply I received:

"All people are special, and all moments are golden. There is no person and there is no time one more special than another. Many people choose to believe that God communicates in special ways and only with special people. This removes the mass of the people from responsibility for hearing My message, much less *receiving* it (which is another matter), and allows them to take someone else's word for everything. You don't *have* to listen to Me, for you've already decided that others have heard from Me on every subject, and you have *them* to listen to.

"By listening to what *other* people think they heard Me say, *you* don't have to *think at all*.

"This is the biggest reason for most people turning from My messages on a personal level. If you acknowledge that you are receiving My messages *directly*, then you are responsible for interpreting them. It is far safer and much easier to accept the interpretation of others (even others who have lived two thousand years ago) than seek to interpret the message you may very well be receiving in this moment now.

"Yet I invite you to a new form of communication with God. A *two-way* communication. In truth, it is you who have invited Me. For I have come to you, in this form, right now, in *answer to your call*."

The point of this exchange is the God is talking to *all of us,* all the time. That point is made elsewhere in CWG material as well. And so I hope this will remove the shock or sting from my own statement that God is talking to me. I am not alone in this category. Everyone is having *Conversations with God* throughout life, perhaps calling them something else.

You Be the Judge

The best part of all this is that you don't have to accept the notion that an actual conversation with God took place in order to receive benefit from the books. It's not even necessary for you to accept the notion that a God exists at all. All I invite you to do is read the material that has come through and let the message speak for itself.

Millions of people have done so, and millions have considered the material extraordinarily insightful, wonderfully worthwhile, and hugely beneficial to their spiritual growth. I am humbled by this result, because I am clear that I had nothing to do with it. I merely took dictation.

With that as a backdrop, let me say that I consider *Communion with God* to be one of the most revolutionary spiritual messages ever placed before humanity. The bottom line of the message is that *all of life is an illusion.*

This is something we have heard before. It's not what you would call brand-new information. What *is* new is that we now have, in this text, a deep and rich *explanation* of the illusion, aspect by aspect, part by part. Here we are told how the illusion works and why it has been put into place to begin with.

It is as if we have been taken behind the curtain, into the backstage area of the Greatest Magician in the universe. We now understand the magician's tricks, how they are done, and why we enjoy them so much.

Before we go further into this, however, I want to eliminate the thought that you may have that all God is doing here is playing a game with us. We are not God's playthings, and God is not toying with us. What we are doing here upon the Earth is far more sacred than our dancing with illusion might suggest at first glance.

We are "up to" something very special here. We are about the business of expressing Divinity. We'll look at more of this as we move through this book. For now, let's get to the foundational thought underlying all of this. Here is . . .

CWG CORE MESSAGE #18

The human race lives within a precise set of illusions. The Ten Illusions of Humans are *Need Exists, Failure Exists, Disunity Exists, Insufficiency Exists, Requirement Exists, Judgment Exists, Condemnation Exists, Conditionality Exists, Superiority Exists,* and *Ignorance Exists.*

These illusions are meant to serve humanity, but it must learn how to use them.

What God is telling us here is that nothing we look at is what we think it is. We live in a world of physical reality for sure, but all of the *meaning* that it has for us is meaning that we have created. To repeat: Every person, place, situation, circumstance, or event is what we *think* it is. And we are creating our meanings as we go along, for a particular and sacred reason.

All the meanings in our lives arise out of the Contextual Field in which they are held. Context creates everything, and we have placed ourselves within a Contextual Field so massive as to include a universe of universes, and so majestic as to express itself in the wonders of a butterfly and the beauty of a rose and the glory of a night sky—to say nothing of the magnificence of a human being.

All of this, every bit of it, is the placement into physicality of Divinity Itself. God has chosen to know Itself not merely conceptually but experientially, and has created physicality as the means by which to do this. You have heard about this before, but now let's take a look at some things you may not have heard before. Let's explore some of these illusions that God and we have created.

It Starts Here

The first illusion of humans is that Need Exists. We had to create the illusion that Need Exists in order for us to create the possibility of creation itself. There would be no need to create anything if we didn't need anything.

The fact is that we do *not* need anything, because we are Divinity Itself. Yet that which is Divine yearned to experience every aspect of Itself, including Its grandest aspect, which is the power to create, the ability to manifest, the joy of producing wonder and glory as far as the eye can see, across and beyond every horizon, past the limitations and boundaries of the most expansive imagination.

The physical "reality" that we imagine ourselves to be observing is nothing more than the limitless presence of God in the unfathomable expanse of the All of Everything.

Now let me explain to you why the illusions are necessary, and why this is particularly true of the first illusion, the idea that Need Exists.

Imagine that you have seen a movie that you loved from start to finish. From the first moment of the story until the final frame of the film, you found yourself in bliss and ecstasy, wonder and excitement, joy and happiness beyond anything you've ever experienced before.

This is the most magnificent, the most special motion picture that you have ever watched. It's so wonderful that you turn to everyone around you when the film is over and say, "Let's watch it again!" And you do exactly that. And then, in the days ahead, one more time. And then, as time goes by, more often still, until you can recite the dialogue verbatim and describe the scenes in terms incredibly precise.

Now imagine that you never get tired of watching this movie—except for one thing. You know the plot, you know how it ends, you know every line of dialogue, you know every scene within it. Nothing can surprise you, nothing can amaze you, nothing can create quite the impact that it created the first time you experienced it.

So even with your very favorite movie, you will finally put it on a shelf some place and decide that you won't watch it again for a while. It may even be a few years before you take it off your shelf, blow the dust off the cover, pop it into the player, and view it once more. If you're lucky, you will have forgotten some of the key parts. If you're lucky, you will encounter many of its moments as if for the first time. You'll say to those around you, "Oh, yeah! I forgot about this part! Wait until you see this!"

Then the joy of what you are seeing is actually *doubled*. You can't *wait* to see it again—*even though you know exactly what's going to happen*. Now the details that you have *not* forgotten are exciting to you, actually *enticing* you to watch everything again, to *experience everything again*.

But for a moment, you had to forget that you've seen this before. For a moment, your Mind had to entertain the idea that at least some of the scenes, some of the dialogue, some of the actions and outcomes were brand new. Or at least *felt* brand new. We've all had this experience. We've all watched a favorite old movie and had exactly this encounter.

I've just explained to you why the Ten Illusions of Humans exist in the way that they do.

The part of you that is Divine delights in the adventure once again, in the glory once again, in the joy once again, in the thrill and the excitement, the happiness and the spectacular expression and experience of self-fulfillment that comes with encountering what you've encountered before, as if for the first time.

Where the Magic Comes From

What allows us to do this, what allows us to create such magic, is the thing we call love. This is an extraordinary energy for which it is impossible to find full and complete words. And the energy is so magical that it can transform the old into the new, the past into the present, the "been there, done that" into the "I wonder what's going to happen next."

Brought into the present moment of life itself, this special magic can make everything brand new and just as exciting as it was the first time it was experienced. Love is what does this, love is what sustains this, love is what makes this magic possible, for the magic is love itself, expressed in wondrous form from moment to moment throughout the whole of one's life.

I have often said (and I don't mean to be in any way insensitive with this observation) that the human sexual experience is a microcosm of life itself. If you have been involved in a romantic relationship with a long-term lover, you can know and you can predict, you can expect and you can be aware of every move that the other person is going to make in the human sexual encounter. The longer you have been lovers, the more true this will be. It will get to the point where nothing can happen that has not happened before. Ah, but *that does not mean it cannot feel brand new.*

This is where love comes in.

And God so loved the world that God gave us this ability to make magic. Not only while making love, but while making the most and the best of every single moment of Life Itself.

I could, of course, be making all of this up. I could be imagining that this is how it is. But if you know of a better way to live, please tell me about it, because I have been searching for well over half a century and had not found it until God told me what I'm telling you.

Bless the Illusion, and Curse It Not

So then, we now understand the reason and the purpose for the Illusions of Life. Again, the first of these illusions is the idea that we need something. Of course, we all know that God needs nothing. And because you are an individuation of the Divine, you, too, need nothing. Yet you step into the illusion that need is part of your reality in order for you to experience the wonder of meeting that need head-on, creating precisely what you imagine yourself to require from moment to moment.

Now the Master is the person who sees all of this, understands all of this, and is aware that none of it has anything to do with Ultimate Reality. She knows she needs nothing. He knows he can be perfectly happy and utterly content with just what is true, just what is so, just what is happening here and now.

From this place of deep peace do all Masters proceed, stepping into the Illusion time and time again in order to demonstrate the wonder and the glory of Who They Really Are, and to assist other souls in claiming their true identity, and then doing the same. This is all that any Master has ever done.

And so we bless the idea that need exists, because it gives us a platform on which to prove that it does not. And that is the greatest magic trick of all time.

All of the other Ten Illusions of Humans emerge from the first. You will see upon close examination that each gives birth to the next. This is fully and completely and wonderfully explained in *Communion with God*. If you have not read that book, you may want to do so immediately. But for now, in this space, let's look at a select few of these illusions more closely—those that I believe to be most critical in the overall scheme of things.

The other illusions that I would like to examine in this book are the illusion that Failure Exists, that Superiority Exists, and that Ignorance Exists.

You already know from your previous reading here that Judgment and Condemnation do not exist. You already know that Disunity does not exist. And it follows then that Insufficiency does not exist. So these things need not be dissected further here.

You also already know that it is an illusion that Requirement Exists. Nothing is required of anyone by anyone—least of all, of *us* by *God*—for the reason that Need does not exist. If nothing is needed, nothing is required. Not even by God.

What an extraordinary idea! Can you imagine a God who has no requirement for anything at all? If you can, you have stepped into Ultimate Reality.

But now, let's look at Illusions that are not quite so obvious.

The Only Thing at Which You Can Fail

Nothing is more negatively impacting upon the daily experience of human beings than the illusion that Failure Exists. It stops more people in their tracks than you might ever imagine. It curtails more efforts, it shuts off more possibilities, it truncates more projects and more promise than any other single condition or circumstance.

Yet what God has come to tell us in *Communion with God* is that there is no such thing as failure. In fact, "failing" is the only thing you can fail to do! (This is what I call a Divine Dichotomy.) Everything that you experience, everything that you do, everything that you express, everything that you create produces forward motion on the journey upon which you have embarked.

Oh, yes, there is a journey. There is a reason for all of this that extends beyond the mere joy of experiencing the Illusions *as* illusions. The journey upon which we have embarked is the Journey of the Soul. It is a process that has been called Evolution.

God, of course, is that which Always Was, Is Now, and Always Will Be. It, therefore, *cannot* evolve. But we can. Each individual Soul has been given the final great gift of God: The ability to become more and more and more and more.

This process is not one of *actually* becoming more, but of becoming more *aware* of what It has *always* been, always is, and always will be. In other words, to "grok it in fullness." (A memorable verbal invention of the late Robert Heinlein, whose classic novel *Stranger in a Strange Land* is a fascinating and often insightful commentary on the experience of living and the searching of a species for an understanding of God.)

"Evolution," therefore, is not really a process of growth, it is a process of remembering.

You Cannot Discover Anything

Again I return to the very human experience of being in love. When we are truly in love with another, we find—much to our delight and much to our amazement—that it is possible to love someone more and more and more, even though you thought you had loved as much as one could possibly love from the very beginning.

The wonder and the glory of love is that it is expandable. Or seems to be. What is actually happening is that you are simply experiencing greater amounts of what was always there. What has expanded is not Love, but your awareness of it. And that is why we can say to our beloved, meaning every word of it: "I love you more and more every day."

So, too, is it with all of Life. And so, too, with God. For God and Life are one and the same. Thus it becomes the most wondrous prayer of every human Soul to speak in gratitude to the Creator itself: *I love you more and more every day.*

And one of the reasons that we fall so deeply in love with God is that God has created life in such a way that Failure cannot possibly exist. We cannot fail to get where we're going. We cannot fail to experience who we are. We cannot fail to remember what is really true and how it really is.

It can surely sometimes seem as if a failure has occurred, but all of this is an illusion. The scientist in the laboratory understands this perfectly. Even the experiment that "fails" is seen as a success, in that it reveals to the scientist more of what she needs to know to move forward with the larger process of discovery in which she is engaged.

In reality, there is no such thing as discovery. That which always was, is now, and always will be cannot possibly be "discovered." We don't *dis*cover, we *un*cover. We uncover life's truths like gems, like long-buried treasures suddenly found. The treasure was always there, buried within Life Itself. We have not discovered it, we have uncovered it.

This is a wonderful way of explaining the whole process in which we are all engaged. God gave me that metaphor so that I could understand exactly what is going on.

So the huge turning point in my life was when I realized that failure cannot exist; that I have not failed at anything at all, from the beginning of my life to its most recent moment. I can now stop beating myself up for all the things I thought that I did "wrong" in the past, and for all the things I imagine myself to have "failed" to accomplish.

Everything is perfect exactly as it has occurred, precisely as it has eventuated, and just as it is arising right now. The Master comprehends this.

If you'd like to know more about how a person can live with such an understanding as a practical matter in everyday life, read anything written by Byron Katie, whose life-changing book *Loving What Is* has been a gift to humanity. Likewise, read anything by Eckhart Tolle, one of the most extraordinary human beings I've ever met, who understands all that I've just said here perfectly, *and lives it perfectly every day*. As does Byron Katie.

How freeing it is to know that everything is happening exactly as it should and that we have failed at nothing at all! This is not a naive excusing of our own past, this is a masterful explanation of it.

Life's Greatest Seduction

I have learned and I have experienced that there is nothing more seductive in human life than the idea of superiority. Yet if failure cannot exist in the life of any human being, then superiority must likewise be an illusion. For in the absence of failure on the part of anyone alive we find the absence of any one person being "better" than another.

It turns out that all of us are equal in the eyes of God—a statement that is astonishingly and breathtakingly true, but a statement that the world's religions cannot accept, cannot embrace, cannot endorse, and dare not suggest to anyone. For all of the world's religions, and all the world's political parties for that matter, and certainly the world's so-called upper classes, depend for their very existence on the notion that somehow, in some way, they are "better" than another religion, party, or class. Take away superiority and you take away that which many people and groups feel is special about themselves.

Superiority wouldn't be so bad if we did not use it as justification for discriminating against others—to say nothing about warring with others. But the idea of superiority is so ultimately ugly that it cannot produce anything save ultimately ugly results. The beauty of a garden is not that one flower is superior to another, but that the *splendor of equal glory* is obvious at first glance. The same is true of the night sky. Tell me which sector is more glorious than another.

Why we cannot see the human race as we see a garden of beautiful flowers or the night sky is beyond me. Yet if we saw the whole of humanity the way God sees us, we would observe precisely the same breathtaking beauty that we can easily observe in all the world around us. There are those who say, however, that we cannot expect to know and understand what God knows and understands. This leads me to the last illusion of humans, the idea that ignorance exists.

The Biggest Lie in the World

Nothing is more damaging to the human psyche than the notion that there is something we not only *don't* know, but cannot possibly *come* to know, cannot possibly *ever* know.

"Mysterious are the ways of the Lord" is the biggest lie that has ever been told. There is nothing mysterious about God, there is nothing mysterious about life, and there is nothing mysterious about you and who you are and why you are here and how you may best experience and express that.

There is nothing about Divinity that we cannot fully know, fully understand, and fully experience. This is God's greatest promise: Seek and ye shall find. Knock and it shall be opened unto you. Would we call God a liar?

Eliminate from your cosmology, from your innermost beliefs, the idea that ignorance and superiority and failure exist and you will have removed the final block to the fullest expression of the greatest glory and the grandest wonder of who you really are.

Applying This Message to Everyday Life

The idea that most of what we understand (or *thought* we understood) is an illusion can be a tough one to find a way to integrate into our moment-to-moment experience. And if it's just an interesting thought that is never explored more deeply, there will be no benefit to us even trying to do so. Here, then, are some things you can do to make this notion more real in your everyday life:

- Create a Ten Illusions Notebook. In the first part of this notebook, make a list of things that you thought a decade ago that you absolutely needed. Next to that list, indicate which needs have been fulfilled and take special note of any need which has not, and which you imagine you still have today.

- Notice that you're still here, you're still capable of experiencing the highest level of happiness, you are still able to joyously express yourself (regardless, by the way, of any present condition). Notice that you did not need what you thought you needed in order to be, do, and have what you are being, doing, and having on this very day.

- In your notebook, make a list of three things at which you feel you have utterly failed in your life. Beneath each of these listings, write a paragraph about what you may have learned from that "failure," or what you may have experienced as a result of it. Do not be surprised if this allows you to see with great clarity that your "failure" was not a failure at all, but merely a stepping-stone bringing you to exactly where you are right now: A place of greater wisdom, greater understanding, greater ability, greater insight, and greater awareness than you have ever experienced before. How can anything that brought you here have been a failure?

- Also in your notebook make a list of any person or group to whom or to which you have felt "superior" in the past. Write a paragraph on why you felt that way. What was the basis of it? Express in a second paragraph how you feel about the person or group today and explain why—even (and perhaps especially) if your feelings have not changed.

- Make a list of people who you sense feel that they are superior to you. Write a paragraph about how this affects you and how you respond to that person when you see him or her.

- The next time you think there is something you don't know and can't possibly understand, allow yourself, as a simple experiment, to do whatever it takes to come to know and understand that particular thing fully. Use the universe as your resource. Use the world as your tool. Now more than ever you will discover that the gathered and accumulated wisdom of our entire species has been made available to us on the Internet. With a press of a button and the click of a mouse we can access anything we think we don't know about. How can ignorance exist?

- If it is life wisdom and life insights that you feel you are ignorant about at any level, simply close this book right now, close your eyes as well, and ask the God of your understanding to bring you to a place of greater awareness and total knowing of what it is you imagine you can't possibly understand. Do not be surprised if even before completing the question you might formulate in your mind, God will have already responded. "Even before you ask, I will have answered" is another of God's famous promises. It has become famous because it is true.

14

The fact that we are living our lives inside of a construction of illusion is a blessing, because only within such a construction would it be possible for each of us to be the creator of our own reality.

If "reality" were static, it would be extraordinarily difficult for any individual to change it, to alter it, to modify it in any way to suit their Soul's agenda. Only within a pliable reality could such accommodations be invited. So our malleable reality is the greatest gift that God has given us.

This does not mean that there are no Constants in our environment. It is quite easy to create a Constant. All we have to do is agree with each other about anything, and that about which we have agreed becomes our Constant Condition.

The question is, how can life be lived within a container that creates both Constant Conditions and Changing Circumstances simultaneously?

We have to "agree to agree" on many things. We call a spoon "a spoon," we call the sky "the sky," we call red "red" and blue "blue" and yellow "yellow." We point to the stars at night and say they are "up there." We point to the Earth and call it "down." From language to language and culture to culture these Constants remain in place. They help us to negotiate the territory.

We think these aspects of our experience remain Constant because they are "facts," but that's not the reason at all. What we call "facts" are merely elements of our physical environment and our emotional experience upon which we have all continued to agree for a great many years. In fact, for centuries and millennia.

(Yet an astronaut who has circled the Earth may not agree that "the stars" were "up there," but may say they were to her left or to her right, and she may feel that she was looking "up" at the Earth, not down! So there you have it. All agreement is contextual.)

And therein lies both the wonder of life and its biggest challenge. Because we are literally "making it all up," depending upon the context within which we have encountered it, and we had better make it up well, or we're going to get ourselves into deep trouble.

This is precisely what we've done.

And here's the big problem: Because we both want and need the Constants upon which we have agreed to *remain* Constant in order for us to express and experience ourselves within the shifting tides created by the moments of our lives, we are extraordinarily reluctant to *alter* any Constant.

Therefore, what we have imagined to be "known facts" about our world have been difficult to change—even when we have discovered that those "facts" are completely inaccurate.

You can't imagine the trouble our species had simply acknowledging that the sun does not revolve around the Earth! We excommunicated a brilliant person from the most prestigious religion of his time because he dared to suggest that one of our Constants was not constant at all but merely an idea that we had, based upon what we *imagined* was true. In a sense, it was an elaborate story that we made up.

It was equally difficult for doctors to admit that germs existed. Or for teachers in some parochial schools to acknowledge that left-handedness was not a sign of the Devil, and that it was therefore not necessary for them to tie the left arm of left-handed students behind their back and force them to learn how to write with the nondominant hand. (*You think I'm making this up?* This actually *happened* in many of our parochial schools in the lives of our grandparents.)

So we see that even in the face of irrefutable evidence that something is not true (to say nothing of it being altogether ridiculous), a belief that we have held as a Constant is extraordinarily difficult for us to shake. We have to be told over and over again across a period of many years that what we thought was a Constant was merely an Illusion—something that we *thought* was true, but that was patently false.

The question in these days and times: Could any of the things that we think of *now* as Constants be, in fact, equally not true? And could any of those things *have to do with God*?

So the big challenge with this blessing that we call the Illusions of Life is that we need to be more willing to create new and more beneficial illusions more rapidly than we have been in the past. We need to be light on our feet, so to speak. We need to be able to "move with the times."

If in Life there are going to be shifting sands, they at least ought not be piled in front of us, placed and shaped as the wind would decree, in ways that make them impossible to traverse, but rather, formed into beautiful castles, that we ourselves can dismantle if and when we choose to.

In short, we need to be creative rather than reactive. If we're going to live within the World of Illusion, let us create illusions that *serve* us, not illusions that stymie us.

What's Needed Is a Decision

Of course we cannot produce that which serves us if we have no
idea what we're trying to do. We must first understand who we are
and where we are and why we are here and what we are "up to"
before we can possibly create an illusion that serves us.

Reaching this understanding has been our second biggest challenge, because even the agenda is something we are invited by God
to create in whatever way we wish. So it is not about reaching an
understanding at all, it is about reaching a *decision*.

In this we find ourselves in something of a hall of mirrors. We
look into the first reflection and see multiple reflections of that reflection behind it. We are a reflection of our own reflections—or, if
you please, of our own thoughts about ourselves.

If I think of myself as being "courageous," then I will see myself
as one who is courageous, and then I may act as a person who is
courageous. In this way my actions become a reflection of how I see
those actions, based on how I think of myself. (What one person
calls "courageous" another calls "foolhardy.") I become a reflection
of my reflection of myself.

If I think of myself as "unlucky" or as "a loser," then I will see
myself as "losing" when certain things happen in my life—even
though the very same things happening in the life of another may
be seen by *them* as "winning."

And so we observe that in Life's Hall of Mirrors we become a
reflection of our reflection of our reflection.

Similarly, our experience of God is a reflection of our own
thoughts about God. Or as it was put succinctly in *Conversations with
God*: "Life is a process that informs life about life through the process
of life itself." And how life informs you about life depends upon how
you informed *yourself* about how that process informed *you*.

This is another way of saying that life is what you think it is.

Stories both old and new, from *Alice in Wonderland* to *The Matrix*, have offered us glimpses into this ultimate state of things. In each and in all of these stories the through line is virtually the same: We are making it all up! A thing is what you say it is.

These glimpses have been essentially metaphorical, dealing with the mysteries of our everyday physical life, but rarely theological, dealing with spiritual realities. We are perfectly content to hold an idea that all of life may be, after all is said and done, a metaphor, but we are in no way content to assume that this could be true about Theology.

Our understandings about God, we have told ourselves, are absolutely complete and correct, even if our understanding of nothing else is.

You can imagine how difficult this makes it, then, to embrace the five-word message to the world that God invited me to share with Matt Lauer on the *Today* show on NBC a number of years ago. You'll recall from the opening of this book the content of that message.

"You've got me all wrong."

This statement is the greatest gift that God could have given to humanity. It offers us a chance to "do it all again" when it comes to the creation of our Most Sacred Story. It invites us to not only re-create *ourselves* anew, but to re-create our *God* anew, in the next grandest version of the greatest vision that we ever held about the Divine.

Dare we do such a thing?

Dare we change our minds about God? Dare we come up with a New Story about the Creator of the Story itself?

If we don't, the story we are now living is not going to have a happy ending. Or to put it another way, if we're not careful, we're going to wind up exactly where we're headed.

And so our species has arrived at what may possibly be the greatest single Choice Point of its entire history upon the Earth: A time when we decide our future by deciding about our past. A time when we choose to notice that what we imagined to be true yesterday is not what we decide we wish to experience today. A time when we construct a new construction in a constructive way, not a destructive way, allowing us to experience and express at last the full potential of who we really are and who we were always meant to be.

This is the moment of the birthing of humanity into the cosmic community of sentient beings, as futurist and visionary Barbara Marx Hubbard put it. I agree with her allegory completely.

Yet what shall we use as the building blocks of this New Story? What shall be the next Constants—at least for a while? Is there anything new that we wish to tell ourselves about everything around us and about All That Is? Is there a different way that we can express and experience ourselves on this planet that may alter tradition, but not trajectory, taking us, instead, exactly where we have always been seeking to go?

Would it be beneficial for us to reconstruct ideas that we have long held to be sacred and certain and true?

Even as we finally let go of our idea that left-handedness is a sign of the Devil, is it okay for us now, at last, to let go of our idea that blacks are inferior to whites? That people of the same gender may not demonstrate their love for each other in sexual ways? That women are lesser than men and should not be placed in positions of power because of their inferiority? That people are not capable of governing themselves freely and without restriction? That God is a violent, angry, vindictive, and punishing deity who will "get us" in the end if we don't do precisely and exactly what He demands, in precisely and exactly the way He prescribes?

Perhaps most daringly of all, is it time for us to let go of the notion that there is such a thing as Absolute Truth?

Conversations with God says yes to all of the questions above, and to many more. It says yes to the question of whether it is time for us to change everything that no longer serves us, but visibly and obviously obstructs us from fulfilling the highest agenda we can imagine, leaving us with only the lowest.

The text of *CWG* places before humanity 25 breathtakingly revolutionary constructions—revisions of our reality and of our theology that, if embraced by humanity, would turn the world upside down. Or is it right side up?

Among these New Stories is the mind-rattling concept contained in . . .

CWG CORE MESSAGE #17

There is no such thing as Absolute Truth. All truth is subjective. Within this framework there are five levels of truth telling:

Tell your truth to yourself about yourself;
Tell your truth to yourself about another;
Tell your truth about yourself to another;
Tell your truth about another to another;
Tell your truth to everyone about everything.

If we accept the notion that is articulated in this message from God, virtually everything we have thought to be so unravels before us. As I've said above, this might just be the greatest gift we have ever received, and this could very well be the perfect moment for all of humanity to receive it.

It is probable that many, if not most, of our currently held understandings of what is "so" could use some unraveling. Not the least of these might be our thought that there is such a thing as Absolute Truth.

If we embrace the idea that Absolute Truth, in the objective sense, does not exist, it would place us into the space of total responsibility for how we perceive and experience the world around us. This does not mean that people who have been victimized in our world, or crushed by life events over which they had no control, are responsible for those creations. I do not want anyone to believe that *Conversations with God* says anything such as that. It does not.

What it does make clear is that the life events that we individually experience are collaboratively created, the outcome and the result of our collective consciousness. This includes victimizations, such as rape and robbery, as well as circumstantial conditions, such as health matters, economic situations, or environmental events.

What it also makes clear is that our internal reactions to such events are entirely under our control—no matter how horrific such events may be. And herein lies our power and our freedom to create our own reality.

There are many people who have experienced the selfsame exterior event—from rape to robbery, disease to bankruptcy—but who have reacted and responded entirely differently to the experience.

If we embraced the idea that Absolute Truth, in the objective sense, does not exist, we would see and acknowledge that nothing is *objectively* "so," and that all "truth" is subjective. That is, a thing is "so" only in the eye of the beholder.

Now if *many* "beholders" see something—a circumstance, condition, situation, or event—in the same way, then they, *by their mutual agreement*, actually *create* what is thereafter *called* "Reality."

When we realize how this "system" works, we come to a startling conclusion: We are, and have always been, far more in control of our collective reality (and therefore, by extension, of our individual experience) than we have heretofore been able to recognize, admit, or acknowledge.

On a collective scale, global warming is a perfect example. Until enough of us *agree* that global warming is "real," it is not. It exists in the "reality" of one person and not in the "reality" of the other—both of whom look at the same exterior data, yet each drawing entirely different interior conclusions from them.

It has been said that when enough people agree on the interpretation of exterior data, "Truth" has been created.

If humanity finally reaches a collective awareness that all "Truth" is interiorly produced based on the exterior data presently at hand, it will at last recognize that the largest mystery still facing humanity—the existence, the true nature, and the desires and requirements of God—rests on a single, simple question: *Is all the data on this subject presently in hand?* Or is it possible that there is still something we do not know about all of this, *the knowing of which could change everything?*

As a newly reconstructed society, we would invite ourselves to the most courageous moment that the members of any species could ever encounter: The time when we decide that *we are the ones doing the deciding,* the instant when we accept that *we are both the creator and the created.*

Only a species that saw itself as Divine could embrace such a notion. Yet what of humility? Is this not the hubris for which God is said to have punished His most promising angel, Lucifer?

According to religious teachings, Lucifer was formerly the Angel of Light, also referred to as Satan, who declared himself to be equal to God. Angered by this affront, God banished him to an eternity in Hades, for he was said to have committed the Ultimate Sin.

Yet do not all parents wish for their offspring that they will equal them in achievement, and even exceed them? And if their offspring do so, have they committed the Ultimate Sin? Or is this, in fact, the Ultimate *Desire* of all loving parents?

Is God, then, less gracious, less generous, magnanimous, and benevolent than our own earthly father?

Only the bravest and most highly evolved species of sentient beings could dare to embrace a concept so sweeping as to include the possibility of its own equation with Divinity.

That would be humanity at this point in time.

Unless it's not.

We get to decide *even that*.

What Is "Truth," Anyway?

The notion that there is no such thing as Absolute Truth is probably best applied initially on a personal level. If we can begin to understand and experience that what we are experiencing internally within us on a daily basis is both controllable and changeable by us, we have taken the first step toward altering our collective external experience as well.

Currently, everything that we do and everything that we experience on an individual level is predicated on what we hold to be "true" about ourselves and the people, places, events, and circumstances around us. The saddest thing about this is that many, many people do not live within the framework of even their own self-constructed "truth." That is, they have a truth and they hold a truth and consider it to be absolutely "what is so" within them, but they too often do not demonstrate this truth in the living and creating of their daily outward experience.

Conversations with God tells us that all truth is subjective. That is, it is "true" only for us. What is true for me may not be true for you. In most cases it probably *is* not.

What we call "truth" is nothing more than our subjective experience of what we assume to be an objective event, circumstance, or condition. Even the objective nature of events, circumstances, and conditions must, however, be questioned.

Quantum physics now tells us: "Nothing that is observed is unaffected by the observer." In other words, the act of looking at something sends energy to it in a way that interacts with the energy of that which is observed. All of *life* is energy, *interacting*. This remarkable revelation from physicists has put into scientific terms the metaphysical assertion that we are the creators of our own reality.

It would be helpful, given this highly malleable state of things, if we could at least recognize and acknowledge *what we have decided within ourselves* with regard to that which we are encountering outside of us. Thus, *Conversations with God* offers us a formula by which we could make ourselves known to ourselves and to each other. This is summarized in the Five Levels of Truth Telling listed above.

It is the idea offered by *CWG* that embracing and practicing the Five Levels of Truth Telling can provide us with a new fundamental basis upon which we can formulate our mutual agreements about Life.

Remember I said that we live by agreement. A spoon is a spoon, a flower is a flower, up is up, and down is down. Of course, if you were an astronaut (an example I used before), your whole notion of what is up and what is down would be dissolved as soon as you found yourself looking "down" at the moon and "up" at the Earth. So we see that even that which we assume to be nonchangeable understandings are merely contextual.

We live within a Contextual Field. And when that Contextual Field changes—or, more correctly, is seen from a broader perspective—our "truth" changes as well. It had better, or we will be deeply conflicted the moment our perceptions of Life expand.

Yet we can't change our truth if we are unable to know or announce, declare or stand for what is true for us now. That is why the Five Levels of Truth Telling can be a powerful tool as we seek to re-create ourselves anew in the next grandest version of the greatest vision we ever held about who we are.

Level One

We are advised by God to first "tell the truth to yourself about yourself." You might think this is easy to do, but it could be the toughest, the most difficult thing of all. It requires us to be totally honest with ourselves.

And so now we see that all of these messages from *Conversations with God* intertwine in a marvelous way, because earlier we were told that honesty, awareness, and responsibility are the three core concepts of Holistic Living. Now we are being invited to apply those concepts in the confronting and the acknowledging of our own truth about ourselves.

Of course, your truth about yourself is going to be constantly changing because *you* are constantly changing. How you were yesterday is not how you are today, and how you are today may very well *not* be how you are tomorrow. Yet how you are today is how you are today, and that's what's true about that.

In chapter 9, I created an acronym for the word "true." I said that, in my experience, that which *I say* is "true" is The Reality Understood Existentially—or, if you will, as an act of individual freedom and personal will. A thing is "true" because I *say* it is. Therefore, it is *true for me*.

When something is "true" in the same way for many people across many years or centuries, humans have a habit of calling it *the* Truth. My acronym for "truth" experienced at this level is: Temporary Reality Understood Throughout History. (Which makes it not very "temporary" at all, doesn't it . . .)

Yet all "truth" *is* temporary, and the sooner we accept this, the better off we are, it has seemed to me, because then we don't get ourselves tied down to a particular truth in a particular way at a particular time—which in our world we tend to call "politics" or "religion."

Stuff You Should Know

So I want you to understand that when I use the word "true" in this book I am speaking of The Reality Understood Existentially. I am speaking of what *I* have decided is true, and what I am inviting you to *explore* to see if it might be true for *you*.

With regard to level one of the Five Levels of Truth Telling, we are talking about what *is* true for you right here, right now. Regarding this, the first level invites you to tell the truth to yourself about yourself. Both the good, and the bad, or what you *call* Good and Bad. Just say what is so about every aspect of yourself and about your relationship with the exterior events and people of your life.

You don't have to share this with anyone. No one else has to know. But *you* should know. You should be clear from moment to moment. Unless you are, you will be interiorly confused about too many of your exterior experiences.

Level Two

The Second Level of Truth Telling invites you to tell your truth to yourself about another.

This may also be easier said than done. I have found in life that people often want to delude themselves about another. A typical example is when they realize internally that they are no longer in love with a person with whom they are sharing their life.

They reject the thought immediately every time it comes up for them, telling themselves that they shouldn't think such a thing, that they are merely upset in the moment, that they are simply reacting to a particular event or situation. And so they remain in a dysfunctional relationship for an extraordinarily long period of time, convincing themselves that what they were telling themselves internally for years was simply not "true."

In this they find themselves in a place of on-again/off-again confusion around the feelings of "love" and compatibility. They think that the two have to be one. When they felt compatible and in harmony with another, they told themselves that they were in love. When they were out of harmony—and especially if this happened over an extended period—they told themselves that they "didn't love" the other person anymore.

I have found that I must reside within a harmonious field for me to be productive, creative, peaceful, and useful to others. I have also found that it is entirely possible for me to love someone *with whom I am not harmonious.*

What was difficult for me was deactivating the idea that loving someone meant I had to cohabitate with them, spending the rest of my days and the entirety of my human journey in an emotional cacophony. I held the notion that if I loved someone, and told them that I did, and committed to love them forever, then I had to stay with them, no matter what, and that to leave them was to announce that I did not love them. In this I confused love with physical proximity.

The result of this is that I created multiple "permanent" relationships, feeling that I had to cohabitate long-term with every person who accepted my love.

I'm not the first person to have done this.

When I finally learned to tell the truth to myself about another, I was finally able to negotiate relationships in a new and more functional way. I'm sorry to say that this wasn't until I had hurt far too many people.

There's no reason for you to fall into—or remain in—that same trap.

Levels Three and Four

At the next level of truth telling, I was invited to tell my truth about myself to another.

This meant revealing everything that I was thinking and experiencing inside of myself with regard *to* myself in open and honest exchanges with another. It was about being totally and utterly naked before them.

It is an intriguing aspect of human behavior that we find it relatively easy and even exciting to stand naked physically before another whom we love, but often enormously uncomfortable and difficult to stand naked mentally and emotionally before that same person.

We are willing to be seen completely on the outside, but not on the inside. The result is that people who have lived together for years, husbands and wives who are celebrating their fiftieth anniversary, can often be virtual strangers to each other in more ways than you might imagine.

This would not be true if we embraced and practiced the Third Level of Truth Telling. Yet such a practice takes enormous courage. We have to be willing to risk being rejected, and since rejection is the biggest fear that many human beings hold, for many it takes the biggest kind of bravery to risk it.

Yet what good is it for us to be accepted by another if the other does not know what's being accepted? How long can we continue to do our dance? How long can we continue to hope that we're not uncovered mentally and emotionally even as we can't wait to be uncovered physically? How long can we ride this train that seems to be going in two directions at once? How long can we say to our beloved other, "Know me completely . . . but don't ask me about *that . . .*"

This leads us to the Fourth Level of Truth Telling, in which we tell our truth about another *to that other*. Talk about courage, talk about bravery, talk about valor! This may require the highest level of all. Yet it becomes the most freedom-giving *experience* of all once we cross over the No Man's Land between two parties who are warring within themselves about how much they want to reveal and surrender to their truth of the moment.

It is vitally important for any other person with whom you have any kind of quality relationship at all to know how you really feel about them in every way. The big things and the small. The obvious and the not so obvious. The important and the trivial. They need to know *all of it*. Indeed, they have a *right* to know all of it.

Life is not a game of poker, in which you place your bets with concealed hands. Life is a game of solitaire. It's played with all our cards on the table, face up, right in front of us. It's a game of solitaire even though we play in pairs and sometimes in groups, because in reality there is only one of us.

Level Five

And this leads us to the final level of Truth Telling: Tell the truth to every*one* about every*thing*.

Now we are really experiencing freedom. When you're free of the need to hide anything from anyone, you are free to proceed with your life in the most joyful, creative, dynamic, fluid, exuberant, and authentic way you could ever have imagined.

Earlier I told you that there are ten illusions of humans, and that the first illusion was the illusion of need. Now I tell you this: *When you're free of need, you're free to proceed.*

The Fifth Level of Truth Telling brings us this freedom. We are now able to proceed with our lives unencumbered by the need to "look good," or to have "gotten it right," or to be "spiritually enlightened," or whatever we have imagined we must be, do, or have in order to avoid rejection.

This is a level of Total Transparency that the world is not used to. When this kind of transparency becomes common not only in our personal lives, but in our entire collective experience, from business to politics to education to religion and everything in between, we will have created the kind of society in which everyone can know anything about everything—and about every*one*.

We are challenged by such an idea to consider the questions: Why should we have a need to keep anything secret? What is the difference between "secrecy" and "privacy"? What in our imagining causes us to think that anything needs to be kept "private"? And why does this thing called "love," when expressed at its highest level, magically erase the need for privacy?

Do we need to keep things from our Beloved Other?

Yes? If so, what would that be? If not, how is it that Love and Intimacy (into me *see*) eliminates the need for "privacy"?

Could it be because Love and Intimacy creates security? We feel "safe" and continually loved no matter what? We feel accepted just as we are? Is it not the fear that we will not be accepted and loved just as we are that causes us to feel the need for "secrets" and "privacy"?

Does this give us a clue about something with regard to how we are behaving with each other on this planet? Does it give us a clue as to how we *might* behave if we desired a totally transformed society?

APPLYING THIS MESSAGE TO EVERYDAY LIFE

I have found that the Five Levels of Truth Telling are easy to understand and hard to apply. At least they were for me. I'm still not there with all of them all the time. But I'm closer than I ever was before.

Here are some suggestions on ways that you can apply Core Message #17 in your daily life:

- Create a Truth Notebook. (Yes, I know, here we go again with the notebook routine. But as I explained to you earlier, designing notebooks for many of the aspects of your life and making important entries in them can be a powerful tool in the re-creation of your life as you have always wished to experience it. So play along here, don't fight this. Just create the notebook!)

- Now . . . in your Truth Notebook, allow your initial entry to be all the truth that you currently know about yourself in every area of your life. Divide your narrative into whatever component parts you can think of. Perhaps they might be: money, love, sex, God, work or career, talents and abilities, children and parenting, appearance and physical attributes, mental attributes, house and environment, and anything else that is true about yourself as you are currently experiencing and knowing yourself in the living of your daily life. This may be a bit uncomfortable if you allow yourself to be honest with yourself. That's okay. Allow yourself to experience the discomfort. Discomfort is nothing more than an announcement that healing is about to take place.

- Now make similar sections in your notebook, with similar narratives, about your present truth regarding another. This could be any other person in your life—your spouse, your offspring, your friend, neighbor, or boss, and even your God.

- Now, take these revelations that you've made to yourself (putting them in writing merely physicalizes your mental experience) and put them "on the street," so to speak. That is, choose to live them. And the first step in living them is to speak them. In this, it is good to remember: "Speak your truth, but soothe your words with peace."

- Decide that from this day forward you will be totally and completely truthful with everyone about everything. This does not mean that you go around telling people that you don't like the clothes they're wearing or the way they've chosen to do their hair, but it does mean that when you are asked anything specifically, or engaged in an open two-way exchange on any topic whatsoever, that you reveal yourself utterly and completely, standing totally naked and allowing yourself to be absolutely seen. When you are expressing yourself and experiencing yourself as Who You Really Are, you will have no fear of this experience. Indeed, you will invite it and eagerly await it. For how can another know us fully or embrace us completely if they can only experience us partially? That is the question before every human being in every relationship. Life invites you to answer that question with the greatest courage, and Life promises you that if you do, you will receive the greatest reward.

- Question every "truth" that your culture, your religion, your society, your political party, your school, and your family has taught you. And question every truth in this book, of course.

- Write down the twenty-five Most Important Truths of your life, and in a column next to it write down why you hold them to be truths, and what, if anything, could change them.

- Do whatever it takes to create a safe environment for others to tell their truth around *you*—and ask them to do the same. Discuss with your Beloved Other what, if anything, you could do to make them feel totally secure in your love no matter what they tell you.

- Practice the "Speak your truth, but soothe your words with peace" approach by writing out ahead of time, in private, any major Truth Telling that you wish to do with another. Often, of course, this is not possible, because the "time for truth" comes up in the moment, spontaneously. But there are times when we know there is something that we really want to say to another, but we're waiting for the "right moment." This is a good time to practice this skill. Write out what you want to say, letting any and all possible negative "charge" that you have on the subject roll out and be released in whatever words best release it. Then, go back over what you have written and look to see if there is a way to say the same thing without losing any of the intent or the meaning, but losing the negative charge or any potentially hurtful or judgmental energy you may be carrying.

- Be aware that *tone of voice* and *facial expression* is just as important a carrier of energy as actual words. So in the mode of peaceful communication of truth, take all of this into consideration.

- Enjoy this little process. Take out a sheet of paper and write down the names of three people who are important to you right now. Leave a big space under each name. In the space, complete the following sentence: "What I'm afraid to tell you is . . ." See what, if anything, comes up for you, and find a way to communicate that to them as soon as you can.

- Do not be afraid to actually *start* any conversation with the phrase, "What I'm afraid to tell you is . . ." Always be sure to ask the person in question whether you may have permission to speak openly about something. Be sincere in this. Don't ask it simply as a matter of form.

- Speak your truth to God every day. If you are angry, be angry. If you are grateful, be grateful. If you are frustrated and questioning, be exactly that. Have a Conversation with God in truth every day. Don't make it only one way. Do it on paper . . . and be prepared to receive some of the most astonishing responses. Be careful, however. Do not do this if you do not want your life to change.

15

When humanity as a species gathers the courage to question everything it has ever accepted about itself and about its God, when humanity is brave enough to believe that it truly *has* been created "in the image and likeness of God," humanity will at last be able to express and experience itself in the way that was always intended, in the way that is open to all sentient beings in the universe.

As we all know, individuals within our species have done this. From time to time, their doing of it has come to the attention of the rest of us who are either unable to do it or, because of our beliefs, are refusing to do it or, because of our understanding of God, are fearful of doing it.

Those few who have done it in highly visible ways have been brought to our attention and are noticed in our histories. We call them saints and sages and gurus and martyrs and heroes, because they have violated the central notion of our species: We are *not* Divine, we are *not* a part of God; we *can* never and *will* never rise to the level of expression and experience that is Divine.

Yet the moment now presenting itself to humanity offers us an invitation to call *ourselves*—every one of our members, not merely a select few—saints and sages, gurus and heroes. It is not only one man who was the son of God, but all men. It is not only one woman who was beatific and blessed, but all women. It is not only one person who is Divine, but every person.

God did not intend to bestow God's magnificence on only one of us or just a select few. It is God's intention to bestow upon all of God's sentient creations all of God's qualities. This God has done, precisely and meticulously. Every sentient being has *indeed* been made "in the image and likeness of God."

Though we've been told about this for centuries, we are just now moving to a place where it seems possible for us to accept it as the Ultimate Reality. To accept it without being called blasphemers or apostates or heretics. To accept it without being labeled mad or crazy or insanely egotistic and self-aggrandizing. To accept it without being marginalized and ostracized and demonized within our community.

The Choice: Breakdown or Breakthrough

Our species stands on the Brink of Breakthrough. Always, breakthrough occurs when break*down* threatens—and never before in the history of our species has total and complete breakdown been threatened in more ways than now.

As we have noted earlier, nothing in our collective experience is working the way we intended it to. We've carefully and meticulously constructed political, economical, ecological, educational, and spiritual systems and solutions, none of which have generated the outcomes for which they were designed, and for which we have so long yearned. Anyone who imagines that our politics, our economics, our spirituality, or any of the rest of it is actually *working* is wildly delusional.

There is a difference between "*de*lusion" and "*ill*usion." An illusion is magic, a delusion is tragic.

Our job, our opportunity, our invitation from life is to make the shift from tragic delusions to magic illusions. We can do this by using the power of pure creation, knowing that all of Life is an illusion, and giving ourselves permission then to create our illusory reality *in exactly the way we wish*, rather than continuing to reside in our delusional reality *as we have been told that we must*.

Yet, as we stand on the edge of this extraordinary opportunity, there is something of which we must all be aware. It was the French poet, priest, and philosopher Apollinaire who wrote the following, which I adapted slightly:

> "Come to the edge."
> *"We can't. We're afraid."*
> "Come to the edge."
> *"We can't. We'll fall!"*
> "Come. To. The. *Edge*."
> And they came.
> And he pushed them.
> And they *flew*.

The Flight Analogy

We must be willing to consider the possibility of flying if we seek to take off at all. And now more than ever it is imperative that we consider this possibility, because we are running out of runway. It's time to either take *off* in new directions or take *on* the nightmarish future that staying grounded in our old beliefs will inevitably produce.

Yet as we move with courage and conviction into the creation of our most hoped-for and dreamt-of tomorrows, it is important for us to understand what we are going to confront along the way. It is important for us to fully comprehend . . .

CWG CORE MESSAGE #16

The moment you declare anything, everything unlike it will come into the space. This is the Law of Opposites, producing a Contextual Field within which that which you wish to express may be experienced.

This element is critical to our understanding of how life works. If we are not aware of this immutable law of the universe, we will be tempted to withdraw, to pull back, to surrender, to avoid stepping off the edge and flying. We will be frightened, afraid, scared to death.

Indeed, that is the nature of the lives of hundreds of millions of people. They are literally scared to death. That is, they live in fear from morning to night, from first to last, from the beginning to the end of their lives.

First they are in fear of their parents. Then they are in fear of their teachers. Then they are in fear of their employers. Then they are in fear of their neighbors. Then they are in fear of their country. Then they are—some of them, many of them—in fear of God.

This is because everything *but* what they are seeking and hoping for is arising all around them.

The Law of Opposites, however, is nothing to be afraid of. Its effect brings us to a place of magnificent power over the course and direction of our lives. For when we witness this effect, we can finally rest assured that we are moving in the right direction at last.

This is, of course, completely counterintuitive. When we see the opposite of that which we are choosing to create, we imagine that we are moving in the *wrong* direction, doing the *wrong* thing, attempting to produce the *wrong* outcome. More often than not, just the opposite is true. That's why this is called the Law of Opposites.

So let's take a look at how it works.

It Is an Imperative

The Law of Opposites is merely a label that was given to me in my conversations with God to allow me to understand why, in the moment that I come to a decision about almost anything, I seem suddenly to encounter some sort of obstacle or blockage at every turn. The "other than" what I seek to express and experience immediately looms large in my horizon, seemingly showing me all the reasons why I should not move forward with my agenda.

What we do not understand is that Life *must* do this. It is an imperative, in order for Life to create a Contextual Field within which we can experience the expression of our choosing.

This has been discussed extensively in the *Conversations with God* dialogues, and has already been explored here in chapter 8. But now, let's look at the on-the-ground encounters with this that I have observed in my own life and in the lives of others, so that we might better see not just *why* it works, but *how*.

The Secret of Ceiving

As I have experienced it, the Process of Personal Creation occurs in three steps. (1) We have an idea. (2) The Universe immediately creates a context within which such an idea may be held, offering contrasting elements within which the idea itself may be singularized, seen, and experienced. (3) We see each contrasting element for exactly what it is—not an *obstacle*, but an *opportunity*, empowering us to move forward with our original creation.

I've referred to this often as the Process of Ceiving.

I know, I know, there's no word like that in Earth's languages. But let us use English as our baseline, and then look further into this fascinating articulation . . .

All creation begins when we *conceive* of a thing. We have an idea of some sort or another. This is the moment of conception. We give birth to a new thought.

The moment we have an idea about anything, the Mind takes a look at it. It explores it and examines it minutely. Thus we *per*ceive what we have *con*ceived.

How we perceive it, how we see it and evaluate it in our Mind, will determine how we experience it. Is this a good idea or a bad idea? Is it functional or is it dysfunctional? Is it possible or is it impossible? Shall we do it and move forward, or not do it and step back?

Thus we present ourselves with the idea again, but not in its original form. Rather, we *re*ceive it. We *ceive* it once again! Now, however, in the shape that has evolved from our *per*ceiving of what we have *con*ceived. This is rarely an immaculate conception, but rather a distorted form of that which we originally conceived.

We must be very careful how we *re*ceive what we have *per*ceived of what we have *con*ceived, because if we are not careful, we are very likely to *de*ceive ourselves. That is, we will *undo* the very thing we thought to do. We will create *deception* because of our *reception* of our *perception* of our *conception*.

More than one person has aborted a great idea after it was conceived but before it was given birth. They have done so because of the Law of Opposites, bringing them face-to-face with what they did not perceive as opportunity but as opposition.

Knowing the Truth

Understanding this, we do well to ignore—or, if you please, to disempower—those things which appear to be obstacles in our life. Those obstacles are merely signposts, indicating that we are moving in precisely the right direction. They are notices that a Contextual Field has been produced within which we can experience what we have chosen to manifest in our reality.

To go back to an example offered in chapter 8, when the darkness comes, we see it as an opportunity to know ourselves as the light.

So when we see these "obstacles" pop up, we should recognize them for what they are—proof that we're on the right path—and keep moving ahead.

Removing this whole process from the realm of metaphysics and placing it inside the container of what we call normal physical life, we would label all of this as simple "determination" or "stick-to-it-iveness." Or as "standing by our convictions" or "exhibiting perseverance." Metaphysically, it is called "knowing the truth."

We understand from a spiritual point of view that nothing can be achieved, expressed, or experienced outside of a Contextual Field in which its opposite exists. This helps us to deal with that opposite in a strikingly different way. Rather than being repelled backward, we are compelled forward. Rather than being turned off, we are turned on. Rather than feeling that the plug has been pulled, we feel that we've been plugged in. And so we advance with all deliberate speed, racing toward the glory and the goal of our next magnificent creation.

Yes, but What If . . .

Now, there are those who ask—and it is a very fair question, by the way—what about when the opposite of what we are attempting to accomplish or experience presents itself repeatedly and endlessly, over and over again without ceasing, over a period of months or even years?

I've had to look at this question myself, as I am certain we all have. So it's fair to observe that there is a nuance around this Law of Opposites that deserves further exploration and explanation.

In my own life, if conditions and circumstances arising continue to make it increasingly difficult for me to achieve what it is I have set out to do, I look at two things immediately:

1. Is there something I am holding as part of my basic beliefs that prevents me from working with the Law of Opposites in a functional way, turning opportunity back into the opposition that I at first thought it was?

   Thus the Law of Opposites provides me with an opportunity to check my beliefs. What am I holding as part of my innermost reality that does not allow me to be, do, or have what I now seek to be, do, or have?

Now, let me be fair and consider the possibility that when you ask yourself this question you find that you are holding no beliefs that would prevent you from going where you wish to go with your life. My experience has shown that this would be unusual, but not impossible. It would be time, then, to ask the second question:

2. Is it possible that I am not moving in the *wrong* direction, doing the *wrong* thing, attempting to produce the *wrong* outcome, but simply going about it in the wrong *way*, or at the wrong *time*?

> This often takes me to a place that I had not previously considered—which is that what may be needed is not a change of destination, but a change of direction. The two are not the same thing.

When we change direction, we are not abandoning our destination, but simply *choosing a different way of getting there.*

Which Is Which?

I think, then, that it is fair to observe that the Law of Opposites can offer us more than a Contextual Field within which to create the experience of our desire. It can also offer us a Soul Sign that either this may not be the perfect time for our manifestation, or the most effective and efficient way to produce it.

Thus, the Law of Opposites is twofold, not singular, in its application.

This, of course, leads to another very fair inquiry: How do we know the difference between the two?

To me it is a matter of emphasis and consistency. If that which is opposite to what I wish to experience presents itself immediately after I make a choice or decision, I normally chuckle about it, laughing into my awareness. I knew that this would happen. I knew that it *had* to happen. Life has no other choice. The Law of Opposites *must* manifest in my life, as the Process of Personal Creation demands it.

Yet if that which appears to be opposing me *continually* reasserts itself over an extended period, and if I can honestly find no place within my personal belief system where I am holding energy that in and of itself renders my greatest wish impossible to realize, then I surrender to the notion that I might, in fact, be being given a Soul Sign that this is not the highest and best for me right now. Again, to reassert, this, too, is a manifestation of the Law of Opposites.

So it's a matter of intensity and longevity regarding obstacles and opposites arising.

More Here Than Meets the Eye?

I want to say something now that might sound a little "woo-woo," but that I must explore if I'm to be completely in service to you.

As you know if you have read *Conversations with God*, all of us live not only many lifetimes (a process that is often referred to as reincarnation), but we can also live the lifetime we are now experiencing more than once. Indeed, many times.

Home with God, the final book in the *Conversations with God* series, tells us that we are gifted with the blessing of being allowed to repeat any particular lifetime as many times as we wish in order to use that singular identification as a means of moving closer and closer to perfection, closer and closer to the Completion in the expression of Divinity in more and more moments of a lifetime. I want to suggest that this is the process by which all spiritual masters achieved mastery.

When we are moving through a lifetime that we have experienced before, we often find ourselves encountering moments that we call déjà vu. Things are exactly as if we have experienced that moment before. This stops us short. We glance about, wondering how such a thing is possible. We may even say out loud to those around us, "My God, I've experienced this whole thing before! Everything is exactly as it was then! You were sitting there, I was standing here, we were saying this . . . I've had exactly this experience before!"

More people than you know have had such moments. Perhaps you have had one or two of them yourself. If you have, you know exactly what I'm talking about here. I've been told in my conversations with God that such moments are "soak-throughs" from a duplicate lifetime onto this lifetime, like a drop of water onto a stack of onionskin paper.

Now, within the context of this discussion about the Law of Opposites, I have often felt that when opportunities are, in fact, obstacles, that this is a physical manifestation of our "other self" signaling to our "present self" that we have tried this particular thing before, and it did not work out very well.

Let me put this another way.

I have an idea that we exist at all places along the Time Line simultaneously. If this is true, then we have a Self in the Future, a Self in the Present, and a Self in the Past.

("Past," "Present," and "Future" do not exist in this cosmology, only Forever Now. In the Land of Forever Now, what we are currently experiencing depends upon where the Consciousness of any particular life expression is focused.

I think it is possible that we are *giving directions to ourselves* as to how best we may proceed with the agenda of our Soul, achieving what we had intended to achieve when we moved from the spiritual realm to the physical realm, through the expression of our sacred Life itself.

If we are truly all One with God, and if our Consciousness is truly expansive to the point where it includes all experiences of everything all the time, it is not inconceivable that a part of our

Mind can have access to the part of our Soul that knows all the adventures it is taking in all those Whens/Wheres of Existence that Robert Heinlein talks about.

It is also not inconceivable that the Soul may not be above "warning" us, like the signs at a railroad crossing, that this may not be the perfect time to keep moving forward in the direction that we're going, but that maybe a change of direction is in order. Or at least a little waiting time. (Unless we want our present lifetime to produce exactly what our other journey in this particular identity is producing—in which case, plow right ahead!)

Belief Not Required

Now I know that that sounds like a way-out thought, a theory so far removed from what so many of us have called "reality" that it may be difficult for you to embrace and accept. So let me tell you that it doesn't really matter whether you accept it or not.

All I want to say to you here is, if the "opposite" of what you seek to experience presents itself in the initial phases of your moment of creation, move right through that apparent opposition and see it as opportunity. Do so with perseverance and determination and commitment. I have done so in my life, and I can promise you that this approach is powerful and that it works.

I would also say to you that if what you see as "opposition" continues to present itself over a long period of time with increasing intensity, it might fall into that second category of Soul Sign, which I have endeavored to describe just above.

That is the wisdom that I can offer you on this subject. It has served me well. And I hope that it will serve you also.

Applying This Message to Everyday Life

Like all of life, the Law of Opposites is more complex than it might seem on the surface, as the above narrative has evidenced. However, it can still be useful to us. There is no question about that.

Understanding this Law discourages me from being discouraged. It stops me from stopping. And there is good in that. So let me give you a few practical suggestions on how this all may be applied in your everyday life:

- Immediately go out and buy a copy of *Loving What Is* by Byron Katie. I have mentioned this book before and I am mentioning it again because it is a powerful tool with which to improve one's life. Begin to engage in what Katie (she goes by her last name with everyone who knows her) calls The Work. This is a simple process of self-questioning that invites you to explore, more deeply than you might normally do, all of your thoughts that are arising. I invite you to do so here specifically those thoughts that relate to or present the opposite of anything that you wish to experience. Ask yourself the questions that Katie's process encourages you to explore. Is it true? Can you absolutely know that it's true? How do you react, what happens, when you believe that thought? Who would you be without the thought? You are then invited to do what Katie calls The Turnaround. It can change your life. If you'd like to know more about The Work as created and then gifted to us by Byron Katie, go to www.The Work.com.

- The next time that you have a wonderful idea or an exciting vision or fantastic dream that you want to turn into reality, *do it no matter what*. That is, *don't let anything stop you*. Certainly, not in the short term—and by "short term," I don't mean a day or two. I would not consider the idea that life is sending you a Soul Sign that you shouldn't be doing something until much time has passed. For me that's usually months or years, not days or weeks. I'm persistent, for sure.

- My motto is, "If there *is* a way, I'll *find* a way." I think that God loves this kind of determination. It sends to the heavens a signal that we know who we really are, that we know what power is ours, that we understand the Contextual Field in which that power can be expressed, and that we intend to let nothing get in the way of our expressing it, even if we follow our Soul Sign to either wait a bit or express it in another way.

- Whether what you are experiencing is a short-term manifestation of the Law of Opposites or a long-term manifestation of a sure and certain sign that you should change direction, always bless, bless, *bless* that which is blessing you by appearing in your life in this particular way. Everything in life, and I mean *everything*, is meant for your own benefit. A friend of mine in France named Jacques Schecroun has written a beautiful book titled *What If Life Only Wanted the Best for You?* It's an extraordinary question—and a question that answers itself. Life *does* only want the best for you. And when we see it that way, we experience it that way. It's as simple, and as wonderful, as that.

I think, before we close, that this business of "expressing it in another way" deserves a touch more exploration.

As I said earlier, changing directions should not have to mean changing destinations. There is more than one way up the mountaintop. Notice that what you wish to experience is always a State of Being, not a process of Doing. What you are Doing—or what you think you *have* to do, is simply and always nothing more than what you think is required in order for you to achieve a State of Being.

Look, then, to see what you think you will *be* should you find yourself able to finish doing what you have set out to do. Will you be accomplished? Will you be famous? Will you be powerful? Will you be rich?

Will you be happy? Will you be fulfilled? Will you be satisfied? Will you be content?

All of these things, and more, are things we are trying to *be* in our lives. The things we are *doing* are nothing more than the ways we think we have to move our Body around, and the ways we imagine we must use our Mind, in order for the Totality of Us to *be that.*

Yet what if there was another way to get to that destination?

To engage this utterly transformational idea in your life, first: (a) Decide in specific terms what it is you have told yourself you would *be* if you could only *do* this or that. Then: (b) Make a list of at least three other ways you can think of that could allow you to be the very same thing. Finally: (c) Elevate what you wish to *be* as a result of any moment, event, or creation in your life to the level of Divinity. Decide that what you wish to experience and express is Divinity Itself; that this is the only reason you came here to physicality.

If this can be "true" for you (and remember that "true" is

defined as The Reality Understood Existentially), measure every hope and every dream and every vision that you have for your life against this yardstick. Ask yourself:

What does what I am wanting to do now have to do with what I am choosing to use my life to express and experience?

What aspect of Divinity do I see being made manifest in physical reality as a result of my taking my time and energy to do this particular thing?

Be aware: Such questions can place your entire life, not only your individual choices and decisions, into a whole new context.

16

I have heard it said that humanity, in its future, will experience a thousand years of peace. It has been predicted by seers and prophets across the pages of history that our species will one day step into a tomorrow of our grandest imagining, claiming at last our true inheritance as cosmic beings and manifestations of the Divine.

It is my belief that this is exactly what is going to happen, and my further belief that we are at the doorstep of this new and wonderfully magnificent expression of life. All we need to do now is knock on the door, for it is as one Master so presciently said: "Seek, and ye shall find. Knock, and it shall be opened unto you."

It does not seem to me to be a coincidence, a mistake, or happenstance that you and I have arrived and are spending our lives on Earth at this pinnacle moment, witnessing and participating in this extraordinary transitional event. I think your soul and mine have come here by appointment, by design, by intention.

I believe we have been here before, you and I. This is not our first visit to physical life on this planet. We have vowed to return, and to *continue* to return, until we have lifted this species to a level of Divinity made manifest in physicality.

Yet the day of the individual "savior" or the single "master" has passed. Our previous saints and sages, saviors and masters all did what they came here to do. They awakened us to the possibility that *all* of us are saints and sages, that *all* of us are saviors and masters. Now they walk among us once again, yet this time not to lead us, but to *join* us in the process of self-realization. Their purpose in their earlier visits was to lead us by example. Their purpose in the present day is to support us through collaboration.

This level of collaboration is resulting in many other human beings experiencing what only "masters" were said to experience in days gone by. And so we see people by the millions living lives of saintliness and wonder. And so we see messengers by the thousands stepping forward to share with their brothers and sisters insights and understandings about Life that these messengers should have no way of knowing, no way of understanding, based on their own individual experience in this lifetime. Yet all people of the Earth are now realizing, one by one in slow but certain progression, that all have been given the ability to reach into the collective consciousness, and to withdraw from it eternal wisdom on a moment's notice.

This is the time of humanity's transformation. This is the moment in which our species is inviting itself to live out, at last, its true identity.

And so it is that among the 25 Core Messages of *Conversations with God* is an idea that forms the basis of everything else the dialogue seeks to share with us and to inspire within us . . .

CWG CORE MESSAGE #15

The purpose of life is to re-create yourself anew in the next grandest version of the greatest vision you ever held about Who You Are.

For as long as I can remember, I have wondered what I was doing here. I can recall when I was seven years old lying on my bed, staring at the ceiling, wondering why I was even alive. Surely, I thought, there must be some purpose or function, some reason for it all.

I took these questions to my parents and, bless them, they did their best to answer. But what do you say to a seven-year-old boy who is bringing to you the Inquiry Of The Ages?

I then took the question to the nuns in the classrooms of my parochial school. But what does a nun say to a first-grader who is asking questions that people are asking in the final year of their doctoral thesis?

So I took the question to the parish priest. Certainly the priest will know, I told myself—especially if he was a monsignor and had those red buttons on his cassock! But what does a monsignor say to a seven-year-old child who is asking questions that the monsignor turns to the bishop, and the bishop turns to the cardinal, and the cardinal to the pope to have answered?

So I exited childhood without a really satisfactory response from anyone. I spent most of my adult years without one as well. Not until I was fifty-three was something said to me that finally rang true to my soul.

It was in my conversation with God. I had the experience that God was saying directly to me, "Okay, fair enough. You've been sincere and honest in your desire to know. You've looked at the question for nearly half a century, since you were just a child. Your search has not been frivolous. Nor has it been meaningless to you. Okay, fair enough, you deserve a straight answer. Here it is."

And then I received the message above.

What We Don't Need to Know

I have come to see that the wonder here is that God doesn't care what my greatest vision for myself is. God has no preference in the matter. So whether I imagine that who I am is a butcher, a baker, or a candlestick maker, the purpose of my life is very simple: to become the next grandest version of that.

(Yet in the end, I have found, it has nothing to do with my occupation. More on this in just a bit.)

The idea that God isn't attached to my choices about my life is remarkably different from what I kept hearing when I was young. As a child growing up inside the Catholic faith I was told over and over again that God had a plan for me. There is a plan for all of us, the nuns in my classroom declared. But they never told me what that plan was, except to say that I was to try to be as good as possible, so that I could get back to heaven.

So I did that.

I tried to be as good as possible.

And when I wasn't as good as I thought I should be, I went to confession and told the priest all the bad things I had done. And then I did the penance that the priest gave me to do, so I could receive his absolution for the sins I had committed. And then I received Holy Communion the next day at Mass. And then I was once again on my way! Free of the encumbrances of my misbehaviors! Inspired again to embark once more on the journey to I did not know where!

If you think that this could be emotionally, spiritually, psychologically, and humanly frustrating, you're absolutely right. Especially for a nine- or a ten-year-old. Even for a twenty-two- or a twenty-seven-year-old. Or a thirty-nine- or a fifty-six-year-old! How can I possibly get to where I'm going when I have no *idea* where I'm going—or even why?

Such was the state of things in my poor mind. And wouldn't it be nice if I was alone in all of this? Wouldn't it be nice if it was just little ol' me simply unable to get it together, suffering the ravages of a damaging childhood, responding to the tragedies of a difficult adult life, and finding it impossible to make any sense of it? Wouldn't it be nice if it were simply that? But it wasn't.

We're All in the Same Boat

For the record, I had a wonderful childhood. I had fantastic parents. I had every opportunity offered to me. No, we weren't fabulously rich. In fact, we were lower middle class. But lower middle class in America in 1950 was doing quite well compared to 90 percent of the rest of the world, thank you very much. So . . . no complaints about that.

And the tragedies in my life as an adult? There weren't any. They simply did not arise or exist in my life. I have been one of the lucky ones. I wish I could say that about all of you, but I can say I've been one of the lucky ones. So *what*, then, *was my problem*?

I want to suggest to you that it was not just simply *my problem*, but a problem faced by millions and millions of people for a wide variety of reasons. Most of us simply have not been given by our parents, by our teachers, by our community, by our global society anything that makes sense as a *raison d'être*.

What, we ask urgently, is our reason for being?

When I called out to God with the question, I received a response giving me the answer in twenty-five words. It's an answer that could work for everybody, and I love the symmetry of it. Among the 25 Core Messages, a single statement that gives us in twenty-five words all that we really need to know about why we are here and how to make our being here purposeful, meaningful, and wonderful.

All we have to do now is decide what *is* the greatest vision we ever held about who we are. And what a freedom it is to know that God is not going to make us wrong for the choice that we make. It turns out, after all is said and done, that God does *not* have a Plan for us. We stand a greater chance of disappointing the expectations of our own parents than we do of frustrating the expectations of a nonrequiring God.

And so all options are open to us, and God has assured us that there is no right way or wrong way to do what we came here to do.

A Real Life Illustration

When I look back on my life I realize that I received this message earlier, in a fascinating way that was astonishingly close to the experience I had in my conversations with God. I wonder if you, too, have been receiving messages from Life all along, and just not syncing them all up.

Let me tell you about my earlier experience, because it's just such a great illustration.

When I was a younger man I had an important job with a large public agency in the state of Maryland. And during one particular period, I was called upon to develop a master plan having to do with how agencies such as ours proposed to proceed in particular and certain interactions with the federal government. This plan was to be submitted to a subcommittee of Congress.

I had no idea how to write this, how to present it. I had never tackled anything like it before. How was I to know how to submit a major document of such consequence to an agency of such austere importance as the United States Congress?

I called my father. I explained the situation. "How am I going to create this document?" I asked him. "I know what our organization is attempting to do, but I don't know how to put that in a written report that we're supposed to send to Washington."

My father listened patiently until I was finished rolling out my frustration. Then he said quietly, "Son, have I taught you nothing?"

I waited for the punch line.

"There is no 'right way' to do anything. There is only the way you're doing it."

I said nothing. I was thinking. Hard. Could this be true? Then Dad went on.

"Trust yourself. Do it the way you would do it if there were no expectations one way or the other. Just do it the way *you* think is best."

I thanked him and hung up the phone. I could hear myself shout to myself in my mind, "Oh, *that's* all it takes? I can do *that*. I thought there were some *rules* here, some way this whole thing had to 'show up' in order to be valid."

So I went ahead and created the report exactly the way I thought it should be created. I sent it on to Washington. A few weeks later, I got a call from a staff assistant on the subcommittee that was to hold congressional hearings on the subject. He said, "We have a request to make of you."

"Yes?"

"We're getting input from other agencies around the country similar to yours, all responding to the same question. We would like to ask those agencies to redraft their input in the format that you've used. My committee members have found your information to be the easiest to access, the simplest to understand, and the most concise in its presentation. We would like to make this document the template for all future submissions of this kind. May we have your permission to do that?"

After I picked myself up off the floor I realized that I had just invented the preferred way—what was now going to be the "right way"—for certain reports to be sent to Congress.

Are you kidding me?

The Step Most Have Yet to Take

I didn't tell you that story to brag. I've long since passed the need to boast about myself. Somewhere between fifty and seventy that need runs out if we're lucky, and I've been lucky. I told you that story because I think it has relevance for all of us. And I have come to understand that what my father said to me years ago is exactly what Our Father said to me more recently.

So the purpose of life is to create yourself anew in the next grandest version of the greatest vision ever you held about who you are, and no one is going to tell you what that has to be, what it should be, what it must be, or what it is required to be, or the "right way" to be it. You get to decide all for yourself.

Yet this is a step that most people have yet to take. When you ask the average person, "What is the greatest vision you have about yourself?" they often can't tell you. Not in specific terms. And if they can, almost always what they have to say relates to something that they're *doing*, or wish to do, in the world. Yet what you're doing has nothing to do with who you are. It is what you're *being* that determines this.

You can choose anything your heart desires. Yet know this: It is a State of Being that your heart desires, not an employment situation. Not a career. That's just *how you've decided to be what you wish to be.*

You can choose to be any aspect of Divinity that you wish, but being *some* aspect of Divinity is what you came to physicality for. You can choose to be wisdom and clarity, compassion and understanding, patience and generosity, inspiration and creativity, healing and love—the kind of love that God has for *you*, flowing through you as you, to all the world. Pretentious? Some people might say yes, but I don't think so. And I know that God does not think so. I'm sure that God says, *Sounds like an exciting choice to me!*

Applying This Message to Everyday Life

It's going to be easy to come up with ways for you to apply this particular message in your daily life, because the message itself is so easy to understand. It drives right to the heart of the human experience. It sings to the soul. It even impresses the skeptical mind (and that's not an easy thing to do).

Here are some ideas—and I'm sure you can come up with many more on your own—for the application of this message in your daily life:

- Decide right now, before another day goes by, what the grandest version of who you are is. And don't be worried about "getting it right." I want you to understand, *there is no way you can get it wrong.* Just decide. Just choose.

- As you make this decision, also do not worry that you somehow have to stick with it until you die. The idea is to re-create yourself anew every day. Or, if you're up for the excitement, every hour. Or if you really want to fly, every *minute*. Notice that each moment of your life is a time of your rebirthing. It's the greatest gift that God can possibly give you: A space in which nothing has yet happened and in which you can decide exactly how you want yourself to be, regardless of all that has gone before. Notice that nothing has any meaning save the meaning you give it. Decide, then, that your past means nothing, except to the degree that it informs your next grandest idea about yourself.

- Notice as you go through the next day and the next week and the next month, having made the decisions that you've made above, that life provides you, surprisingly and consistently, with the perfect stage upon which to play out the scene of your own authoring. Here's that fellow Shakespeare again. He said it perfectly, didn't he? "All the world's a stage, and all the men and women merely players: They have their exits and their entrances; and one man in his time plays many parts."

Life's invitation to us all: Play your part well. Have *fun* with it. And when it does not seem like fun, bring wisdom to it. And when wisdom fails, bring patience. And when patience is in short supply, bring acceptance. And when acceptance is difficult, bring gratitude. For gratitude reverses any idea that something that is going on should not be happening. And then, we have found peace.

17

I've chosen to move through this list of the 25 Core Messages of *Conversations with God* in reverse for a reason. Viewed in their original sequence, as the messages are presented in chapter 2, one thing leads to another in logical progression. But as we analyze them and explore them more deeply, I have started with the last messages and worked backward in order to allow you to more clearly see *how we got there*.

As with any theology, the building blocks of thought and insight and wisdom upon which the study of God is based are important. But it can be especially revealing if we play the movie in reverse, so to speak. I'm at a point in my life where I do that a lot in my own thinking. I know where I've ended up (so far), and it's always instructive for me to look at how I got here, event by event, decision by decision, choice by choice, moment by moment, from the most recent moment to those that preceded it.

When I look back on it, I don't think of my life in the order in which it was experienced. I don't view it from birth to now. Rather, I look at it from now to yesterday, and then the day before that, and

then the months and the year before that, and then the longer period of my preceding adulthood, my youth, and my childhood.

In this way I often experience what I call an "aha," because I see
in advance the impact of each card that fell when the cards that fell
after it are shown. I realize how it is possible that I could be playing
the hand I'm playing now—and I see the *impact* of those previous
cards on the development of my present hand.

To get a better sense of this experience, play an entire game of
chess and record each move you and your opponent make as the
game goes on. Then play the game you've just finished *backward*.
Watch how each previous move created the situation you found
yourself in at the end of the game. (This is a great way to learn how
to master chess, by the way. And it's a great way to understand how
looking at one's life in reverse can give us great insight as we move
forward.)

So in looking at the spiritually revolutionary cosmology of *Conversations with God*, I've chosen to offer you an opportunity to explore it from the end to the beginning, allowing you to see how
each Core Message emerged from a previous articulation, thus creating a series of "aha!" moments that would not be possible moving
from beginning to now, for the simple reason that you wouldn't
know where you're going to be ending up.

We are looking, then, at humanity's new cultural story and a
proposed new spiritual paradigm as a detective would look at a
mystery. He arrives upon the scene and knows exactly what has
happened, but he doesn't know how or why. So he starts looking for
clues, signs, indications that will tell him just how what has occurred *has happened*.

You Are a Spiritual Sleuth

As you have joined me here in looking at what God said, you get to be a detective, arriving at the scene of humanity's present experience and unraveling the mystery of how we got to this place of seriously offering humanity another idea about itself and an opportunity to re-create its entire story anew.

That's what we're up to here, of course. The *CWG* cosmology winds up being an open invitation to the entire human race to rewrite its cultural story, to decide again who we are as a species, to choose anew what we are doing here on the Earth, and to announce why we are doing it—thus to lay down a new basis, a new foundation, upon which we may build our individual and collective future. Or as Robert Kennedy said in his memorable phrase: to seek a newer world.

Of all the messages in the three-thousand-plus pages of the *Conversations with God* dialogues, none struck me as part of that newer world as much as the one we are going to explore next. When we look at it closely, which we are going to do now, you'll see how it became possible for us to come to the conclusions that we reached in our preceding chapters.

I should warn you, however, that the present chapter may not be easy to absorb in one fast reading. What I have been shown here is not something I was able to just breeze through when I first heard it. It may be challenging for you as well.

Allow yourself to take some time with it, then. You may even wish to read certain passages more than once. Go slow, take it all in, and think deeply about what is being said as you go along. For now comes the great "aha" that allows you to understand more deeply, more richly, and more fully how I could have made the statements that have already been made here.

Let's take a look at a stunning announcement from God to humanity . . .

> *CWG* CORE MESSAGE #14
>
> Your life has nothing to do with you. It is about everyone whose life you touch, and how you touch it.

It had never occurred to me until over a half century into the experience that life had nothing to do with me. Like just about everyone else whom I observed, I assumed that of course my life had everything to do with me.

I was not so presumptuous as to imagine that *all* of Life around me was about me, but it seemed perfectly reasonable for me to assume that the largest part of life that I was personally experiencing was about me. Now, here was the God of my understanding telling me just the opposite; that my life had nothing to do with me and that if I thought it did, I was missing the point.

What an astonishment. What a shocker. What a waker-upper.

At first, I wanted to argue with it. How could my own day-to-day experience have nothing to do with me? *What was I expected to do with that information?* How was I to understand this functionally in my life?

Now, after living with this Core Message for more than fifteen years, I can tell you that it has been one of the most rewarding to implement in my day-to-day experience—and one of the most challenging.

It changed everything. It changed my reason for getting up in the morning. It changed my purpose for moving through the day. It changed my understanding of the day's encounters when I placed my head on the pillow at night, staring up at the ceiling, wondering what I had accomplished and what any of it meant.

It is, for sure, a new and radical way of looking at life. If I began considering my life with the proposition that I *needed* something, then I would assume that I would have to pay attention to my needs, spending time in making sure that they were fulfilled. Yet if I spent my time on activities having nothing to do with myself, those needs would go unmet. So the idea that life had nothing to do with me required me to embrace a separate notion about myself: that on a personal level I required nothing at all.

As I looked deeply into this possibility, I began to see the difference between requiring and desiring. I understood that the fact that I *require* nothing at all did not mean that I *desire* nothing at all. In the past, I had seen my desires as requirements. The two had become one, almost as if I had created a new word: "desirements." I had come to feel that if my life did not fulfill my desires, I could not be happy. This meant that fulfilling my desires was *required*.

Exploring this further, it suddenly became clear to me that the human race has been making the exact same mistake with regard to God. We have concluded that because there are things that God *desires*, there are things that God *requires*. Only when I finally came to realize that God needs nothing and that God's Essence included, by definition, everything that is, did I begin to pay closer attention to the difference between what God *desires* and what God *requires*.

There is *nothing* that God requires, but there are things that God desires. Desiring something does not only mean that one does not have it, it can also mean that one *has* it and loves it so much that one chooses to experience more of it.

In this way a God could be perfectly happy and desire to be happier still!

So, too, with us. We could even desire to be *Happier Than God*. And that is what the book by the same name is all about. In this book, which I believe I was inspired by God to produce, I found that I, too, could *desire* something without *requiring* it in order to be happy.

This was not an insignificant "remembering."

Why the Masters Said It

When I remembered who I really am, when I understood that my Soul is the presence and the evidence of God within me, I came to see that I couldn't possibly require anything, because everything that I could possibly desire was easily within reach—within *me*.

That's the last place, of course, that I had originally imagined I should look. I had spent the first fifty years of my life searching outside of myself for what it was that I desired. And when I couldn't find it, the increasing pressure to acquire what I "desired" turned it into something that I "required." At some point it began to seem as if I *needed it* in order to be happy.

When God told me that my life had nothing to do with me but with everyone whose life I touched and the way in which I touched it, my eyes were opened in shocked realization of what I then remembered was *always* true: I needed nothing—and the way to *experience* that I had everything I once imagined that I needed was to simply give it away.

"Havingness" is experienced through "givingness," not through "receivingness." It is not what we *get* out of life, but what we *give* to life, that brings us the experience of what we *have* in life—and through that experience the fullest realization of who we really are becomes possible.

I suddenly understood why all the spiritual masters through all of the ages have all said, each in their own way: "It is more blessed to give than to receive."

Yes, yes, I had heard that through all of my youth, but no one ever explained to me why I should accept this as true. No one ever explained to me the metaphysics of it. Not my parents at home, not the nuns in school, not the priests from the pulpit, not the elders within my community, not the larger society in which I lived, not the world that I observed. I was being instructed by no one and nothing around me as to why or how it could be "more blessed to give than to receive." It sure *sounded* nice, but no one ever told me—or seemed to be able to tell me—why it was true.

Then, after over a half century on the planet, I had my wonderful conversations with God and I was told something so simple that it now seems almost embarrassing to share it as if it were some Great Hidden Truth. Yet here it is: It is in *giving* we demonstrate, and thus experience, what we *have*.

Bingo! I had made the connection! Then I understood that we needed to *reach* out for *nothing*, but to *give* out *everything*, if we wished to experience ourselves in fullness.

This notion depended on a prior understanding of no little significance. We had to know that we possessed everything for which we had a desire; that it was, in fact, all inside of us all along.

Yet how could we embrace such an idea when the whole of our experience from birth seemed to have shown us that exactly the opposite was true?

The Biggest Challenge Facing Humanity

This has become the central question facing our species. How can we imagine, embrace, or accept the idea that we are in need of nothing when our day-to-day experience appears to evidence that this is not true?

The answer is astonishingly simple. We have to use our very existence as a single unified being called Humanity to demonstrate our ability to meet the needs of Humanity.

When each of us meets the needs of all of the rest of us, then none of us have *any* needs, and the promise and the prophecy of God is fulfilled: Humanity is without needs.

This is precisely what God does. When God experiences a desire of any kind, God simply satisfies that desire with what God already has. Thus, God "needs" nothing.

Yet in order for Humanity to experience this, we would have to *understand* ourselves to, in fact, *be* a single unified being, all of us but parts of a single body. We would have to decide that We Are All One is not merely an aphorism, but the way we were designed, the way we were intended to experience ourselves, and the way we were to *function*, in order to express our Divinity.

Yet is it realistic for us to conclude that if we act as if we are all one—that if we are there for each other and share with each other and care for each other—lack and need and suffering will disappear from the face of the Earth?

Well, of course, we have no way of knowing, since we've never dared to try it. At least, not on a wholesale basis. There have been cultures, of course, that have acted exactly like this, living in community, operating as a whole, where "all for one and one for all" was a given. We note that in such cultures and societies, the level of human happiness skyrockets, leaving us to wonder what life could be like across the entire planet if the whole of humanity lived this way.

Oneness Is Not an Objective, It's a Method

Yet the creation of such a collective experience is not the specific purpose of the Soul. The intention of the Soul in coming to physicality is singular and simple: To express and experience, to become and to fulfill through physicality, that which is Divinity Itself. The practice of Oneness is simply the fastest way to do it. It is a method, not an objective.

Life is God made physical, and each aspect and element of physical life expresses Divinity in Fullness when it reaches its particular form of expression in Completion.

A rose expresses Divinity in Fullness when its growth and blooming is complete. There is nothing more for it to do. It has done what it appeared in the Realm of the Physical to do. There is no reason to feel sad when the process is complete, but only to celebrate.

A star in the night sky expresses Divinity in Fullness when its growth and blooming is complete. There is nothing more for it to do. It has done what it appeared in the Realm of the Physical to do. There is no reason to feel sad when the process is complete, but only to celebrate.

A human being expresses Divinity in Fullness when its growth and blooming is complete. There is nothing more for it to do. It has done what it appeared in the Realm of the Physical to do. There is no reason to feel sad when the process is complete, but only to celebrate.

We don't live to fulfill our needs, we live to express our potential. The two are not the same.

We most fully express our potential when we demonstrate it as our reality, not as something we are *needing* to experience but as something that we are *choosing* to experience right now.

And *that* is why my life has nothing to do with me and everything to do with you and everyone else whose life I touch. And I have discovered that by living this way, all of the things for which I was yearning and reaching and striving in years past have come to me without effort.

(And if that isn't reason enough to embrace this message and give it a try in your life, then I don't know what is.)

APPLYING THIS MESSAGE TO EVERYDAY LIFE

Life affords us endless opportunities from day to day, hour to hour, moment to moment to place Core Message #14 on the ground in our daily experience. Here are some ways that we might be able to do that:

- Watch all the little things that you are doing today. Not the big things like going to work or heading to the doctor for an appointment or bringing the car to the garage for a tune-up or whatever other activities are consuming your moments this day, but the little things. The rinsing out of your glass in the sink after using it. The petting of the dog. The grabbing of a bite to eat. The words of hello or good-bye that you share with a loved one. All of the little things. Just take a look at them.

- Now ask yourself why you are doing them. Are you doing them for yourself? Are you doing them for an-

other? If you see yourself doing them for yourself, notice how you feel about that. If you see yourself doing
them for another, notice how you feel about *that*.

- Decide that everything you are doing from this day
  forward has nothing to do with you. You are doing
  what you are doing but not because you need to, not
  because you have to, not because it is required of you,
  but because every single thing that you do is seen as a
  contribution by you toward another. Conceive of it, if
  it makes it easier for you, not as a *direct* contribution
  toward another, but a contribution toward another
  nonetheless. Then explore deeply why and how what
  you are now doing contributes to another. Ask yourself
  if even asking another for something is you giving
  them an opportunity to experience themselves in a particular way. Once you reach this understanding and
  this awareness, hold your every action in that place
  from this day forward.

- Begin to make not just indirect but direct contributions to the life of another more frequently, more flu-
  idly, and more intentionally as each day goes by. Decide
  that you need nothing—not wisdom, not knowledge,
  not understanding, not love, not happiness, not patience, not compassion, not fulfillment, not anything
  at all to make you happy. Decide that all these things
  exist already *within* you, and that your only job in life
  is to allow them to pour forth *from* you into the life of
  another—a person who is still living within the illusion
  that they need these things and must depend on some
  exterior source in order to get them. Allow yourself to

become the Source. Watch what this does to you. Watch what this does *for* you.

Ah! Now we see the circle is complete! So it turns out that what you are doing is being done for you *after* all! Of course that's true, because there is only one of us. Therefore, what you do for another, you do for yourself, and what you fail to do for another, you fail to do for yourself. So it turns out that life has everything to do with you. But with Big You, not with Little You; with Universal You, not with Local You.

The purpose of life is to do what One desires. But not Little One. Rather, Big One. The only One. When you understand this fully, you will be able to live fully what has been called the Divine Dichotomy. And that will change everything in your experience upon the Earth.

18

If we are to truly engage in the process of manifesting on Earth what One desires, it would be necessary for us to have some control over the events of our lives, some modicum of jurisdiction, at least some small ability to command and to create the circumstances of our day-to-day experience.

Most of us have experienced our lives as an expression of exactly the opposite. It seems to us that we have very little control over anything. We are told that God is in charge and that God will decide what is best for us. And if we don't believe in God, then we imagine that we are at the mercy of Fate. If we are not a fatalist, then we think of ourselves as simply moving through a random series of random events in a random universe that offers no guarantee of any particular outcome whatsoever.

Once again, we turn to humanity's great metaphysician William Shakespeare, who captured the dilemmas of these conflicting ideas perfectly in his soliloquy: "To be, or not to be, that is the question. Whether 'tis nobler in the mind to suffer the slings and arrows of outrageous fortune, or to take arms against a sea of troubles, and by opposing, end them?"

What to do, *what to do*? And does it even matter what we do? Are we just kidding ourselves here? Are we deluding ourselves and each other in thinking that we are even in some small way in charge?

Most of our theology tells us not to even worry about such questions but simply to depend on God. It tells us to pray without ceasing and to have faith without limitation. This presents us with an interesting dichotomy. Why bother praying if we have limitless faith that the outcome that we prefer will occur? Yet we are told to have faith that we will be given what we ask for, but first we must ask for it. And of course, we must be in good standing with our Deity. If we are not in good standing, all the prayers in the world will not do us any good at all.

This is largely the message of most of the world's religions. It's a primitive rendering of it, but that's largely the message. The communication that comes to us from God in the New Spirituality is somewhat different and is captured in Core Message #13.

CWG CORE MESSAGE #13

You are the creator of your own reality, using the Three Tools of Creation: *Thought, Word,* and *Action.*

This is at once one of the most exciting and one of the most dangerous teachings of the world's New Thought Movement. It suggests that we are totally in charge, and in this it is entirely accurate.

However, the suggestion has been taken to mean that being in charge of our outer reality is a singular experience. That is, a unilateral quality and ability. We have been led to believe that we are singularly responsible for the reality that we are encountering in the world around us.

That is not accurate—as you have no doubt learned.

What Has Not Been Explained

It is not often explained by those who tell us that we are the creator of our own reality that we are doing this *collaboratively*. The "we" that we are is the One that we are. If we do not start from the proposition that we are all one, we will dangerously misunderstand the process by which we are creating our own reality.

The three tools of creation are, in fact, thought, word, and action, just as is noted in this Core Message. But it is the *collective* thought of *humanity*, the *combination* of *all* the words that we speak, and the actions in which *the lot of us* are engaged that produces our exterior experience of life on Earth.

And so the good news is that you are not singularly responsible for the wars in the world and the disease and pestilence that causes massive suffering and the poverty that creates such sadness around the globe or any of the other physical manifestations, good or bad, that we daily witness.

This is also the bad news, because it seems to, in fact, confirm our original assessment that we *aren't* in control of our experience, that we *have* no jurisdiction or authority over our lives, and that we *are* relegated to suffering the slings and arrows of outrageous fortune.

Yet *Conversations with God* makes it clear to us that we are in no such position. How, then, to reconcile these two views of the world?

Defining Our Terms

We begin by understanding what is meant by the phrase "your reality." This phrase must, in our new lexicon, refer to how we are each interiorly *experiencing* the manifestations of our collective exterior physical life, not to those outer manifestations themselves.

This is not the first time this point has come up on these pages. But let's look at it now more closely.

God is telling us that it is not what is occurring outside of us that creates our experience and thus our reality with regard to who we are and the way in which we are manifesting this, it is our interior *decision* about this that is doing so. It is our internal choice. It is our separate conclusion, our individual assessment.

Put simply: Everything is what we say it is. Or as has been ironically noted by some: One person's profit is another person's poison. One person's trash is another person's treasure. One culture's highest values are another culture's rejected and discarded notions.

There is great power in this, although it may not be immediately apparent. The power that is contained here is the power to separate ourselves from the apparency of external appearances and turn within to create *our own experience of them*.

Difficult as it is to believe, there are some people who actually enjoy boiled spinach. No, it's true. I've actually seen people eat this stuff—and ask for more! Apparently they're experiencing something on that fork that I am not. *What is that all about . . . ?* It is about our individual ability to label our collective experience whatever it suits us to individually label it.

The rain on Saturday is simply the rain on Saturday. It is an objective event. It is something that is occurring. It is "what is arising," as my friend Eckhart Tolle would say. What you think of the rain—and thus, how you experience it—is your business.

When "Reaction" Becomes "Creation"

Now there is an even greater power here than may be immediately obvious. Because when we are in a position to experience and to create our inner reality of any outer circumstance in the way that we wish, we begin to generate an enormous amount of internal energy that, *when projected into our exterior world*, begins to impact that world in such a way that the exterior reality becomes a closer and closer reflection of the interior experience of the spiritual master.

If we hold no animosity toward or negativity about any exterior person, place, or event, the energy that we project into the exterior person, place, or event begins to *transform* that person, place, or event. And if enough of us remove animosity and negativity from our interior experience of exterior events, we begin through the collection of our individual expressions to produce a collaborative impact on the group creation itself. It has been noted that in this way one person can change the world.

Thus it has come to pass that people such as Mother Teresa and Martin Luther King Jr., Lech Walesa and Gloria Steinem, Harvey Milk and you and me have had more effect on the collective reality than any of us might ever have imagined.

I included you and me in that group of widely celebrated people because the only difference between them and us is that they were aware of what they were doing while they were doing it, while many of us are not.

Many people have no idea what they're doing. I admit that I have found myself in that group many times. But I know now that the way I am moving through the world is impacting and changing the world around me. I didn't always understand this. Certainly not on a broad scale. I didn't know that the way I was choosing to inwardly hold the exterior manifestations of life affected those exterior manifestations.

Many people—perhaps most—think they have no control over those manifestations, and that their only response is to react to them. Yet we have the power to not simply react but create our responses. And this is what is meant by: "You are the creator of your own reality."

Your Power Is Greater Than You Think

Make no mistake about this. There is no end to the power of an individual to alter the collective known as humanity. And wherever two or more are gathered, that power is increased exponentially. Not in a 1–2–3–4 progression, but in a 2–4–8–16–32 progression.

If you think the sun makes the paper hot by beating down on it at high noon, watch what happens when you put a magnifying glass between the sun and the paper. If you want to set the world on fire, choose to magnify the highest thoughts that God is beaming down upon us.

You'll find those highest thoughts not in your Mind, but in your Soul. Why not the Mind? If you listen to your Mind, you will find thoughts of survival and what it takes to do that, thoughts of fear and what it takes to assuage that, thoughts of power and what it takes to express that, thoughts of anger and what it takes to release that, thoughts of threat and what it takes to avoid that. You will find none of these thoughts in your Soul.

I have said before in my writings and I will explain here again that your Mind is the repository of this life's experience. Your Soul, on the other hand, is the repository of your eternal knowledge. Your Mind can only respond to what it observes to be occurring based on what it thinks is occurring. Your Soul responds to what is occurring based on what it *knows* to be occurring. Your Soul knows what's occurring because your Soul has engaged collaboratively with other Souls in the creation of what's occurring. It does not seem to your Mind that this is what's happening. So what your Mind tells you often has nothing to do with the occurrence at hand. We only think that it does.

Even if what's occurring externally appears to be something damaging to you or hurtful to you, or injurious to your person in any way, your Soul knows that this is merely an evaluation made by the Mind based on its extraordinarily limited understanding of who you are and what you're doing here. (Your Mind thinks that who you are is your Body, and that what you are doing here is trying to survive.)

The Soul knows that even if the Mind's assessment and prediction with regard to what is occurring proves to be what you would call "true" concerning your Body, your Soul still has not been hurt, damaged, or injured in any way, because such a thing is impossible given the totality of who you are, and such a thing would not be allowed to happen, given what it is that this totality is doing here.

Therefore, to be the creator of your own inner reality at the highest level, you are invited by life to create from your Soul's knowledge and not from your Mind's experience.

We are, indeed, creating our own reality. But the process is not as simplistic as the words might seem to indicate. It is not about simply producing a new car in the driveway or diamonds around your neck or a shiny new bicycle outside the front door (all of which were sadly used as demonstrations of your personal creative "power" in the movie *The Secret*). No, the Power of Personal Creation is about producing a shiny new You. It is not about acquiring or achieving things, it is about expressing and experiencing things. Indeed, the *highest* thing you could express and experience. It is about expressing and experiencing Divinity.

Over and over again this message is given to us in *Conversations with God*. Over and over again it appears here on the pages of this very book. That message awaits your embracing. Or you can go on living your life exactly as you have been in the past. The choice is yours.

APPLYING THIS MESSAGE TO EVERYDAY LIFE

I don't want to make it sound for one minute that all of this is very easy, that all of this is very simple, that all of this is like rolling off a log, that "there's nothing to it." I would be lying to you if I told you that this was my experience, and I do not want to suggest in any way that that will be yours. This is challenging. And it is challenging because it is transforming.

And yet, after a while, it does become easier. Saints and sages and gurus of all of our wisdom traditions have told us so. The process of personal transformation becomes easy as we go along. But I want at this juncture to paraphrase a marvelous articulation from John F. Kennedy in his inaugural address:

"All of this will not be accomplished in the first one hundred days, nor in the first one thousand days, nor, perhaps, even in our lifetime. *But let us begin.*"

How to begin becomes the question. Here are a few humble suggestions from one who has just begun the real work himself:

- The moment anything occurs in your life that begins to upset you or cause you to worry or throws you into mental anguish or emotional turmoil, watch what your mind is doing with the data that has been incoming. Then, *change your mind about that.* You can do this. It is simply a case of Mind over matter. You instruct your Mind to think its highest thought, rather than its lowest. (This process is wonderfully explained in the book *When Everything Changes, Change Everything.*)

• Practice at least three times a day inviting your Mind to access the knowledge of the Soul. This can be done in any number of ways, and here is one that I use: Ask your Soul if it knows anything at all about what is now being encountered by your Body and your Mind. Ask your Soul: "If you hold any knowledge that can expand upon the experience from which my Mind is drawing to reach its conclusion, what would that be?" In other words, simply ask your Soul a question! This is how I began my conversations with God. I didn't know I was doing it at the time, but this is how the entire experience began. My Soul is my direct link to God. So my dialogue with God began with the process that Byron Katie calls Inquiry. Ask your Soul what's true about what you're thinking about what's happening. Your Soul will tell you the truth. Always.

• Know that the doorway to the Soul is opened very easily, but first the Mind must agree to knock on that door. Without this agreement, the Mind will attempt to block everything. And no, you cannot access the Soul by trying to go around the Mind. It's impossible to turn your Mind off, but it is not impossible to redirect it. A description of how to use the Mind to access the Soul can be found in *The Storm Before the Calm*. The relevant chapter is posted at www.TheWaytothe Soul.net.

- Choose in every moment that you can manage it to make life an experience of creation rather than reaction. When something that does not feel welcome arises in your life, don't ask yourself, "What does this mean?" Ask yourself, "What do I *want* this to mean? What do I *choose* for this to mean? What did I *intend* for this to mean?" Then don't look to your Mind to give you the answers. *You* give the answers to your *Mind*. This is called "making up your mind." Most people let their Mind tell *them* what to think. Masters tell their Mind what to think.

- In at least three places where you will see it often, put a sticky note that says: "Nothing has any meaning save the meaning I give it." Perhaps you'll put that in your closet or maybe on your vanity mirror or maybe on the dashboard of your car—or maybe all three of those places. I know a man who actually had a bracelet engraved with those words. Whenever life would bring him a moment or a circumstance in which he was tempted to be discombobulated, he would watch the feeling arise within him, reach over and touch with his right hand the bracelet on his left wrist, allow the energy from the message that was engraved there to course through his body, and move to a place of greater peace almost instantly.

- Give yourself permission to understand what we are doing here, to become clear about the purpose of life and the opportunity that our day-to-day experience presents us. If you are, you will see each incoming event as a blessing, no matter what it is. In such moments, you move toward completion on the journey of your Soul. You can reach completion more than once in a lifetime. That is the beauty and the wonder and the glory of Completion. You never can be, and never want to be, "completely complete" with this process. Rather, you want to experience being Complete over and over and over again. That is why life is "showing up" the way it is.

- Write down in a separate place the point I have been making here, which is that because the Master understands this, the Master's inner experience of her outer reality begins to affect and re-create that outer reality, such that certain negative encounters and experiences in the outer world begin weakening in their impact, reducing in their frequency, and ultimately receding altogether.

Someone once described me in the most unusual way. "You walk around with a bluebird on your shoulder," they said to me. I am not sure this was meant as a compliment. I think it was perhaps a mixture of mild annoyance and envy. And I think that the person who said this imagined that I was lucky to have such a nature, that it was a by-product of my fortunate upbringing, or simply a gift of genetics. They did not realize that I also played a role in nurturing this.

We are all the creators of our own inner reality. Shall we put a bluebird on our shoulder?

19

One thing that helps me to keep that bluebird flying along with me, dancing all around me, and hopping onto my shoulder at every opportunity, is the fact that I am deeply aware that there is only one true emotion, one true experience, and one true identity.

I'm not referring to my identity only, but to the identity of God, and for that matter, the identity of everything on Earth, all that there is in the heavens, and our entire universe.

Call me a cockeyed optimist, but I have always felt from the earliest moments of my life that life itself was on my side. I didn't see life as that which was opposing me but that which was composing me. Several times when I was young I was given the advice to "compose yourself." I took this to mean that I should "get myself together." As my life went along, I began taking this quite literally. I am seeing my life as a symphony, and every minute is like a movement in that musical piece—and I am composing it as I go along. And with each passing year I have become more and more convinced that life is not opposing me but composing me. It is joining me in my process of "making it up the way I want it to be."

It just never occurred to me that life would oppose me. I couldn't figure out any reason why it would do that. I imagined myself to live in a friendly universe. Now I admit that much of this may have been due to the fact that I grew up in a wonderful family with wonderful surroundings and happy experiences wherever I turned.

I had a stay-at-home mother who actually got down on the floor with my brother and me to play with our toys, made us peanut butter and jelly sandwiches for lunch, and whose entire life seemed to be devoted to my brother, myself, and my father. And I had a father who was hardworking, never missed a day at the office, "brought home the bacon," kept us safe and secure, and played the appropriate role for a father in the '50s. He became a leader of our Boy Scout troop, took us fishing to Canada, showed us how to use an ax to chop down a tree in the backyard, and played softball with us. (Actually, Mom played softball with us, too! It was usually Mom and me against my dad and my brother.)

If you think this seems like a scenario straight out of a '50s television sitcom with Jane Wyman and Robert Young, you'd be right. As I've explained earlier in this narrative, we didn't have lots of money—we would have been defined as lower middle class—but we never lacked for anything that it seemed really important for us to have, and most of all we had our parents' love, their attention, their obvious devotion, and their presence in our lives in a large and meaningful way.

Not everyone on this planet can speak in this way of their childhood, and I am clear that I am very fortunate to be able to do so. And this situation, without question, has much to do with why I grew up with such a positive attitude about life. Life *was* on my side, as far as I could see, as far as I could tell, as far as I knew.

So I owe a huge thanks to my parents and an enormous debt of gratitude to God for placing me in such an environment, for putting me in such a blessed space, for giving me such a glorious opportunity to experience life's Better Side so early in my journey on the Earth.

It Didn't Go on Forever

That having been said, a sweet and loving childhood is no guarantee that somebody will grow up with a positive attitude. More than one person has had precisely the same kind of upbringing, only to move into adulthood with a feeling of *entitlement*. And when they don't get what they feel themselves to be entitled to, they become anxious, upset, and negative. Ultimately, this can turn into bitterness and anger, and a long-term feeling that life may have been on our side at the beginning but has since turned against us.

For my own part, I saw early in my adult life that the road was going to be much bumpier outside of that safe container in which I spent my childhood. The rough-and-tumble of finding a job, earning a living, keeping myself going in romance and in the other arenas of my day-to-day encounters was certainly vastly different from my experience on Mitchell Street in Milwaukee, Wisconsin, where all was well all the time—or certainly seemed to be.

And as I moved even more deeply into my adult experience, pushing into my thirties and forties, I began to realize how hard my parents must have worked to create for me such a wonderful environment. Yet as difficult and emotionally challenging as my own life began to be, I somehow never lost my early thought, never set aside my beginning assumption, that in the end, all would always work out, everything would be okay, there was nothing to worry about, and life was on my side.

And by golly, that was exactly how it was turning out. Then, in one quick snap, I was given an opportunity to see the other side of life.

A Pain in the Neck

As many of you are aware if you know my story, I was driving down the road one day when an elderly gentleman crashed into me, causing an accident in which I fractured my seventh cervical vertebra posteriorly.

Not a good thing.

To put this into context (and to make sure you know that I am not exaggerating), let's look at what the encyclopedia has to say about such an event:

> A cervical fracture, commonly called a broken neck, is a catastrophic fracture of any of the seven cervical vertebrae in the neck. Examples of common causes in humans are traffic collisions and diving into shallow water. Abnormal movement of neck bones or pieces of bone can cause a spinal cord injury, resulting in loss of sensation, paralysis, or death.

Amazingly, I escaped all three. Apparently my neck fractured in just the right place to avoid those outcomes. I could not, however, avoid two and a half years of rehabilitation.

I was unable to lift so much as a half gallon of milk with my arm extended, I walked around in a Philadelphia collar for two years, unable to remove it for any reason whatsoever—not even a shower, not even to sleep at night. My neck was to be kept immobilized. And if you don't think that will radically limit your life's possibilities, think again.

Still, I was alive, and had no complaints. Except that I couldn't work for a living, the other driver's insurance took longer than two years to pay off as the company tried to negotiate me down, and I was utterly without income, with benefits from the social welfare system (food stamps, disability income, etc.) running out before new income was available to me.

Making a long story short, I wound up living on the street. Outside, in the air, with only a tent for shelter and with no means of personal transportation. (You will not believe this, but within weeks of the accident, my car was stolen. God, it seemed, was going to show me that life *wasn't* always a bed of roses, that some people had it a lot worse than others, and that I was going to be one of those people from now on.)

I wound up living in a homeless park, a stretch of open land that other transients had taken to occupy. Each of us had our own little campsite or area. Some of us only had lean-tos or makeshift shelters. Others of us were lucky enough to have a tent to at least keep us out of the weather. I was in the second group, but all I had in addition to my tent were two pair of jeans, three shirts, one pair of shoes, and a camper's stove with a couple of pots and pans. I felt like I was on an extended campout that would be over very quickly. How long could it take me to find a simple job somewhere, even with a therapeutic collar around my neck?

I couldn't have guessed that the answer would be: two weeks shy of a year.

Nobody wanted to hire somebody who was a walking unemployment insurance claim. After thirty-six weeks I found a weekend job at a little radio station that brought me four hundred dollars a month—which, I need to tell you, to a person living on the street is a fortune. I could eat again without Dumpster diving for soda bottles and beer cans to turn into cash for their redeemable deposits, hoping that I had enough to buy a bag of french fries.

Ironically, it was after I got off the street, rented myself a little cottage behind someone's larger luxury home, and found a full-time position at another local radio station, that I realized I had reentered a world of utter meaninglessness.

Reality Hits

I was putting in ten and twelve and sometimes fourteen hours a day, bringing home just enough money to scrape by, and trying to rebuild my life at the age of fifty. I can remember screaming to myself inside my mind, "A half century on the planet, and *this* is what I have to show for it?"

I could find no purpose in what I was doing other than to simply survive. Sure, I could grab a little bit of happiness here or there—catch a movie now and then, play a CD that I enjoyed, maybe even make love with a willing new friend once a month if I was lucky. But this was supposed to be it? This was going to be my life? I was supposed to start over after a half century, working my way up the ladder *again*? No, thanks. Thank you very much, but I don't think so.

And it was during this depressing "comeback" that I had my first conversation with God, which appears word for word in the books that have since been published. And then Hollywood made a movie of the entire drama.

That quick description of a multiyear experience is my way of telling you that, yes, there is a bluebird on my shoulder . . . and on the shoulder of all of us. Because after all was said and done, I found my way back to so-called "regular life" . . . then created the life of my dreams.

And, having said that, I want you to know that I understand, given the extremely challenging and difficult circumstances which so many people face (most often through no fault of their own), that it sure may not seem that way. I know this now not merely conceptually but from *experience*.

Yet it is my own difficult and challenging life experience that qualifies me to share with you now what I deeply understand about . . .

CWG CORE MESSAGE #12

Love is all there is.

Oh, really? So car accidents and broken necks and a year on the street don't count? Or, even more implausibly, they're all demonstrations of God's love?

So love is all there is, eh? So how do you explain my experience? It's true that I had pretty smooth sailing from birth to nineteen and not really much going on in terms of horrible outcomes or difficult challenges even from the age of twenty to the age of fifty. A pretty good life, in all, until that older gentleman decided for no apparent reason to drive right into me.

Sure, I had my relationship challenges, creating life events that left me and others feeling sad and disappointed, and sometimes downright angry with each other. But I could deal with that. Sure, I had my career ups and downs. But I could deal with that, too. And yes, I had a few minor health challenges along the way, but nothing I couldn't handle.

All of this fit easily within the framework of a relatively normal life. There were no major catastrophes, just the normal stuff that goes on with so many people in one way or another.

Ah, but now comes a situation that places me *on the street*, living the great human nightmare. My relationship was broken, so I had no place to go there. I didn't want to turn to my father or my family of origin because I was embarrassed—and I really did think that I would pull out of it within a few weeks.

So there I sat with my pride and my empty pockets in the home-less park, panhandling on the street for dimes and quarters to get through the day. This is what God's love is all about? Life is on my side? Love is all there is?

Sure.

The College of the Sidewalk

Only in hindsight have I been able to say that it was one of the most loving things that life could ever have done to me; that love comes in all shapes and sizes and in many different forms.

I learned more in that one single year of trudging down the sidewalk asking people if they could help a person down on his luck, I acquired more insight into human nature and more aware-ness of who I really am at the core of my being, than I could pos-sibly have done in any other life situation or circumstance.

It was the College of the Sidewalk. It was what my father would have called "a liberal education." I don't recommend it, mind you, but I certainly am grateful for it.

If I had acquired even a smidgen of a sense of "entitlement" as a result of my golden childhood, or had developed even a tiny bit of complacency about the flow of life's goodness to me, all of that was quickly washed away. In its place came a new appreciation of just how rough this experience called Life can be—as well as a new understanding, a new awareness, a new expression, a new experi-ence of who I really am, of what life is really about, and of why we are all here in physical form.

I learned that my time upon the Earth had nothing to do with what I was accumulating in life. It was not about personal success or achievement or power or wealth. In fact, I learned that life had nothing to do with *anything* that I thought life was about.

This produced two interesting effects: First, it pulled the rug right out from under me, leaving me wobbly and working to keep my balance. Then, it created a platform upon which I could stand far more steadily than I could on the carpet of my misunderstandings. I knew that I would never have to worry again about falling, because this platform would never be pulled out from under me. It was the platform of my True Identity, of my Real Purpose, of my Oneness with Life and with God.

Divinity's Mirror

I'm surely not the first person to have encountered an experience that I thought, as I was encountering it, was the worst thing that could possibly happen to me—only to find months or years later that it was the *best* thing that ever happened.

When this occurred in my experience, however, it changed everything for me. I personally encountered the fascinating proposition that it was possible that *all* things that happen in life are for our highest benefit, even if we are not clear about what that benefit is.

It was while exploring this idea that I first looked at the larger possibility that I was, in fact, embarked on a Journey of the Soul having nothing to do with my Body and Mind except insofar as the latter were tools, devices, *vehicles* with which to undertake that journey, and to achieve what the Soul had set out to achieve along the way.

My conversations with God convinced me that I was an *eternal* being on an *eternal* journey, engaging joyfully and adventurously in a process that might loosely be called "evolution." That is, the process of *becoming*.

And becoming what? Becoming the next grandest expression of

who I really was: That Which Is Divine. Life is God realizing Itself as Itself, in moments of ever-increasing awareness.

Have you ever looked at yourself in the mirror and realized something about yourself that was always there, but that you suddenly saw as if for the first time? And if it was something positive, did a smile not come to your face?

Tell the truth. Have you ever looked at yourself in the mirror and with a blink of your eyes realized, "Hey, you know, I'm not bad-looking. And I'm a pleasant and nice human being. I like me!". . . ?

If you've had that experience, you may also have had this one: You deny your own beauty and goodness, telling yourself, "Well, this must be just a good day for me. It's a good hair day. And nobody knows me as I really am."

Still, the point is that we have the ability to become aware of ourselves, and to appreciate that of which we have become aware. We have not suddenly *become* good-looking. We have not suddenly *become* a pleasant and nice person. We always were. But suddenly we have become aware of this—even if we then immediately deny it or diminish it.

Surely you must be among those who have experienced moments in which you recognized your own compassion, your own patience, your own deep understanding, your own wisdom, and your own truly loving self. Surely you must have had moments, as have I, when you step back from yourself and appreciate yourself through a deeper awareness of yourself. This is a delicious and wondrous and glorious and very special human experience. Surely you have had it at least once.

This is what God experiences all the time.

Unlike us, God does not then deny what God is, but *delights* in the experience. And how is God creating this experience? *Through us*, and through every other expression of life in physicality—all of it magnificent, all of it wondrous, all of it incomprehensibly majestic, complex, and beautiful.

All of it Divine. All of it, Love expressed.

God's Most Unexpected Message

And now I want to share something very unusual that God said to me. Warning: It will seem more than unusual at first. It will seem radical. You're going to have to dive to the deepest level of understanding to really "hear" it. Yet it's something your Soul desires for you to hear, because it will give you a wondrous new view of life and of others *in* your life.

I have said that God is Love. I have said that Love is all there is. Well, then, what of fear? What of anger? What of hatred? What of evil? What of violence and killing? Surely, this can't be an expression of Love! *But it is.* And here is the most unusual, the most striking, the most unexpected message in the *Conversations with God* series of books: *Every* expression of Life is an expression of Love.

If you didn't love something, you couldn't hate something else. If you didn't love something so desperately, you couldn't even begin to think of using desperate measures, such as violence or killing, as a means of getting it, keeping it, or protecting it. If you didn't love something intensely, you could never be angry about either not having it or having it taken away from you.

Thieves act out of love. They love something so much that they desperately want to have it, and they know of no other way to get it, so they steal it.

The same is true of people who commit other actions that we call "crimes." Even the most horrific crimes. Rape. Murder. All are acts of love. Deeply distorted acts, for sure. Utterly unacceptable acts, without question. Not condoned or approved of or excused in any way by me, by society, or by the explanations in *Conversations with God*. No, not excused, but *understood*. And thus, *held* in a new way.

Nobody does anything that is not an act of love, however distorted and unacceptable that expression may be. If they didn't love something, they simply wouldn't have done what they have done. This is something that God understands completely.

God sees us as little children, without the emotional or spiritual maturity to truly understand or care about the impact and the consequence of our actions. And there is a tiny percentage of us who do things that are ugly beyond measure, totally unacceptable, and from a human point of view, utterly unforgivable.

It would take a saint to forgive some of the things that some people have done. Or perhaps, a God who is so saintly that forgiveness is not deemed necessary. For the message here is not that all things are forgivable from God's point of view, but that, difficult as it may be for us to embrace, all things emerge from a single energy in the universe that in our language we call Love, and so, are understandable. And understanding replaces forgiveness in the Divine Mind.

Even in your mind it does. You don't have to "forgive" a baby for crying at three in the morning, because you understand why the baby is doing so. You don't have to "forgive" a small child for knocking over the glass of milk while reaching for the pie, because you understand how it could happen to a child. You don't even have to forgive adults for certain things that they do which may make things awkward or difficult, when you understand why they have acted as they have acted.

Understanding replaces the need for forgiveness.

The only reason you would call anything "unforgivable" is that you *don't understand how anyone could do such a thing.*

But God does.

You see? It is all very simple. God does.

The Distortions Will Disappear

Now the remarkable insight that all action is birthed by Love creates a space within which we can finally and fully understand how certain things can occur, opening to an awareness that it is through extreme distortion of the Essential Energy that people do what we call "bad things."

It is very much like nuclear energy. This extraordinarily powerful force within our physical universe can be used in a way that is beneficial or nonbeneficial. Love is exactly like that. It is the most powerful energy of the entire cosmos, physical and nonphysical, and it can produce what we call "good" and what we call "evil."

Used without the distortion of a twisted or damaged mind, the Essential Energy of the universe is our best friend, creating a milieu within which we live and breathe and have our being, producing an environment that supports our every desire and perfectly generates from moment to moment the exact conditions necessary for us to complete the Soul's agenda.

Yet are the things we do to each other on this planet sometimes producing twisted thoughts and angry responses? Yes. Does humanity's very biochemistry sometimes produce damaged minds even at birth? Yes. Do both of these conditions sometimes produce both long-term and short-term mental illness, and what even our legal system understands as "temporary insanity" or "diminished capacity"—and for this very reason declares us *innocent?* Yes.

As humanity grows and evolves and increases in its understanding of the entire process by which life expresses itself, those distortions will become fewer and farther between. First, because our new understandings will cause us to behave in a remarkably different way with each other, making mistreatment and cruelty of every kind virtually disappear. Second, because our increased awareness of the long-term effects of every aspect of life will cause us to clean up our environment, alter what we consume, change other of our personal habits, and modify our lifestyles in ways that will drastically reduce and eventually all but eliminate biochemical imbalances in our species at birth.

Taken together, these alterations, as part of our evolution, will produce a new kind of human. Not only will blatant crimes disappear from our collective experience, but so will other blatant distortions of the Essential Energy. For it is not simply the crimes that are committed by humanity, but the many *legal* actions of human beings (speaking harshly to a beloved, ignoring what those close to us have to say or what they request, betraying life partners, etc.), that demonstrate on a daily basis that we simply have not learned how to love each other.

The Essential Energy *is* Love, and life calls us to express it, in only its purest form, in us, through us, and as us in every moment. When we evolve to the point where we understand and embrace this, our species will be very clear that creating an economic system in which 5 percent of the world's people hold or control 95 percent of the world's wealth and resources is simply not an expression of love for all of humanity. It will understand that a political process based upon ruthless absolutism, ugly name-calling, marginalization, and demonization is not in any way an expression of love. It will see that allowing over six hundred children to die of starvation every hour is not an expression of love. It will see that creating a "winner take all" society, a "to the victor go the spoils" culture, is not an expression of love. It will see that creating and encouraging second-class citizenship for persons of particular religions, nationalities, races, or sexual preferences is not an expression of love.

Life's Current Invitation

While we are clearly not there yet, I have found that it is possible to live an individual life knowing that the ever-present Essential Energy—that God in its highest form—is available to me at all times. This is the "bluebird" that some people say that I have on my shoulder. And the reason that I took the time to tell you—even though you may have heard it before—a bit of my life story here is that I wanted you to know that I am not speaking to you as someone who has spent his life on the mountaintop, but as someone who has known the devastation of losing everything and living a life of complete abandonment by society, struggling to survive not just month to month or week to week, but day to day and hour to hour in a cold and wet, windy and stormy world without warm shelter, without a guarantee of even your next morsel to eat, and with no one to hold your hand, give you a hug, and walk by your side through it all.

We remember that Love is all there is by allowing each moment of our life to be a demonstration of this, causing nothing but Love to flow through us to every person in every situation that life presents. This is exactly what Nelson Mandela did during the over quarter century that he was kept imprisoned in South Africa—to use one striking example of what human beings are capable of. It is said that his jailers wept when he was set free. They had lost their best friend.

And so we are invited by Life to create a new personal ethic, a new personal expression, a new personal experience. We are invited by Life to stand as an exemplar, a living and continuing presentation of the highest truth of life: Love is all there is.

All we have to do to step into such a possibility, such a demonstration, such an extraordinary expression, is to invite our Mind to move into a place of deep understanding of the "why" behind the "what" of human events.

When we understand why the robber robs, why the terrorist terrorizes, why the cheater cheats, why the killer kills, we then take a giant step toward the place where Divinity dwells.

With understanding comes not only the lack of a need for forgiveness, but a remarkable level of awareness that allows us to say: "When we know better, we do better," in the wonderful words of Maya Angelou.

Until I know better, I will do the best I can. And I'll begin by loving every person, place, and thing that I encounter, understanding that it was placed in the space of my life so that I might express and experience my True Identity—and that if I can do so without distortion, I will reach the place of self-realization at last, realizing that this has been, after all is said and done, the purpose of my entire life.

APPLYING THIS MESSAGE TO EVERYDAY LIFE

Challenging as it may be, it is possible for ordinary human beings to rise to the levels of understanding and awareness that I have been describing here. Nelson Mandela did it, Mother Teresa did it, and many other ordinary people as well. So we can do it, too. We begin in small ways. We take baby steps. And we get to where we want to go with little advances that result in big strides ultimately. Here are some small ideas that might help you along the way:

- Express the love that is all around you by loving your-self first. Notice the things that you yourself do that are not considered completely acceptable or totally won-derful by the society in which you live. Have you lied? Have you cheated? Have you hurt others? Have you looked out for yourself first and put others second at least a few times in your life and felt shamed in the aftermath as you saw what you had done? Have you shown up in life as less than you know yourself to be more often than you wish? If you are like me, the an-swer is yes. But if you are like me, you will also have moved into a place of understanding and loving your-self and allowing yourself to do what it takes to know better, and then to do better.

- Having found a way to understand and love yourself, even through the worst of your own behaviors, look then to see if there are persons around you to whom you can offer the same gift. It is the irony of many lives that we often find it possible to give that gift to others more easily than we can give it to ourselves. Yet if we can learn to give it to ourselves in the first instance, we find that it becomes even more possible and immensely more natural to offer that gift to others.

- Right now, think of three people in your life to whom you may give this gift. It begins in the human heart. It begins in the interior of you, where you give the gift at first silently. Then, you can speak it aloud in open and caring, compassionate and loving communication with the other. Do it this week with the three people you indentified above.

- As you move through your daily experience and come face-to-face with the moment-to-moment encounters of your life, ask yourself this question: *What would Love do now?* I have found this to be an extraordinarily motivating and deeply energizing inquiry. I use it all the time. And remember that we are talking about love for yourself as well as love for another. The two are not mutually exclusive. That is the most important thing that I've come to understand in my life. Loving myself and loving another at the same moment is possible. So be sure to do it, and don't feel you have to sacrifice one for the other.

- When you see a person behaving in a way that does not appear to be "loving" by our standard definitions, ask yourself (and ask that other person, if the opportunity arises) what is it that the other person is loving so much that the only way they feel they can express it is by distorting love itself? Look to see if the answer to this question brings you to a new level of understanding.

- Decide the next time you leave your house for any reason that you're really not stepping outside to perform any task or undertake any particular function, but rather, that you are simply giving yourself an excuse to express and to share your love with the world. Make this the very reason that you spend time doing anything. Imagine that everything you are doing was intended to be a form of love. See if this changes in any way how you move through the day and how you feel as you are performing ordinary tasks.

- Finally, choose to rely on the fact that love is available to come *to* you every bit as much as it is available to flow *through* you. See if you can find a way to move to a place where you simply know that Life and God want only the best for you, and seek in every way to flow love to you. Come to depend on it. Allow yourself to rely on it. Move to a place where you are certain this is what is going to occur. You will find, if you are in any way like me, that the power of such positive thinking can change your life.

20

We're beginning now to move into some of the more esoteric understandings and explanations with regard to life that have been offered to us in the *Conversations with God* dialogue. And nothing is more abstract than . . .

CWG CORE MESSAGE #11

There is no such thing as Space and Time; there is only Here and Now.

What *CWG* is telling us is that space and time—or what fantastic futurist Gene Roddenberry dubbed the space-time continuum—is purely a figment of our imagination. It is a construction of the human mind. It is a way that our species has created to organize the environment in which we find ourselves in order to make some sense of it, given our limited but ever-growing understandings—and, more important, a way to have it serve our purpose.

I envision a future in which our species will expand its consciousness and enlarge its awareness to include the possibility of living within a framework where it is clearly understood that Space and Time are manufactured realities, simply perceptual constructions allowing us to experience Always Here/Ever Now in a way that provides us with more opportunities than we could have guessed to know and experience our Divinity.

When discussing concepts such as Space and Time—and especially when discussing the *absence* of such limiting and conditional life expressions—it is necessary for us to suspend disbelief and to step outside of our comfort zone, moving beyond the territories within which the Mind most easily travels.

The Mind, it must be understood, holds only the data it has gathered since the moment when its biological mechanism was activated, between conception and birth. The Soul, on the other hand, is the repository of the full and complete awareness and the total knowledge of eternity.

As the Mind begins to access and absorb the vast and very different information held by the Soul, its own understandings and holdings, creations and constructions begin to fall apart. We find ourselves moving into esoteric explorations that cannot be supported or sustained by reason or logic or any evidence whatsoever. In such a discussion, conjecture replaces conclusion, possibilities replace probabilities, fictions replace facts. So it is within that framework that we proceed here.

The Nature of Things

I have been caused to understand that the whole of Ultimate Reality can be conceptualized as existing in three forms: the Realm of the Spiritual, the Realm of the Physical, and the Realm of Pure

Being. All three of these expressions of life exist simultaneously and always in a single "location." That's another way of saying that in Ultimate Reality, it is always Here and Now. In addition, in Ultimate Reality all there is is Love.

Physical life is based on an illusion through which we separate the inseparable—at least in our minds—thus permitting That Which Is Whole to be observable and experienceable in its aggregate parts. It was *intended to be* experienced in that way, in order that the Whole may be fully expressed.

Let me use a metaphor here in order to break that idea down just a bit.

Consider the beauty of new-fallen snow on a hillside at the break of dawn. The sun glistens upon the fresh blue-whiteness, creating a sight breathtaking to behold—but awesome *only because of the awesomeness of that which comprises it*, only because of the breathtaking beauty of its individual parts.

This is clearly evidenced when we collect a bit of that snow, separate each snowflake, one from the other, then look at them under high-intensity magnification and experience their wondrous beauty.

What stops those individual snowflakes from melting instantly on the hillside is the fact that they are one with the snow itself. They *are* the snow. The snow is not separate from them, the snow is the *sum total of them*. It is the lack of separation from the other snowflakes that allows all the snowflakes to form and sustain the whole.

The snow is the snow is the snow, and it is magnificent in its wholeness. It is even more magnificent in its aggregate parts. But one must know the beauty and the wonder of the aggregate parts in order to experience this.

That is exactly what God is doing with us.

You Are No Less Than a Snowflake

What makes all of God *experienceable* as God are the individual and disparate and aggregate parts of God, each of which is as magnificent as the Whole itself, and all of which *create* the magnificence that the Whole emanates.

Do not be tempted to use your powerful imagination to think that you are somehow less when compared to God than a snowflake is when compared to a mountain of snow. What we see all around us is *exactly how life is.* Ironically, we think this is how life is with regard to flakes that make up the snow, drops that make up the ocean, stars that make up the night sky, and just about everything else that makes up God . . . except *us.*

It is time now to stop that. It is time now to declare that *everything* in life is an expression of Divinity, not everything *but you.* Yes, you are an individuation of God, and individuation is not separation.

The illusion of Space and Time is what makes our individuation possible. And the absence of Space and Time in Ultimate Reality is what allows God's pure-as-snow Souls to remain "unmelted" forever.

The separation of All That Is into its individual parts is simply a process by which All That Is allows Itself to look at Itself and experience Itself in the aggregate wonder of Its Totality, through the use of Space and Time.

Now it could seem that the notion that there is no such thing as Space and Time has no practical application in your day-to-day life, but just the opposite may be true. It is my truth that in order to live in this *Alice in Wonderland* universe of ours, it is useful and necessary to conceive of things as existing in Space and Time. Yet knowing that both are an illusion can be metaphorically and metaphysically helpful in a number of ways.

First, we don't put too much negative energy on the passage of time, but allow ourselves, rather, to know that we exist in All Time. The urgency that the concept of limited time presents to us in our lives can thus be removed from our thinking and from our experience. We can become more peaceful, more calm, more centered, more relaxed, and thus more capable of creating in our individually experienced reality the kind of lasting tranquility and serenity for which we yearn.

As well, the esoteric understanding that there is really no space but Right Here allows us to consider the fictional spaces into which we move, and from which we emerge, as all the same place. Namely, the Kingdom of God. Or if you please, heaven. This is not an unimportant consideration.

Turning "Hell" into "Heaven"

The knowing that every place is the same place has been enormously helpful to me when I have found myself in physical locations that for one reason or another I judged to be unpleasant or unwelcome. In those places I have tried to bring the blessing of a deeper comprehension of Ultimate Reality to my current notion of what is right in front of me. And—in some strange and fascinating way—that larger comprehension often alters and transforms my present experience of the "location" in which I find myself. Put another way, my interior experience begins to color my exterior experience. I start to like where I am—*wherever* I am. I start to like what I am doing, *whatever* I am doing. I start to like who I'm with, *whoever* I am with.

I have a notion that this is the way all Masters walk through life. Not that I in any way claim to be one of those Masters, but I am studying the ways in which they have been known to move through their daily experience.

In the last chapter I brought up the example of Nelson Mandela, about whom you can find out more with a quick Internet search if you do not know who he is. You'll discover why he stands as such a striking example of this level of mastery.

Mr. Mandela spent over a quarter century in a prison for the "crime" of wanting to set his people free. Yet he turned his space into a wholly acceptable location, realizing that no matter where he was, the space became what he made it. He realized that there is really only one space, simply demonstrating different characteristics, and that those characteristics are nothing more than what we call them.

These kinds of esoteric understandings challenge us and invite us to consider whatever Space or Time we are currently occupying to be paradise—and to *make it so* by how we perceive it and how we experience it. And again, I want to make the point that it is our interior experience that affects the exterior reality in which we find ourselves, not the other way around.

Mr. Mandela's holding of his incarceration in a particular way altered the entire exterior environment in which he was involuntarily placed. His guards became his friends. They grew to admire him, and even to love him. They sought his counsel about life matters on the "outside" and he gave it to them willingly, happily, and even joyfully, understanding that he was exactly *where* he was *when* he was in order to be exactly *who* he was.

The same thing is true of all of us, no matter where we are or what time it is. And *that* is the applicable and practical life tool that is given to us in Core Message #11.

APPLYING THIS MESSAGE TO EVERYDAY LIFE

As divorced from our presently understood reality as the notion that is being discussed here may be, there are some ways that you may apply it to your daily encounters. Try these:

- Look around you right now. Stop everything you're doing, even put down this book, and look around you. Decide that where you are right now is heaven, and that things couldn't be any better if you wanted them to be. Notice that everything is perfect just the way it is. See that everything is supporting you magnificently in providing you with an opportunity to announce and to declare, to express and to experience, to become and to fulfill Who You Really Are.

- The next time you find yourself in a space that does not seem wholly pleasant to you, use your imagination. Just decide that it, too, is a little spot of heaven. Call it okay just the way it is, no matter how it is. And then see and feel and touch and smell and experience fully the wonder and the glory of that particular environment. Watch the space in which you find yourself transform right in front of your eyes.

- One interesting way to do this is to decide whether you would rather be where you are, as unpleasant as it may seem to be, or whether you'd rather be dead. (I know that there is no such thing as "dead," but I use the fiction as a metaphor to make this experiment work.) I've actually done this. I've actually found myself in spaces that were not totally pleasant for me, but when I asked myself if I would rather be there or be no longer among the living, suddenly everything around me looked not only acceptable but preferable.

• Now it is arguable that some people might say, "No, I'd rather be dead." And that, too, is a choice. It's okay to make that choice in your Mind. It's okay to stay in your negative energy about whatever you're experiencing in any particular space. There is no Right or Wrong around this. There are no rules here. Everything is just what it is. It's just what you create it to be. But notice how your life is enriched the moment you decide that whatever space you're in is perfect just the way it is.

• Now notice how time works in your life. Notice how some moments seem to stretch themselves out and some moments seem to shorten themselves. Take a close look at why you often have this experience. Which are the moments that move more rapidly and which are the moments that seem to extend themselves endlessly? Looking at both, ask yourself what point of view or frame of mind or state of being you are injecting into a particular time that gives it the quality of extending itself or shortening itself. Just take a close look at this. Notice it. Then look to see what that tells you about yourself. Oh, and have a good "time" doing this.

21

For many people there is nothing more powerful in its emotional, psychological, or spiritual impact than the contemplation of their own death. The idea that we somehow one day won't be part of life, that life will go on without us as if we were never here, can rattle the mind and shake the psyche to its core.

If we are simply biological creatures who live and then die, no longer existing in any way, the reason and purpose of life escapes us. We simply don't understand. Why bother doing anything in any particular way if it has no consequence beyond our death? Should the in-this-life consequences be enough to motivate us? Why bother even living, for that matter, if our life has become nothing more than a series of difficult and challenging and even tragic experiences? Why bother going through the pain? Why bother going through the turmoil?

There are, it should be noted, many people who believe that the prospect of nothing at all existing or occurring after death can itself provide sufficient motivation to life, bringing us a sense that it is "now or never time," that what we do here is all we will ever have a chance to do, all we will ever have an opportunity to experience, so we had better do it and experience it now.

Someone once ruefully noted that nothing makes a person more efficient than the Last Minute. Translated into lifelong terms, that observation might read: Nothing makes each moment in a person's life more meaningful than the notion that Nothing Follows This Life.

So the idea and the concept of humanity's confrontation with death has carried with it a dual-edged fascination from the beginning of our species' experience on the Earth. That's nothing new and you already know this. Yet here is perhaps a new idea expansion of this age-old topic . . .

CWG CORE MESSAGE #10

Death does not exist. What you call "death" is merely a process of Re-Identification.

What may be new is the second half of that message. No one ever told me anything before about "Re-Identification." We'll explore what that means here presently.

The first part of this message we have heard from multiple sources for many, many years. Virtually every religion on the face of the Earth proclaims that life goes on beyond the end of the existence of the Body and the Mind. Even before—actually, *way* before—organized religion, our species had developed notions and thoughts and ideas about this thing we have come to call "death," and many of those thoughts included the expectation that our personalities somehow remain intact after our demise, and that life went on in some mysterious way for reasons unknown, but unquestioned.

Some among us have said that these ideas are all nothing more than the yearnings and wantings and desires of our species to not believe that we simply cease to exist at any level when our Mind ceases to function at every level.

Life after death is nothing more than wishful thinking, these people say, and the best we could do for ourselves is simply get the idea out of our head and move on with life as if this is really all there is, allowing it to be sufficient.

Yet the largest number of people on this planet through the largest number of years that we have existed on the Earth have held to the idea that there is something more going on here than simply our physical life. And now along comes *Conversations with God* to confirm that understanding.

The Questions That Arise

I was not surprised when God told me that death does not exist, but I *was* surprised when He told me about the *process* of death— and what that process actually amounted to.

While, as I've noted, no one had ever defined death as a process of Re-Identification before, when those words first came through to me, they made perfect sense.

God had said to me previously that we are all living a case of mistaken identity. We don't know who we really are. It's not the awareness or the experience of most people that we are all God in individuated form. Many people like to think (or hope) that we are, at least, all spiritual beings (which some of us call "souls") created *by* God, who live beyond life in the physical. But if that is our true identity, we come upon other questions that such an idea produces.

Why does life go on? What is the purpose of its continuation? What is the purpose, as well, of our physical life to begin with? What happens after death, and what is the relationship between what happens in life and what happens following our physical experience? Do we really have more than one such physical experience, or is reincarnation a myth? If we have more than one, what is the point of that? If we have only one physical life, what is its purpose?

Are we really residents of a Reward and Punishment Universe, in which "good" receives kudos and "bad" receives condemnation? If so, who decides what is "good" and what is "bad"? And what is the nature of the "reward" and the "punishment"?

All of these concerns are what all of humanity's religions seek to address, of course. If we feel they've been addressed to our satisfaction, we become a member of that particular religion. Our fears, concerns, and questions have been satisfied, and we can lay the matter aside, at least for the time being, and move on with the living of our lives. What we believe happens *after* our lives will, however, have a dramatic impact on *how* we live our lives. This is, therefore, not an unimportant matter.

At Last, the End to Our Dilemmas

If we think that God is going to punish us with everlasting damnation because we have become a member of the wrong religion, we will forever quake in our boots wondering if we have made the right choice, desperate to know if we're going to be okay in the eyes of our Deity or are going to be sent to hell.

If we imagine that certain behaviors are "abominations" in the eyes of the Lord, we will shiver with fear even as we struggle deeply with an inexplicable attraction to thoughts and actions that are deemed "corrupt" or "immoral."

If we believe we have to "pay for our sins," whatever we may imagine them to be, we will approach the end of our days with anxiety and foreboding, dismay, and maybe even panic, wondering what worse can happen to us than what we have already gone through in this life.

Religions have, of course, sought to resolve these dilemmas. They do not seem to have been successful. Our dilemmas have continued.

Now comes a new theology called *Conversations with God*, which agrees with old theologies in their declarations that death does not exist, but which disagrees with just about everything else old theologies have to say about what occurs after we die (and, for that matter, what they say about the meaning, the purpose, and the function of life *before* we die).

The *CWG* cosmology ends our dilemmas, bringing us answers that at last make sense. The final book in the nine-book series, *Home with God in a Life That Never Ends*, describes the experience of the Soul after death in great detail. It says nothing of judgment, condemnation, and punishment. The groundwork has been laid throughout the *CWG* theology for this lack of anger or retribution or need for "justice" on the part of Deity. We've already discussed much of that here.

This theology asserts that there is no separation between us and God, that God and we are One. Thus, we see that if God were to punish us, God would be punishing Itself. Such a thing can make no sense, and so, in order to make judgment, condemnation, and punishment real, standard-brand religions must dismiss out of hand the notion that God and we are One. It has no other choice.

Yet if we embrace the message that God and all of life's elements (and that includes us) are One, the definition of death as simply and wonderfully a process of Re-Identification pulls everything together, answering our end-of-life questions, ending our end-of-life fears, squelching our end-of-life turmoil, and allowing us to Rest In Peace not just after we die but while we are approaching our death (which we are doing, of course, every day).

What Happens After Death

Conversations with God tells us that in the moments following the end of this physical encounter, we come at last to fully understand, fully experience, and fully express our unity with the Divine. It is the illusion of our separation from God that is over, not life.

We have come home.

Once at home again, we join other members of our spiritual family, realizing at the same time that there is really only One Member of this family, and that we are all joined in that Sacred Membership. We become members once again. We, quite literally, re-member. We are glad to see all the other forms of "us," and we are even happier to know something we have always felt and hoped was true about those we deeply love: that we have never been separated at any time from any of them.

And so we identify ourselves with who we really are, finally and without equivocation, without doubt and without question. The experience of our Oneness is full and complete, even as the experience of our individuation as a particular expression of the Oneness is more gloriously experienced than ever before.

We live into the Divine Dichotomy, experiencing our individuation and our reunification simultaneously. It is like your right hand shaking your left. It is like your own arms giving yourself a huge embrace, a big hug, and in that embrace realizing that you are hugging every other expression of life, and that all of life is embracing you as well, with massive love.

In this Divine and glorious moment of self-realization, everything loves everything and everyone loves everyone and all there is is love—which has been the truth from the very beginning. There is no judgment, there is no condemnation, there is no punishment. There is no need for such primitive responses and barbaric reactions from a Deity who is everything, has everything, creates everything, experiences everything, expresses everything, knows everything, understands everything, includes everything, and wants and needs and requires nothing at all.

Paradise on the Planet

All that remains in the evolution of our species is for us to place on the ground, in the everyday moments of our physical life on Earth, the same awareness, the same understanding, the same experience that is ours after death. Then we shall have created heaven on Earth.

We have the ability to do this. We have been promised that we have that ability. We do not have to wait to "die" to know how to live. All we have to do is remember, recognize, and demonstrate Who We Really Are right now. It is as simple as that. But this would require us to embrace a whole new theology, a brand-new kind of spirituality, the different identity which emerges from that, and an even more wondrous God.

God's message to the world—"You've got me all wrong"—looms larger than ever in importance if such a new theology is to be even explored or investigated, much less accepted and embraced by the human race.

Dare we imagine that such a thing could be possible? Could we actually have made a mistake about God? Is it even conceivable that God loves us without condition eternally and forever, has never separated us from Itself, and never will? And could holding the idea of a God who loves us so much, who loves life so completely, who loves the expression of Divinity so absolutely, actually be a sin?

APPLYING THIS MESSAGE TO EVERYDAY LIFE

It has been said that when we no longer fear death, we no longer fear life. I have found this to be true. Here are some ideas that might be helpful as ways that you may apply Core Message #10 in your life:

- Make believe that you have been told you are going to die next month. Just pretend this is true. Then make a list of things you are going to do, given this information. This device was used as the idea for a movie titled *The Bucket List*. Make your list realistic and doable, given your life circumstances, but make the items on your list personally important to you. Be sure to include on this list everything you've ever wanted to say to everyone you've ever wanted to say it to. Review the list, and do everything on it.

- Now make a list of things that you'd like to do even if you *weren't* going to die but are afraid to do because of other consequences you think might occur in your life. Ask yourself what would happen if those consequences *did* result from what you want to do. Take a look at what it would take to go out and do what you really want to do anyway. Then decide to do it. Then *actually* do it.

- Make a promise to yourself to read at least three biographies of people who have accomplished extraordinary things in their life, then look to see what quality or qualities they demonstrated in the achieving of what they did. Now call forth, nurture, and express those same qualities in your own life at the next highest level.

• Make an "I Stopped Myself" diary. (Really. Call it that and make it that.) At the end of each day, write a paragraph or two about things you stopped yourself from doing that day that you really wanted to do, and the reason you stopped yourself from doing those things. If there is nothing that falls into that category on a given day, congratulate yourself and write a paragraph or two instead on the most important thing you will achieve tomorrow.

22

As we look backward in the hall of mirrors that fill the corridors of our belief systems, we see that one understanding that we have held about life and how it works leads to another, which leads to a third, which produces a fourth, which generates more and more and more, and finally, the totality of our larger understandings that we might call our cosmology or our theology.

In the *Conversations with God* theology we see that this progression is also present. And so it is not surprising that the notion that death does not exist and, more importantly, that death is merely a process of Re-Identification, emerges from a prior Core Message—specifically . . .

CWG CORE MESSAGE #9

There is no such place as hell, and eternal damnation does not exist.

This particular idea does not require a great deal of extensive explanation. The message speaks for itself. Yet its ramifications and its implications and its inferences hold many nuances that it could be beneficial for us to explore.

If there is no such place as hell, we might ask, where is the system of eternal justice reconciled? What is the "payoff"? And what are the consequences of our actions during life here on Earth?

If there are no consequences to any particular actions, choices, or decisions, what is the point of any of them? What difference does it make what actions, choices, or decisions we take? Why not just do everything and anything that it pleases us to do, regardless of how or whether it damages another?

Why bother following any kind of moral or spiritual guidelines? And what kind of a God is it who has no sense of justice or morality or right or wrong, but simply allows us to run rampant, doing whatever we want? What kind of a parent would raise a child that way? What kind of Deity would create such a universe?

Those are all very good questions. So let's take a look at what this idea of an absence of hell or damnation could mean in terms of the Ultimate Reality in which we are being told that we find ourselves.

Looking Again at That Contrasting Element

Conversations with God tells us that the purpose of life is not to be ultimately rewarded or punished, but for life itself to experience itself in never-ending and ever-increasing wonder and glory. That is, God's purpose in creating physicality was to use it as a device through which Divinity could know Itself experientially, and could increase Its knowing of that experience without end or limitation.

Put in another way, God simply wants to express Itself in the countless ways that are available to It, and to expand Its experience of those endless expressions in ways that produce more glory and more wonder, more joy and more happiness, more of what God really is—love—in every conceivable form.

Given this desire on the part of God, the notion that God would make Itself wrong for any one of Its expressions—to say nothing of condemning Itself and then punishing Itself with everlasting torture, unremitting pain, and eternal damnation—is absurd.

The key here is understanding how the thing we call evil could be given rise to. How could anything that is not our notion of a wondrous and glorious and joyful and loving God possibly manifest itself in physical reality, given what we are to understand is God's ultimate purpose and singular intention?

The answer lies in the fact that nothing can be experienced in the absence of its opposite. And this is a point that is made repeatedly in the *Conversations with God* cosmology. Indeed, you have heard it several times in this narration.

Life must produce a contrasting element in order for any aspect of Itself to be experienced. And so, Life Itself has created (actually, *is*) a Contextual Field, within which all expressions of Itself become possible—and, indeed, are occurring—always, simultaneously, eternally.

Life has devised a second aspect of Itself, found in its Individuations, which allows those Individuations to *experience* all of the expressions of Life that are possible. That second way is what we, in human terms, might call "selective amnesia."

By limiting the amount of data of which each Individuation of Life is consciously aware (that is, by imbuing physical Life Forms with varying levels of *consciousness*), it is possible for the All to behold the Contextual Field through limited perspectives, and thus have experiences of Life that would not be possible were the Total Perspective of Life available to each Individuation all of the time.

To explain this further . . .

When we move from the Spiritual Realm to the Physical Realm as part of our eternal and cyclical journey through life, we undergo a process of physicalization that involves the embedding of our Consciousness within the limited confines of the collective reality into which we have inserted our Self. During this process the level of awareness within our Consciousness contracts to fit the space in which it is being held.

It must be understood that Consciousness is nothing more than energy. Everything is energy. You. Me. Everything. Everything that we are is energy. Everything that *is* is energy. Thoughts are energy. Emotions are energy in motion. Ideas, concepts, awarenesses—all are energy.

It must also be understood that all energy impacts other energy. That is, the energy of life is interconnected. One energy affects another. Physicists have found a way to describe this interactive process as it relates to quantum physics by saying: "Nothing that is observed is unaffected by the observer." In other words, the simple act of looking at a thing has a material effect on the thing being looked at.

Put another way, we are creating what we are looking at by the way that we look at it and the place from which we are observing it. What this has to do with what I call "selective amnesia" is this: The movement of our Unlimited Consciousness into the environment of physicality produces a Limited Point of View of Ultimate Reality. This Limited Point of View reduces our awareness. Our Consciousness remains unlimited, but our awareness of all that our Consciousness knows is significantly reduced.

This is something like putting blinders on a horse.

Putting blinders on a horse does nothing to impair the horse's eyesight. It simply impairs the horse's ability to *use* its eyesight completely. The horse's awareness is thus impaired. He is less "aware" of all that is around him, of the reality in which he exists. This makes his surrounding no less the reality, but his lack of full awareness allows less of it to be brought into his *experience*. The horse thinks that what he is experiencing is the reality that exists. Only when you take the blinders off does the horse realize that there is "more here than meets the eye."

In human beings, Consciousness is the eyesight of the sacred being known as You. It is unlimited and sees everything. Physicality is the blinder of Consciousness. When you "put on" physicality it is like putting blinders on a horse. You limit your ability to see everything that the unhindered Consciousness is able to see. Your awareness is impaired. You are less "aware" of all that is around you, of the reality in which you exist. This makes your surrounding no less the reality, but your lack of full awareness makes it less of your *experience*. You think that what you are experiencing is the actual reality. Only when you take the blinders off do you realize that there is "more than meets the eye" to the reality in which you exist.

Unlike the horse, you can do something about this. You can take the blinders off even as you are continuing your journey. The "blinders" of physicality can be removed all at once, or a little at a time. In the second instance, we see more and more gradually. In the first instance, we see everything all at once.

Sometimes we see everything all at once and then *lose sight of it*. This can happen when seeing everything all at once throws us into "psychic shock," and it can also happen when we voluntarily withdraw back into "limited eyesight" in order that we may more gently and effectively confront and deal with all the data, the *unlimited* data, that was made available to us in our moment of Expanded Awareness.

Physicality "squeezes" our field of vision. As we squeeze our

Unlimited Self into the extremely restricted space of physicality, we shift our point of view dramatically, obstructing it in the process. Greatly obstructing it, I might add.

None of this is accidental. None of this is a mistake or an unfortunate condition of having a physical body. It is all quite by design. Without this "squeezing" of our field of vision, we would "see" more than our Mind is equipped to process—or even *desires* to.

To give you another example of what is being said here, let us use an experience common to humans, not to horses: a scary movie.

If you know every scene in a "horror film" before you see it, having been told all about it by friends (including exactly how the story ends), it will be very difficult for you to be frightened by the film. If your object in going to see the movie is to experience the rush and the exhilaration of fear, shock, and surprise, you will say to your friends, "Stop! Don't tell me anything about it!" Even though it is *possible* for you to know, you will not *want* to know all there is to know.

Life on a larger scale is not very much different. But because in Life everything that has ever happened, is happening now, and ever will happen is known to our Soul already, there is no way for us to say to Life, "Don't tell me anything!" Yet we *can* say to Life: "Help me forget what I know."

This is something that Life (read that: God) is happy to do. Thus, as individuated souls we are given the gift of temporarily "forgetting" who we really are in order that we might re-experience various aspects of who we really are that it pleases us to experience.

To the soul, the most joyful aspect of our True Identity is that we are The Creator. Yet if we wish to *experience* ourselves (and not merely *know* ourselves) as a creator, we would have to *forget* that all that ever was, is now, and ever will be *has already been created*. Only then would the process that we call creation, and thus the experience of our highest self, be possible. We do not really "create." We simply make ourselves more aware of the "already-thereness" of something.

So we see that the two Divine Devices—the Contextual Field and Selective and Temporary Amnesia—are used together to produce the experience of Life that you are now living.

Theater of the Mind

The wonderful part about all of this is that we are not required to take part in any way in the so-called "negative" aspect of the physical reality that has been created in order to form the contextual field within which we can experience our Divinity.

That so-called "negative" aspect of the contextual field merely exists as a placeholder. It is like what actors in the theater call the "fourth wall." Thespians routinely refer to the invisible divider between themselves and their audience with this term. The back wall, of course, is the upstage wall. The side walls are the right flats and the left flats. The fourth wall is the wall that's not there. It is the space between the actors and the audience. That wall is not real.

What the audience is looking at from its point of view as it sees the stage is not real. It's all a play. And both the audience and the actors agree to pretend that there is a fourth wall. The audience, therefore, gets to experience itself as a "fly on the wall," observing the lives that are taking place on the stage as if they were real, and imagining that they as the observer cannot even be seen, although they know full well that in real life the actors certainly can see the audience, but simply *pretend they cannot.*

This is a pretending within a pretending. The actors are pretending to be someone else, then they are pretending that they cannot see the audience watching them *be* someone else!

You Belong to a Resident Company

It's not necessary for us as souls to step *into* and make *real* any negativity or evil in order for us to use the illusion to create a context within which the experience that we truly seek (that of our highest desire for the expression of Divinity) may be experienced.

If we do fully step into the illusion of negativity and evil, it is because we have made a choice to do so, forgetting that evil was simply a placeholder, and imagining that we have no choice but to experience it, and even in some ways to express it through us, as us. (I will explain how and why it happens that we do this in just a moment.)

Still, when all is said and done, it is, was, and always will be an illusion, as is everything in our physical life, and we will come once again to know this.

When the play is over, the director does not walk up to the actor who portrayed the villain and throw him into a jail cell backstage, refusing him food and water and causing him to be tortured day and night for the rest of his life because he gave such a good performance. Nor does the director take the hero of the play and put him into a paradise, throwing roses at his feet and placing bonbons in his mouth, surrounding him with beautiful music and whatever else he desires, because his performance was equally realistic and powerful. The director does no such thing to his actors. He simply congratulates them on a very realistic performance.

But there is something unusual about this particular company of Thespians. It's a resident company. And its residency is in heaven. Now in resident companies, as you may know, *actors change parts*, assuming different roles from play to play.

The director may assign the player who portrayed the villain in one script to play the hero in the next, and the actor or actress who played the hero or heroine in the first show of the season often winds up playing the villain in the second. And so all of the actors play many parts in order that the illusion might be fully expressed and experienced in ways that allow the season ticket holders who are watching *to experience within themselves* emotions generated by the illusion that they are witnessing.

This is a very loose description of what is happening on Earth. And we are both the actors and the audience—and yes, even the director. The evil we see and the evil we experience feels very real, but it is an illusion—as is even the idea that death is the end of our life. *All* of it is an illusion, and many Masters have understood and demonstrated this, Jesus being one of them.

Relating This to Everyday Life

Now, to that explanation I promised you a moment ago. Because if none of the above can be related to life "on the ground," right where you are, there will be no meaning, no purpose, and no benefit to your having read it. So something must be said about the senseless killing of innocent children by a madman, or the ruthless disregard for human life by some who are more concerned with their own greed/self-interest. We experience this suffering as very real. How does that fit in, and how should we relate to these situations?

Those are fair questions. These situations don't seem like "the wonder and glory of life" when we're faced with them. Isn't it precisely at this moment that "selective amnesia" fails us? you might ask. And it would be perfectly natural for you to question why God would create these things and make us suffer through them.

And so first, let us be clear that "God" is not a separate entity, creating things. Every kind of behavior created within the human experience is being created by human beings. "God" is not some creature high in the sky creating horrible human circumstances, foisting them upon us, then looking down from on high and watching us squirm to get out of them.

Human beings act the way they act because they have heard, embraced, and lived out complete stories ("scripts," if you please) about who they are, who God is, and what life is about that are utterly untrue. These stories are not part of the "Divine Forgetting," not part of what we have called here "selective amnesia," but rather, mistaken notions that we have passed on from generation to generation that run counter to everything that human beings *do* remember about who they are, what God is, and how life works—but that humanity nevertheless has rejected as being *too good to be true.*

For instance, most of us know, deep within our hearts, that We Are All One. This is an instinctive knowing, a cellular encoding, a base-of-the-spine understanding that causes us to run into the burning building to save the baby. Our survival is not the issue in such moments. Who We Are and what we Know To Be True takes over for nearly every human being.

Most of us feel this in our bones—yet interestingly, most of us ignore this most of the time. Unless we see someone else facing a crisis situation, most of us think our basic instinct *is* survival.

This has nothing to do with forgetfulness. Most of us know full well that what is good for one of us is good for all of us and what is not good for one of us is not good for all of us, that what we do for another we do for ourselves, and that what we fail to do for another we fail to do for ourselves. We know this so well, in fact, that *this is exactly how we behave with those we love.*

So our day-to-day behaviors have nothing to do with selective amnesia, they have to do with *selective application* of what we already know to be true. It has to do with *selective surrender* to our true basic instinct: the expression of Divinity in us, through us, and as us.

We know full well, at the core of our being, that "humanity" is "divinity" expressed. That is why, when we *do* see someone else facing a crisis situation and we do nothing about it, we are said to have *lost our humanity*. People shout at us, "Have you no *humanity?*" People beg us, "Have some *humanity,* man."

We understand perfectly well that the quality of "humanity" we are talking about is a quality that we ascribe to "divinity." There is no mistaking each other about this. We know exactly the quality of being that we are talking about.

And so, the senseless killing of innocent children by a madman, or the ruthless disregard for human life by some who are more concerned with their own greed/self-interest, and all the other worst scenarios of human life, are not events and experiences that "God" creates and makes us suffer through. They are things that we create and that we suffer through out of our abject refusal to *believe* the highest and grandest reality about Who We Really Are, Who and What God Really Is, and How Life Really Works—and our belief in the fictional "script" that we have been acting out instead.

We are behaving as if the "play" is real. We have acted our roles so well that we have fallen down the rabbit hole, where the Mad Hatter is pouring tea into a cup with no bottom, insisting that what is "so" is not so and that what is "not so" is so. And we think that God is going to punish us with everlasting damnation because we have behaved as if the illusion was real.

Yet the truth is, we don't know what we're doing. The level of our collective consciousness, while continuing to expand, has not reached the point where the largest number of us understand clearly Who We Are, Why We Are Here, and what the experience called Life is all about. We can't even let the smallest number of us propose a different idea about Life (to say nothing of a different idea about *God*) without marginalizing them as dreamers or lunatics—if not outright condemning them as blasphemers.

The truth is, of *course* there is no such place as hell. Of *course* eternal damnation does not exist. Why would it? We're simply all experiencing life within a contextual field that allows us to do so.

God desires to know Itself experientially in Its grandest and most magnificent expression, and desires for you to grow in your awareness of that expression, using all the possibilities contained in the limitless boundary that is Divinity Itself.

Which Story Do You Wish to Believe?

Now, you may say that what you've read in those last two paragraphs (and throughout much of this book, for that matter) is just a story that has been made up and that it has nothing to do with Ultimate Reality. Yet is it any less real (or does it *need* be any more real) than the story we have made up of a God whose angel Lucifer angered Him and was thus sent to eternal damnation, from which he is allowed (even *invited*) to tempt men's Souls for the rest of eternity, causing many of them to succumb to his temptations to join him in hell, rather than be with God in heaven?

Is it any less of a made-up story than the idea that God and Lucifer are in an eternal battle that never ends? A battle for the Soul of Humanity?

Do we really believe ourselves to have a God who is so impotent that God could *lose* the battle for your Soul? Is it our understanding that God says to Himself whenever the Devil triumphs and a person is condemned to hell, "Well, win a few, lose a few . . ."?

Which of the stories is more absurd? Which of the stories is more beneficial for humanity to embrace? Supposing none of the stories is true. Which one would you rather believe? Which one would you feel brings you more peace of mind, more of a desire to express your life in a particular and wondrous way?

Which one brings more love to your heart, more excitement to your life, more joy to your experience, more wonderment to your every encounter? Which God do you choose? Yesterday's God, or tomorrow's?

Applying This Message to Everyday Life

Here are some suggestions on how you can apply Core Message #9 in your daily life:

- The next time you imagine that you're going to be punished by God with eternal damnation because of something you've done, tell yourself that you're an actor who has walked backstage after giving a brilliant performance in a play. Simply say to the director, "I don't want to play that kind of a role anymore. Cast me in the role of a hero. Have that put in my contract. I never want to play a villain again." Remember that you're such a good actor, the company has no choice but to honor your request. You're given a new contract. From now on you play nothing but heroes.

- The next time you are tempted to condemn anyone else for anything, to pass a judgment about another, try to remember that they have simply forgotten who they really are. Judge them no more than you would judge an actor in a play that you are watching from the audience.

- To continue with the illusion, pretend that one of the actors on the set has forgotten his lines, so he starts ad-libbing. He's doing a pretty good job; he's managing to get through the scene, even though he's not saying what he was supposed to remember. Imagine that the person that you are now judging or condemning is simply an actor who has forgotten his lines. Know that in his next performance he'll remember them again. And he won't forget the discomfort he experienced when he lost his place in the script and didn't know what he was doing. Maybe you could even imagine yourself to be a stage manager in the wings whispering the actor's next cue, *to help him to remember.*

Wouldn't it be interesting if that's your job in this company of actors? Maybe you're just the stage manager running from one wing to the next reminding the actors of their lines. While you're at it, take a look at the script yourself so that you can know where in the play we all are.

23

There is another reason that there is no such place as hell. There is another reason that eternal damnation could not possibly exist. It is because we have done nothing wrong.

I understand that "wrongdoing" is part of humanity's cosmology of life. We really do think that there is such a thing as Right and Wrong. After all, God has told us so. Our religions have told us so. Our parents have told us so. Our culture has told us so. Our societies around the world have made it clear that some things are Right and some things are Wrong.

Yet now here comes this new theology arising out of *Conversations with God*, which brings us . . .

CWG CORE MESSAGE #8

No one does anything inappropriate, given their model of the world.

This is a tough one for many people to embrace. You may be among those who have a real "pushback" to this idea. Yet, as with all of the spiritually revolutionary messages being explored here, the invitation is to allow yourself to examine the idea closely, rather than reject it out of hand, to see if you agree or disagree with the spiritual rationale behind the statement.

The underlying basis of this declaration is the observation that it is people's understanding of their actions, choices, and decisions that creates their formulations of what is "right" and "wrong." From these understandings, humans create an entire model of their world. This is, they convince themselves, "how things are," and it is from that perspective that they tell themselves what is "right" and "wrong."

This all begins with fairly innocuous declarations and decisions—a few of which we will explore presently, to offer an example of how one's world model informs one's values. But it ultimately and inevitably progresses to far more important—and dangerous—notions, which produce concepts of "right" and "wrong" that cause the whole world consternation and throw people everywhere into confusion and despair. Yet we don't seem to know how to get out of this trap of our own creation, and so can't even agree from one place to another on what is "right" and what is "wrong." That is how malleable those terms are.

One culture says it's right for women to cover themselves from head to toe and not allow any parts to their body to be seen in public other than their eyes, through a small slit in their garment that allows them to watch where they're going. Another culture says it's totally okay for women to show *everything* there is to show, to even walk on a nude beach completely naked, to appear in movies in exactly the same way, and to stroll down a public street wearing clothes that leave very little to the imagination. Indeed, in some cities nudity even on public streets is legal.

Which is right and which is wrong? Which is good and which is bad?

In some places, having a sexual experience with another person who is not your spouse is considered immoral, and to do so for money is considered more than immoral. It is thought to be the worst thing that a person could possibly do to defile their sacred being. In other places, such an activity is considered very okay, is legal, and is actually regulated by the government to ensure that health and safety standards are met.

Which is a more holy place? What city or country is more sacred because of its laws and customs and which is a den of iniquity and the hallway to hell?

Some people can eat whatever they want and other people are required by their beliefs to eat only certain foods or particular foods at particular times in particular ways.

What is the right way to eat? What is the wrong way?

Some people can sing and dance and play music and be clean-shaven or bearded as they wish, and in other places on the Earth the playing of music is strictly prohibited except certain songs devoted to God. In some places the growing of a beard is *required* of all men, while dancing and many other forms of entertainment are strictly prohibited.

Which is okay and which is not okay? What does God want? What does Deity demand? What is appropriate? And what is inappropriate? Who makes up the rules? And who says that the rules being made up are the right ones?

Legislating Morality

Of course, humanity has been arguing about this for centuries. Now along comes *Conversations with God* to bring us a startling answer: No one does anything inappropriate, given their model of the world. "Right" is what we say it is . . . and so, too, is "Wrong." We are the ones declaring what is "good" and what is "evil," what is "appropriate" and what is "inappropriate," what is "right" and what is "wrong." And we *change our mind about that* regularly. Then we call our ideas "law." We literally legislate morality.

In China a law has been passed to make it illegal for children to fail to frequently visit their elderly parents. Parents can sue their children in court if their children do not visit them often enough in their later years. I am not making this up. Autocratic and dictatorial as it may sound, *this is the law in China*.

In certain states in America, people who love each other deeply and have declared their love by marrying each other will not have that marriage recognized for any legal purposes if they happen to be of the same gender. None of the rights of married couples are accorded them. I am not making this up. Primitive and antediluvian as it may sound, *this is the law in many places in America*.

Other laws in other places have similarly attempted to codify Right and Wrong, to make it a matter of legislation, to make it not simply a point of view, but a point of law. Yet here is the irony: Nearly every culture has declared on a spiritual level that *God* has determined what is Right and Wrong and all we are doing is trying to obey God's Commands.

The problem is that even those supposedly clear-cut Commands are difficult to obey when the interpretation of them shifts and changes from time to time, from place to place, and from culture to culture. Which interpretation, then, of God's laws to obey? For that matter, which *God* to have faith in?

The Answer We Refuse to Believe

The extraordinary answer is that God gives us complete freedom in these matters, desiring us to create our own reality and experience it as we wish. Thus, every act is an act of self-definition and every choice is an expression of individual will. We have been given Free Will.

This is God's intent, for God wishes every sentient being and all of life to have the grandest opportunity to freely express and experience the fullest level of Divinity that a life-form's consciousness will allow.

That opportunity, of course, would not be available to humans if we were simply following orders, doing as we are told, responding to demands. For the nature of Divinity Itself is total freedom and complete power and absolute authority, and if humans are to experience Divinity, they must be able to experience the same unlimited liberty and ability. Simply following orders and responding to commands would not be the same thing at all. Logic alone, therefore, tells us that God has given us Free Will in all things.

Thus, we see that it is one's model of the world that determines whether one imagines or creates one's actions as being "appropriate." If we then find ourselves in the space of a person or a group of people acting in a way that we judge to be inappropriate, our opportunity is to invite that person or those people to rethink and to modify their model of the world, for it is *this* that is sponsoring their behaviors. Yet we do not do this. Rather, we punish others for not acting in accordance with *our* model of the world. And we do this without even wondering where they picked up their ideas in the first place.

The irony is, they often picked them up from us.

The Contradiction We Fail to See

In much of human society we, ourselves, demonstrate one model of the world, then demand that people watching our demonstration subscribe to another. This is the "do as I *say*, not as I *do*" method of creating a society. And this is also where our own model of the world slides us down the slippery slope from the innocuous to the dangerous.

We kill people in order to deter people from killing people, and wonder why the killing goes on. We terrorize people who terrorize people, and wonder why the terrorizing goes on. We become angry with people for becoming angry with people, and wonder why the anger goes on. We abuse people who abuse people, and wonder why the abuse goes on. We hate people who hate people, and wonder why the hatred goes on. We condemn people who condemn people, and wonder why the condemnation goes on.

We avoid utterly the injunction to do unto others as we would have it done unto us. In fact, we turn this completely around, doing unto others what we do *not* wish to have done unto us. And we fail to see the contradiction.

Yet God does not. Nor does God engage in such contradictions. It is for this reason that God has made it clear that there is no such place as hell, nor any such experience as condemnation and damnation—because in a world in which sentient beings are given total freedom to create their own model of what is appropriate and inappropriate, and to produce their own demonstration of who they really are, punishment and damnation for making a free will choice would be a contradiction in terms.

What the world needs now is simply to change its model, alter its ideas, rewrite its cultural story. All sentient beings ultimately do this when they stop looking to others for their direction. The people of Earth are in the process of doing this right now.

That process is called "evolution," and it begins with a brand-new understanding of God Itself. Out of this understanding arises a story about Tomorrow's God that is quite different from our story of Yesterday's God.

Our Future Deity

In order to move forward in our evolutionary process, we will re-linquish our attachment to the "God of our fathers." The rules and regulations and guidelines and commandments of that God are no longer functional or applicable to life in the twenty-first century, and we are now seeing that clearly.

Tomorrow's God will not be really a new God but simply a new and expanded understanding of the God who always was, is now, and always will be. In the book *Tomorrow's God*, humanity has been given a wonderful preview of what is now evolving and of how we will view and experience this "new" Deity. That text says:

1. Tomorrow's God will not require anyone to believe in God.

2. Tomorrow's God will be without gender, size, shape, color, or any of the characteristics of an individual living being.

3. Tomorrow's God will talk with everyone, all the time.

4. Tomorrow's God will be separate from nothing, but will be Everywhere Present, the All in All, the Alpha and the Omega, the Beginning and the End, the Sum Total of Everything that ever was, is now, and ever shall be.

5. Tomorrow's God will not be a singular Super Being, but the extraordinary process called Life.

6. Tomorrow's God will be ever changing.

7. Tomorrow's God will be needless.

8. Tomorrow's God will not ask to be served, but will be the Servant of all of Life.

9. Tomorrow's God will be unconditionally loving, non-judgmental, noncondemning, and nonpunishing.

APPLYING THIS MESSAGE TO EVERYDAY LIFE

No conversations about God can have any practical value unless we place the ideas that are presented in them "on the ground" in our everyday experience. We need to try them out. See if they work. Explore their ramifications. Deeply study their implications.

Our life on the Earth right now is giving us a wonderful chance to do so. Here are some ideas on how you might wish to undertake this challenge:

- Start an Appropriateness Notebook. In this notebook, make a list of three things that you may have done in your life that were considered to be inappropriate by another. It should be relatively easy for you to do this if you've led a relatively normal life. Underneath each of these listings, write a short paragraph explaining why you did this "inappropriate" thing anyway, even though you knew it would be considered inappropriate by those around you. Or, if you did not know that it would be considered inappropriate until you found out by doing it, ask yourself what would have been appropriate. Explore deeply this whole question of what you've come to understand and know is appropriate and inappropriate within your present model of the world.

• Continuing your work in the notebook, ask yourself if you've ever made the switch back and forth between appropriate and inappropriate more than once. That is, look to see whether something you thought was appropriate at one time in your life was declared by others to be inappropriate, which caused you to stop the behavior, only to find yourself changing your mind about that and calling your previous behavior appropriate once again by your own definition.

The best example I could think of is the one that we used in the narrative above. Namely, nudity.

As a child, we thought there was nothing inappropriate about running around naked, and we did it all the time. Then we learned that, as an adult, it wasn't appropriate for a wide variety of reasons—a list much too long to get into here. But we knew, we were told unequivocally, that it was not appropriate to walk around naked.

Then, even later in life, some of us did it anyway. We found others who agreed with us and joined us in the behavior. And not just in our homes with our loved ones, but even total strangers in places like sunbathing colonies and on certain public beaches.

So we found that "appropriateness" is a moveable feast (to borrow a sweet phrase from Ernest Hemingway). What is appropriate is what we say is appropriate—and we get to decide.

- In your Appropriateness Notebook, make a list of behaviors about which you made the switch back and
  forth—things that you once thought were appropriate,
  then thought were inappropriate, and have now decided once again are appropriate. Write a short paragraph about what this tells you regarding yourself, your
  culture, your model of the world, and for that matter,
  your understanding of God and of Right and Wrong.

- If someone does something around you that you have
  decided is inappropriate, and if they wish to change
  their behavior but say that they just don't seem to know
  how, ask yourself what you might do to invite that
  person to explore a new and different model of the
  world.

- Decide to join with others around the planet in designing and authoring a new model of the world as
  a proposal for the whole human population to consider. (You may do this right now at www.TheGlobal
  Conversation.com.)

24

I fully realize that it is difficult for us to imagine a Deity such as that which is described in the nine sentences describing Tomorrow's God in the preceding chapter.

We are used to having a commanding God, a demanding God, a condemning God, a punishing God, a God of needs—or at least, of requirements. Yet I do not believe this is the God of Ultimate Reality, and it is not the God that humanity will experience in its tomorrows when we understand, accept, and embrace our Actual Identity.

When we do, I expect that many people will see and will experience that all that has been said in the *Conversations with God* dialogue (an inspiration put into writing no less worthy than other inspirations put into writing through the centuries) is definitely worth serious consideration. Not the least of its messages is . . .

CWG CORE MESSAGE #7

In the spiritual sense, there are no victims and no villains in the world, although in the human sense it appears that there surely are. Yet because you are Divine, nothing can happen against your will.

Everything that is being brought forward in these messages is based upon our Actual Identity, rather than who we have imagined ourselves to be.

If we are, in fact, nothing more than biological entities, then this entire discussion may as well be over. Nothing that is being said here applies to any being or entity who is not spiritual—and whose spiritual nature is not a derivative and a duplication, in individual form, of the Divine.

If we are not the Divine, very little of what has been brought to us in the *Conversations with God* dialogues will make sense. Virtually none of it will be acceptable. Most of it will be considered inaccurate, if not outright blasphemous.

On the other hand, if we accept the notion that we are emergent from the Divine, that we are singular expressions of God—or, if you please, Singularizations of the Singularity—then all of what is being shared with you here could make *perfect* sense. It could also create a perfect world.

This is the intention of the Divine and it is the result that is experienced by all evolving beings in the Universe as they move through the process of achieving greater and greater awareness and deeper understanding.

Perspective Is Everything

Only from this place of deeper understanding could one dare to suggest that there are no victims and no villains in the world. As the message itself says, in the human sense it appears that there surely are. Yet this statement is meant to be taken in the spiritual sense. It is meant to be considered from the viewpoint of the Divine. That viewpoint resides in you, because it *is* you. Therefore, it is accessible by you.

In the spiritual sense, there are no victims and no villains in the world because nothing can happen to us that is not collaboratively created by all the souls involved, in a way that meets the combined agenda of every Soul that comes to *know* about any particular event, situation, or circumstance.

As an illustration, I was not involved in World War II, but I have come to know about it. I was not involved in the stock market's ups and downs, but I have come to know about it. I was not involved in my friend finding a terrific job, but I have come to know about it. All of these things—what I call "good" and what I call "bad," have created the context for my own continuing life experience and expression.

All of this is another way of saying that life is designed to be expressed and experienced by every Soul on the planet during every moment of Earth's history in perfect alignment with life's perfect purpose: the creation and the expression of Perfection Itself.

It can be very difficult to see this when viewed from up close. Not just up close in terms of Space but up close in terms of Time. We have discussed these elements of life before. Space and Time are precisely the same thing in the cosmology of our imagined reality. Therefore, looking at any particular "space" on our planet or any tiny moment in "time" in our history is the same as looking at any particular thread in the tapestry that pictures Ultimate Reality.

If you place your nose right up against the tapestry, its interweavings will make no sense at all, nor will they hold for us any interest or any beauty whatsoever. They will look, rather, like nothing more than a mishmash of colored threads moving in every direction, none of which reveal a pattern or make any sense at all. Only when you stand back from the tapestry can you see the whole picture.

Such is also true when you look at any single moment or sequence of moments in the everlasting and only moment of time that we call Now.

Therefore, it *looks* as if there are "victims" and "villains" in our world because of the ways in which the threads of human behavior are interwoven with each other. Only when we stand back from any particular moment or period and view the totality of human history as a single tapestry can we see the perfection and the beauty of the interweavings and the necessity of the crisscrossings of the threads of experience in order to produce the outcomes that we view as a perfect part of evolution from the standpoint of Always Here/Always Now.

Jesus Said, "You, Too"

It is fair to ask, as we have done now a number of times in this narrative, why we need to experience what we call suffering in the process of these interweavings. The answer is that from a spiritual perspective we understand that "suffering" is experienced only when we do not fully comprehend what, exactly, is occurring in our lives and why. When we see the *reason* for the occurrence, suffering ends. A woman giving birth understands this perfectly. She is in pain, but she is not suffering. Indeed, she is weeping with joy.

Simply put, pain (both physical and emotional) is an objective experience, but suffering from that pain is a result of our decision that something that is happening should not be happening. This is not a decision that anyone looking at life from a spiritual perspective would ever, or could ever, make.

A prime example of this from the human story is the demonstration made by Jesus Christ. It is regrettable that so many people have turned this extraordinary human being into God in the way they have done. What is sad is not that they have declared his Divinity—which is certainly an accurate statement—but that they believe and declare that his identity was singular.

"There was no one else like him and there never will be another like him," many humans have told themselves as a means of reconciling his miraculous deeds with our seeming inability to duplicate them. Yet it was Jesus himself who said, "Why are you so amazed? These things, and more, shall you do also."

He wasn't referring in that statement to a few of the things that he did. He meant that about all of the things he did. He didn't say, "Some of the things that I have done here, you'll also have a chance to do, too." He said, "These things, *and more*, shall you do also." We simply haven't believed him. Yet the day will come when we will. That will be the day when we accept our Actual Identity, even as he did his. It will be the moment when we embrace the reality that we are one with God, one with Christ, one with each other, and one with all of life.

Jesus clearly understood that he was not the victim of anything, and he also understood that there were no villains perpetrating evil upon him. He knew that nothing could happen *to* him and that everything was happening *through* him. He also knew that this is true about every single human being who ever lived and who ever will live. His special mission was to show this to us.

There Have Been, and Are, Many Masters

I honestly don't think that Jesus thought or imagined that we would "get this" immediately. Or even in the short term. I think he very well understood that it would take humanity many generations and many centuries—which in the life of the universe is a veritable blink of an eye—to fully comprehend, completely accept, and totally embrace what he was inviting us to experience. In this, Jesus was millennia ahead of his time, and he knew it. And that is why billions have declared him to be Divine. (It is also why he was crucified.)

Now, "time" has caught up with one of Divinity's most spectacular demonstrations, providing in humanity's present moment the opportunity to fully self-realize. Many have done so since the time of Christ, and before. Throughout the human story we have seen demonstrations of Divinity by many others in many ways.

For instance, people are healed by other people, and even "come back to life," all the time. We call these miracles the result of modern medical technology and marvelous medical science, yet who is to say that medical science and medical technology is not one of the ways in which we now choose to demonstrate our Divinity?

As well, many people have healed themselves and healed others with no physical technology at all, simply using their faith, and their faith alone, as their miraculous tool. An entire religion was created around this experience by Mary Baker Eddy, who called it Christian Science.

Many people who have walked among us—both before and after Christ—have shown us to ourselves, holding a mirror before humanity so that we might see a reflection of our own Divinity. Lao Tzu did it. Buddha did it. Bahá'u'lláh did it. Many, many others have done it as well, those recognized and remembered and those not remembered specifically by human history. Not all who have done it have had their message and their teaching perfectly understood and accurately interpreted.

Is God Really Battling Satan?

Those who have stepped into this level of Divine demonstration never for a moment thought of themselves as being the victim of anything or anyone, nor did they see anyone as a villain. They *did* see a world of people who did not understand or comprehend who they were or what was going on or the purpose of life or the process through which it is expressed or the reason for the process. They *did* see a world filled with judgment and condemnation, punishment and unforgiveness, anger and hatred, violence and killing, and the barbaric behavior of sentient beings who lack expanded awareness.

Indeed, we see precisely this to the right and left of us even today. Everywhere we look we see it. And so we wonder, could it perhaps be true? Could this be who we really are? Is this the fundamental characteristic of human nature? Were Lao Tzu and Buddha and Christ and Bahá'u'lláh and all the others merely anomalies, counted among a tiny handful of human beings who really *were* Divine out of the billions who have lived and live today? Or are all of us Divine, while only some of us know it and believe it at a level sufficient to experience it and demonstrate it? Or are some of us, in fact, *demonstrating Divinity every day* at some level, in some ways, in some moments here and there, as we move closer and closer to doing it always, reaching completion on this Journey of the Soul?

Are there really villains and victims—not just in the human

sense, but in the spiritual sense? Is there really a battle raging on the planet between God and Lucifer? Are the evildoers in our world the minions of Satan, and those who are attempting to put an end to evil the soldiers of God?

More intriguingly . . . when we use hatred to end hatred, violence to end violence, war to end war, killing to end killing, and evil to end evil, whose side are we on?

Dare We Take Jesus up on It?

If Jesus thought there were evildoers in the world, minions of Satan, villains of the highest order, why would he have said, "If a man slaps you on the right cheek, turn and offer your left"? Why would he have said, "Bless, bless, bless your enemies"? Why would he have suggested to do good to those who do evil? What was *that* all about . . . ?

Could it be that Jesus deeply understood that what we call evil is merely the distorted and mangled expressions of love of those whose misunderstanding of who they are and what is happening in life is total?

Could it be that he knew that the ultimate healing of the world would not be achieved by condemning or punishing those who acted in ways that we call villainous, but rather, by changing the *model of the world* from which their choices and decisions and actions emerged?

Could it be that all we need to do today is to carry out Jesus's very clear and very simple instructions to love our enemies and bless those who persecute us, for they know not what they do?

It seems that all the world's great spiritual Masters have told us the same thing, each in their own way, and it appears that *very few of us are listening.*

It has been said before and I will say it again: The question is not, "To whom is God talking?" The question is, "Who is listening?"

If we listen to the messages of *Conversations with God*, we will come to understand that even in the moment of the greatest villainy (as defined by humans), if we refuse to identify ourselves as victims, we will alter our own personal and deep inner experience of those events. It is in this way that we create our own inner reality and begin to project energy into the world that ignites the process by which exterior events change as well.

This is the highest benefit and the greatest miracle of being Divine: No matter what anyone does to us, we can experience it in the way that we choose and, therefore, nullify any negative outcome that another may have hoped to impose upon us. There are many human beings who have demonstrated this precisely, and you can be one of them. And that is the point, ultimately, of Core Message #7.

APPLYING THIS MESSAGE TO EVERYDAY LIFE

The power of this message is that it can transform your life overnight. It can do so with regard to every event, situation, and circumstance that you are now experiencing, as well as any that you may have experienced in the prior moments of your time upon the Earth. Here is a practical suggestion or two on how you may apply this message in your daily life:

- Take a look at all the moments in your life when you have felt victimized in any way, both large and small, and look to see what was ultimately presented you. How many of your prior victimizations have resulted in your presently receiving benefit from the experience? This may not be true of every single incident you can remember, but can you think of a time when it was true? Have any of the moments when you felt wronged turned into opportunities for you to step into the most marvelous outcome you could ever have hoped for or imagined? Look closely and be honest.

- If the above is true, looking back on it, would you still claim yourself to be a "victim" in the original scenario, or simply a sacred being undergoing a multilevel process involving a collaboration of souls producing a singular outcome experienced in a variety of ways by the collective participating—all toward the end that Evolution and Perfection may be served?

- Think of a time when you became a villain in someone else's story. Surely there must be one time that you can remember in the whole of your experience. Perhaps more than one. Looking back on that event, ask yourself now whether you felt like a "villain" when you perpetrated this "wrong" on another, or whether you felt in your own mind that you were doing what you needed to do, what you had to do, what you chose to do in order to best express what you wanted to experience in any particular moment. See if you can imagine another person having the same kind of motivation when they villainized you. If you can, offer that person in your mind and heart the forgiveness that you have offered yourself. If you have not offered *yourself* forgiveness for your own past misdeeds, do so now as your first step in recontextualizing and sanctifying your own experiences, both incoming and outgoing, of so-called "villainy."

• Allow yourself to comprehend that the fact that "there are no victims or villains in the world" does not mean you intend to stand by and watch certain things occur without doing anything about them. The Master does not do what the Master does because what someone else does is "wrong." The Master does what the Master does in order to seize the moment that is allowing that Master to express and experience the highest level of Divinity that resides within. So we have been advised: "Judge not, and neither condemn."

• It is not necessary to make someone or something else "wrong" in order for you to demonstrate who you are. In fact, quite the opposite is true. That is *why* Jesus said what he said and offered us the path that he laid out so clearly: "Love your enemies, and bless those who persecute you. Be a light unto the darkness, and curse it not."

Live each day of your life this way and watch the world around you slowly begin to change, first in your innermost circle, then in a widening arc, and ultimately, touching hundreds, thousands, then millions. If enough of us do this, the World Entire will change entirely.

25

The Core Message we have just reviewed is surely one of the most difficult of all the insights we have been invited to consider in the *Conversations with God* dialogue. When we understand the basis of that insight, however—when we look closely at the foundation upon which it rests—it becomes more clear to us how it could be even possible that there are no victims and no villains in the world.

This clarity emerges from a deep understanding that we are offered in . . .

CWG CORE MESSAGE #6

There is no such thing as Right and Wrong, there is only What Works and What Does Not Work, given what it is you are trying to do.

If we thought we were confronted in a major way with Core Message #7, this one moves us to the next level. Once again the

Mind begs to know, how can this be true? How can there be no such thing as right and wrong? Why not pull *all* the rugs out from under us? Shall we simply abandon all of the understandings that all of humanity holds all of the time?

No, my own Mind said when I first heard this, *surely right and wrong must exist at some level.* Surely there must be *some* guidepost, some yardstick, some standard or criterion with which we can measure or determine whether particular choices and behaviors are appropriate or inappropriate, are good or bad, are best taken or best ignored.

The human race seems to agree. People have stuck to their guns about this—and I mean that quite literally—for many, many years. We are absolutely certain that there *is* such a thing as Right and Wrong, and we are absolutely sure *that we are right about that.*

If It Were Only That Simple

We have examined this topic earlier. We do so again now as we move in reverse through the Core Messages of *Conversations with God* so that you can see clearly how we arrived at the place announced earlier.

The difficulty and the problem has been that our ideas of Right and Wrong change from time to time, from place to place, and from culture to culture, as we have noted here repeatedly. The result: What one person or culture says is Right, another person or culture says is Wrong. And—to make the point again—this is the source of more than a small or trivial amount of the conflict and violence, killing and war that we have seen on the planet, much of it, ironically, in God's name.

Not only can we not seem to be able to agree on what is Right and Wrong, we can't even agree to *disagree* about this. We don't seem capable of observing our differences and calling them simply that. We apparently feel the need to make each *other* wrong for holding views different from ours. We can't even agree to openly explore the topics on which our beliefs diverge, with all possibilities on the table, with compromises at least considered. No, there can be no compromises when we are *right*. One does not compromise one's principles, one does not bargain with the Devil—and we have already demonized each *other*, not just each other's views, so there you have it. We are left with our disagreements and our absolute inability to overcome them.

Worse yet, we are left with our righteousness about them. We imagine we are so right about what is Right and Wrong that we are willing to belittle others, to criticize others, to persecute others, to judge and punish others, to attack others and even to kill others—all of which *we* would consider Wrong *if others did it to us*. The interesting thing about Right is that it is always on our side.

The Problem Is with the Model

The statement was made earlier that no one does anything inappropriate, given their model of the world, and we see now how this becomes functional. It is this model that tells us that things are *morally* right and *morally* wrong—and, billions believe, that it is *God* who has said so. If God says that something is Right or Wrong, who are we to contradict that, or even to question it?

So our model of the world leaves no room for discussion, no room for debate, no room for exploration of any possibility other than what we have been told and commanded by the God of our understanding.

Yet even God can't get things straight from one culture to the next, or even from one moment in history to the next—or so it seems. In one culture we are told that God said we are to take adulterers to the town gates and stone them to death. In another culture we are told that God said to forgive people their sins and have mercy, and never to kill anyone deliberately. What, then, to do? How to resolve these contradictions?

The answer is to build a *new* model of the world, based on a *new* understanding, brought to us by Tomorrow's God. And that new understanding is that there is *no such thing* as Right and Wrong, there is only What Works and What Does Not Work, given what it is we are trying to do.

Our measurement should have nothing to do with moral *righteousness*, but simple and practical *effectiveness*, given our agenda and our intention regarding the outcomes we wish to produce in our experience.

Even that we can and will disagree on, but this takes the moral absolutes out of the equation, substituting for them a simple observational inquiry: Is it working? Is what we have chosen to do working to produce the outcomes we say we wish to produce?

Should Results Make a Difference?

Right now, very little of what we are doing on the planet is producing the outcomes for which it was designed—another point that has been made unceasingly. What is astonishing about this is not that this lack of desired results has occurred, but that it doesn't seem to make any *difference* to us. The utter lack of intended results is having no effect on the actions that we continue to take.

Humanity simply doesn't seem to care. It would rather suffer unintended results, even results that work in direct opposition to what we say we are wishing to experience, than change its beliefs.

What God is advising us to do is take a close look at what it is that we now intend to do in our world. Do we intend to create peace? Do we intend to produce prosperity? Do we intend to guarantee our safety and the safety and security of others? Do we intend to generate the kind of life that can offer basic dignities to all? *What are we trying to do here?*

And what do we see as the difference between what we're *trying* to do, what we say we *want* to accomplish, and what we are actually *achieving*?

Are we capable as a community of sentient beings to admit and acknowledge to ourselves that how we are going about what we say we are intending to do is simply ineffective? And that it *has* been ineffective now for several thousand years?

Do we really think that following the old rules from millennia ago about what is morally Right and morally Wrong is all that we need to do to create the kind of life on this planet that we say we wish to create?

Morals or Function, Which Shall It Be?

I've used this illustration in other books, and I'm going to use it yet one more time here: If you are driving westward in the United States and you are approaching the Pacific Coast, it is not morally wrong to head south toward San Jose if what we're trying to do is get to Seattle. It is simply functionally ineffective. We do well to not confuse morality with functionality.

We are doing this presently and have been for quite some time. Thousands of years, actually. We think Right and Wrong is a question of "morals" (which change from place to place, from time to time, and from culture to culture), when it's simply a question of *effectiveness* (a thing either produces the result you want or it does not—no matter *what* place or time or culture you are in).

Things are not *inherently* Right or Wrong, and that is an idea we would benefit from releasing.

There is no evidence to suggest that people who play volleyball naked on a beach in a sunbathing community are somehow less moral or worthy in the eyes of God than people who wear coverings from head to toe and do not allow a single inch of their body to be seen by anyone outside the home for any reason or at any time whatsoever.

We have no reason to conclude that people who eat only vegetables are somehow morally more advanced or can be depended upon to make higher critical and spiritual choices than those who eat the flesh of dead creatures—such as Jesus, who apparently ate fish, and gave away tons of it for people to eat before his Sermon on the Mount.

There is nothing in our experience to suggest that people who are gay are inherently, inevitably, and invariably morally, emotionally, intellectually, philosophically, and spiritually abysmal, while people who are not gay are inherently, inevitably, and invariably morally, emotionally, intellectually, philosophically, and spiritually advanced.

As absurd as these and other notions are, countless people call them "truth" and live by them. There *are*, they say, rules and regulations regarding proper behavior, and those who do not follow them *are* Wrong for not doing so.

Could We Survive Without Rules?

Yet sometimes the very lack of what we declare to be Right works better than all the rules and regulations in the world. Anyone who has ever driven around the Arc de Triomphe understands this perfectly.

There is not a single traffic director or policeman at this historic monument in Paris, around which a circular roadway revolves. There are no pavement markings or traffic lanes. There are no signs or signal lights. This is one of the busiest, most congested travel routes in the world, with hundreds of cars whizzing in and out of that circle every minute, and yet there is nothing at all to indicate where one is supposed to go, what one is supposed to do, or how one is supposed to do it. People enter that wild conglomeration of vehicles at their own risk.

And that's the point. When they, themselves, are at risk, they take care of themselves and others. They don't need traffic cops. They don't need traffic lanes. They don't need painted signs and they don't need flashing lights. *They know what it is they're trying to do.*

They're trying to get to the other side of the circle in one piece. It's all really very simple.

When you know what it is you're trying to do, the preferable and beneficial action to take becomes instantly obvious and very clear to you. That's why there are fewer traffic accidents on the circle around the Arc de Triomphe than there are on the Champs-Élysées a hundred yards away, where traffic lights abound, lanes are clearly marked, and the way to proceed is guided by rules and regulations.

The Question No One Will Ask

If the idea of nothing being *morally* Right and *morally* Wrong (as opposed to *functionally* efficient or inefficient) is frightening or anxiety-producing to people, it is merely because the sentient beings on this planet have not jointly and universally decided what it is that they are trying to do.

Are we trying to create freedom, or do we believe that a free people are a dangerous people? Is life a case of the one with the most toys wins, or have we defined "success" in life in another way?

And what of our spiritual journey? Are we seeking to create the experience of Divinity in, through, and as us, or are we merely trying to make it from birth to death with the least amount of offense to God? Does our spiritual experience have anything to do with anything at all? If so, are the lane markings and the blinking lights and the traffic cops of our spiritual world making it easier or more difficult to get to where we say we want to go?

Let this be our question for the day.

APPLYING THIS MESSAGE TO EVERYDAY LIFE

Let's see if there might be some practical ways to apply Core Message #6 in our everyday life. Try this list of suggestions:

- Invent a list of three things that you believe you did "wrong" in your life and ask yourself, do you hold the idea that you were wrong in doing them because they did not achieve the result you intended? Or is it because they may have very well achieved the result you intended, but you colored outside the lines and violated what someone else told you were the rules and regulations? Or have you called your actions wrong because you felt in retrospect that they were hurtful or in some way damaging to others?

- Take a look at some things that you feel others have done "wrong." Have you ever done anything like it, or even similar to it? At any point in the entirety of your life, have you ever found yourself engaged in the same *kind* of behavior, if not the precise and exact action? If you see another cheating, ask yourself: Have I ever cheated at anything? If you see another evading or lying, ask yourself: Have I ever evaded the truth or told an outright falsehood? If you see another being hurtful or cruel, ask yourself: Have I ever been hurtful or cruel in my life?

• Type this out into your computer:

On the day that I release judgment of myself for anything that I imagine myself to have done "wrong," I will automatically and gracefully release my judgment of others. On the day that I release my judgment of others, I begin to express Divinity. On the day that I begin to express Divinity, I begin to do what I came to life on Earth to do. Everything else is merely a way of doing it.

• Use this as your desktop or screensaver. Print out several copies and place them everywhere . . . on the refrigerator, on your bathroom mirror, as a folding tent on your nightstand, on the inside door of your closet, on the dashboard of your car, on the wall in front of you in the shower . . . *everywhere.*

• Make a list of five things that you would very much like to do before this year is out. Perhaps they were on your list of New Year's resolutions, or maybe they are emerging in your consciousness now as a result of a new determination to achieve certain results before time runs out. Whatever the case, write out this list and then ask yourself under each of those five items what it is exactly that you are trying to do. What are you trying to accomplish? What are you seeking to produce? What do you hope for as an outcome? And then, with regard to each item on the list, ask life's most important question: *What does this have to do with the Agenda of my Soul?*

- Concerning your spiritual beliefs, make a list of at least three things that you believe that God absolutely finds "wrong" under any circumstances or conditions whatsoever. After making this list, look to see if any of these things have been done by anyone—by any person or country—that you admire, claiming that they have been done in the name of good or in the name of God. Write a small five-paragraph essay on what, if anything, this reveals to you.

26

The entire foundation of the idea that there is no such thing as Right and Wrong emerges from an awareness that I was given about life itself at its most fundamental operational level.

I can honestly say that this particular idea was one I had never heard before, thought of before, or imagined before. But when I finished with my conversation with God around this topic I felt that I finally understood, at a deeper level than ever before, how everything works on this planet.

I invite you to take a look now at what I was invited to look at then . . .

CWG CORE MESSAGE #5

There are Three Basic Principles of Life: *Functionality, Adaptability,* and *Sustainability.*

What I was told is that all of life, everywhere in the Universe, operates on the same basic principles. Whether it is the life of a human being or the life of a tree or the life of a planet, we're talking about an identical process.

At all levels of its expression, life is functional, adaptable, and sustainable—or life does not exist at all. This is the order of things. This is how physicality demonstrates. This is how Divinity manifests. This is how life *is*.

Life is always functional. It is always adaptable. And it is always sustainable in one form or another. Life always was, is now, and always will be, for this very reason.

Now what this means in practical terms is that life works in a way that renders itself functional eternally. Nothing that exists ceases to exist, ever. The Essential Energy that is Life Itself merely changes form, expressing in an endless variety of ways depending upon what is required for the expression itself to continue.

On Earth as It Is in Heaven

This might be, in broad general terms, a spiritual articulation of the physical principle that Charles Darwin described as "natural selection."

What Darwin uncovered is what has been expressed in very simple, but not necessarily simplistic, ways in *Conversations with God*, and that is that *life has no intention of ending*. Ever. Therefore, when any expression or form of life is threatened, it immediately adapts itself, thus rendering its expression sustainable once again.

The Earth is doing this right now. There is a theory running about that suggests that the Earth itself is a living organism. It's even been given a name: Gaia. This organism is said to function and operate under organizing principles that reflect a high level of universal intelligence found in all life-forms, both large and small.

An idea has been put forth by some environmentalists that

the increasing number of geophysical incidents on this planet—from tsunamis to earthquakes to hurricanes and other physical phenomena—is Gaia's response to humanity's threat to the world's survival.

Nobody really expects the world not to survive, but very few people expect it to survive in the same form and in the same way that it has appeared for these many centuries and millennia. The Earth as a biological system is without a doubt shifting and adjusting to conditions that have been placed upon it by its inhabitants.

The life-forms hosted by the planet itself are doing exactly the same thing. They're constantly adapting themselves so that they can sustain the expression of Essential Energy that flows through them.

It would be a mistake to assume, however, that the adaptations that life-forms make guarantee that their physical expression or appearance will remain the same or nearly the same. We all know that there are certain life-forms that have been rendered "extinct" on the Earth. So, in the common usage of Earth's many languages, this means that they no longer exist. But what is true is that they simply no longer exist *in the form* that they took before. All things that exist continue to exist; it is merely a question of how they do so.

The Parable of the Log

In the book *The Only Thing That Matters* will be found a wonderful parable or analogy illustrating this. It's the story of a log burning in the fireplace. It looks to us as if a huge log was resting in the fireplace and then, after a number of hours, it was no longer there—reduced, as it were, to ashes. And so, that which was, was no longer. And there are those who would say the log no longer exists, except in the form of the few ashes it leaves behind. Yet according to the parable, that which we once called a "log" has simply transmogrified, literally going up in smoke. Its energy was expressed, as well, as heat and light and ashes. Yet this revised expression of its energy is not its extinction, but merely its transformation into other kinds of energy. Part of the log still exists in physicality (the part that we call "ashes"), but 95 percent of the log moved, through the expression of its energy, into what we call the invisible universe.

So, too, do you, after what you call "death." In precisely the same way, I might add. That is, you transmogrify. (The dictionary defines "transmogrify" as: "to transform, especially in a surprising or magical manner.")

In this process the physical part of you, which is the smallest percentage of your energy's manifestation, may remain behind in the Realm of the Physical in some form—perhaps itself reduced to ashes, as in cremation, or more slowly changing form over a longer period of time in a casket somewhere. But by far the largest percentage of who you are moves on in transmogrified form to what has been called the Realm of the Spiritual.

It is in this way that the life-form that expressed itself as You adapts and, thus, continues to sustain itself. Smaller versions of this cycle of Functionality, Adaptability, and Sustainability evidence themselves throughout your tenure in your present physical form and during the life of everything around you as well.

I know a man who found it totally functional to consume crabs and lobster on a regular basis. Then he developed what his doctor called a spontaneous allergy to shellfish. He exhibited adaptability by limiting his seafood intake to salmon and trout and other non-crustacean creatures of the sea. In this way he generated sustainability within his physical being.

Anyone who has dealt with weeds in their backyard garden understands how certain life-forms demonstrate cycles of Functionality, Adaptability, and Sustainability!

So this rather simple and elegantly effective formula explains a lot of what we see happening all around us in life on Earth, and also what we can expect to see as we continue in the living of that life. You can expect life to always be functional, adaptable, and sustainable.

What is important for us to understand is that these differing expressions of the Essential Energy are not in any of their characteristics "right" or "wrong," but simply "this" or "that." There is also no such thing as one expression of the Essential Energy being "better" than another. It is simply "other than" or "different from."

It is we who overlay value judgments on the perfectly elegant process of life. We call storms bad and beautiful sunrises good. We call death bad and birth good. We mourn one and celebrate the other. Yet in truth *all* of life is on our side, as every event works toward our personal and collective evolution.

The American poet Em Claire captured this understanding perfectly when she wrote:

> God says for me to tell You This:
> nothing needs fixing;
> everything desires
> *a Celebration.*
>
> You were made to bend
> so that you would find
> all of the many miracles at your feet.
> You were made to stretch
> so that you would discover
> *your own beautiful face of Heaven*
> just above
> all that you think you must shoulder.

When I appeal to God to speak to me,
I'm feeling just as small and alone as you might be.
But this is when, for no particular reason at all,
I begin to
shine

Being at Cause in the Matter

To borrow the sentiment in Em's artistry, we begin to shine when
we *engage* in the process of life, and not simply *observe* it. We can
be the cause of the adaptations that life makes, not merely the witnesses of them. We are, in fact, the cause of them right now.

As I just mentioned a moment ago, the adaptations that life has
made on the Earth thus far are largely the result of what we have
instigated with our behaviors. From global warming to earthquakes
to tropical storms to tornados to heat waves and droughts and
floods and other so-called "natural disasters," we see that humanity
has been hugely impactful on, and largely responsible for, the ecology on this planet.

We don't like to admit that this is true, of course, and so there
are those who absolutely refuse to acknowledge the participation of
the human race at any level whatsoever in the ecological response
of Earth to life on its surface as we have been living it and creating
it. However, scientists with a more neutral position are very clear of
the impact humanity's behaviors have had on our delicate system
of ecological balance.

We can, as a species, affect the planet and its adaptations with
equal power in a positive way. The first thing we would have to do,
however, is admit to ourselves that we are *capable* of having an impact, good *or* bad, on the Earth to begin with. If we declare our-

selves to be in no way responsible for any of the environmental adaptations that we label as negative, then we can't possibly hold a thought that we can have a positive effect on the Earth's ecology.

So life invites us to be a cocreator, an active participant, a conscious collaborator in the use of the Three Basic Principles of Life as tools with which to fashion our own future.

Simply because such a formula by which life itself expresses throughout the Universe exists does not mean that we must stand aside from the formula and be placed at the effect of it. All sentient beings everywhere in the Universe have learned ultimately that the opposite is true.

Our opportunity here is to become a conscious (rather than an unconscious) *part* of the formula by actively and intentionally *creating* functionality, adaptability, and sustainability rather than simply witnessing the playing out of this formula without our intervention or participation of any kind. All intelligent, highly evolved species understand this perfectly.

Do we?

Applying This Message to Everyday Life

Here are some practical ways that you can overlay the Three Basic Principles of Life on your everyday experience:

- Create an ecologically friendly household. Ways to do this are innumerable and can be found in countless books, pamphlets, brochures, and bulletins published

by a huge number of organizations worldwide. Learn
the rules of environmentally friendly behavior and follow them.

- Apply the principle of Functionality, Adaptability, and
  Sustainability to your own personal health. Immediately stop all behaviors that threaten to render the
  particular expression of your life-form no longer functional. You already know what those behaviors are. If
  you're smoking, stop it. If you're consuming sugar in
  any but the smallest amounts, stop it. If you're drink-
  ing alcohol more than you should, stop it. If you're eating foods high in starch or fat, stop it.

- Conversely, immediately *begin* activities that you know
  will be helpful in sustaining the functionality of your
  body. A modicum of exercise, for instance, would be an
  obvious one. Getting plenty of sleep would be another.
  Controlling and then eliminating emotional outbursts
  and dramatically reducing stress would be a third. And
  the list goes on. We all know what we can do and what
  we are better off not doing in order to maintain the
  optimum functionality of the human body. Will we
  pay attention to these things? That's the question. It all
  depends on the adaptation that you want the being that
  is you to make.

- You will never cease to exist. You are an eternal entity
  and an expression of Divinity. But whether you continue to express the Essential Energy in the form that
  you now call your present physical personality is another

matter. That is totally up to you. You will, ultimately, "adapt" your physical expression in a way that we call "death," but that time can come later rather than sooner if you wish it to. It all depends on what other "adaptations" you're willing to make right now.

- Decide to pray, decide to meditate, decide to shift your ground of being at every level, to expand your spiritual experience and your spiritual expression. Explore visualization and guided imagery. Read quietly. Stop watching noisy movies with images of exploding bodies flying all over the place. Play nice, soft, gentle music in the house for a change. Yes, your children or your grandchildren may call you an old fuddy-duddy, but at least you'll be an alive fuddy-duddy and not a dead fuddy-duddy (in the common human usage of those words).

In all of this, pay attention to what you're *doing*, pay attention to what you're *being*, pay attention to what you're *having* in these days and times of your life.

I don't watch horror movies, because I'm having none of it. I don't listen to ugly or inciting lyrics in angry music, because I'm having none of it. I don't eat junk food, because I'm having none of it.

- Look to see what *you* are being, doing, and having. Start now. Not tomorrow, not next week, not after you get back from your vacation or when you get a few extra moments or when you reach retirement. Start now. Take control of your life. We've been given all these tips before. Wouldn't it be wonderful if these ideas offered us something new? But the fact of the matter is, we've heard all of this over and over again from a hundred different sources across a thousand different moments in a million different ways. Do we care enough about the expression of life that we call ourselves to guarantee the functionality of our present lifeform by making the adaptations that render that form sustainable for the maximum amount of time? That's the question.

If you can't find the motivation to do it for you, do it for those who love you. I'm sure they would really like to have you around for a lot longer than the behaviors that you may currently be exhibiting might allow.

I could be wrong about this, of course. Only you will know for sure as you're reading this. And as you know, there is no such thing as Right or Wrong in all of this. There is only what works and what does not work, given what it is you're trying to do. Are you trying to stay in your physical form longer? Bingo.

And so the principles of life given to us in the *Conversations with God* books hang together quite nicely. One thing leads to another in a perfect sequencing, producing applicable wisdom at every turn.

27

Sooner or later you decide to lead a God-centered life.

It happens to everyone. It is not a question of *whether* but of *when*. When this occurs, everything will change.

Your reason for being here will change, your reason for thinking, speaking, and doing will change, your countenance and appearance will change, your tone of voice will change, your clothing and eating habits will change, your work in the world will change, your friends will change, your purpose in life will change, your expression of life will change, your experience of life will change, and the world you touch will change.

Your decision to lead a God-centered life may occur over the course of many months or perhaps many years or even many lifetimes. You can cause it to happen or wait for it to happen, you can ask for it to happen or demand that it happen—demanding, of course, of *yourself* to allow it to happen at last—but it *will* happen, without question and without fail. Sooner or later you will decide to lead a God-centered life.

When you do, you will be clear about . . .

CWG CORE MESSAGE #4

God talks to everyone, all the time. The question is not: To whom does God talk? The question is: Who listens?

Listening to God means listening to ourselves. Embracing this realization takes enormous courage, because it says something about you—and about how you hold yourself and your experience *of* yourself in the world—with which people in the world around you may disagree. They may even actively oppose you. They may even crucify you.

None of this will matter. Even if those things should occur, they will have no affect on you—for you will have assumed your new and your true identity, and once that happens, nothing of this world will mean anything at all.

Now you may ask, if nothing will matter ultimately, why bother with experiencing anything in particular? Why bother with solving problems, or confronting challenges, or enduring pain, or withstanding the seemingly unending onslaught of day-to-day living and the struggles it entails? Why bother with life at all?

Yet when you complete your journey you will know that these struggles were simply stepping-stones leading to the full experience you are having at your place of completion, and that the only reason they seemed like struggles to you is that you did not know what they really were meant to be. They were meant to create opportunity, not opposition, regarding aspects of Self that you wished to experience.

Have you ever struggled with anything, only to find out later exactly how it is done, and then marveled that you ever struggled with it at all?

Of course you have. Everyone has. Everyone has learned to tie their shoes. Billions have learned to ride a bike. Everyone has learned in one way or another *to do what seemed like the impossible* until they learned how to do it. *Then* what seemed impossible was that *they ever had any trouble doing it at all.*

What is true about shoelaces and bicycles will one day be true about all of life, for everyone.

The "Shoelace" Formula

What we experience to be a hidden secret about Life will no longer be secret. It will be widely known, because it will be widely remembered. It will be widely remembered because people everywhere will be reminding everyone. We will be reminding each other of what we always knew to be true: Life was meant to be happy. All we have to do is share. And love. And know that everything works out for the best, that life is on our side. And help each other when we forget. And listen to God when God talks to us and through us.

That's all we have to do. That's all we've ever had to do.

God is talking to all of us, all the time. There is not a moment, not a nanosecond, in which God is not communicating with us. Life is a process that informs Life about Life through the process of Life Itself. God is a process that informs God about God through the process of God Itself.

You may not have thought about things in this way before, so this idea may be new to you. Stop, then, and see how it feels. See how it feels to hold the idea that . . .

. . . God is a *process.*

This is why I said earlier that the words "God" and "Life" are interchangeable. God is a *process* that we happen to *call* life.

This process is simple when understood. Yet we have been allowed to temporarily forget that we know how it works, in order that we may work the process once again. This temporary or selective amnesia is the greatest gift we ever gave ourselves, because it has allowed us to experience all over again our greatest joy: the process of pure creation.

As you move into full remembrance it will be clear to you that everything that ever was, is now, and ever will be, *is now*. You will know once again that there is Only Now and Only Here and Only Us and Only This. Yet in order to fully and grandly experience such a reality we divided Now-Here-Us-This into Then-There-Them-That.

We then allowed Our Selves to forget this, so that we might re-member Our Selves once again. The process of re-membering God—that is, of acknowledging once again that we are members of the Only Thing There Is—brings great joy, almost indescribable bliss, as we turn loneliness into *ownliness* once more.

Yet why cause Our Selves to experience separation and loneliness to begin with? If it is so blissful to be One, why forget that we are, and cause ourselves to imagine that we are more than One, and separate from The One? Why is this necessary to the process of re-membering?

This has been explored now several times, so please forgive the repetition. Just give yourself permission to experience the explanation one more time, so that you may always remember it.

The Reason Behind It All

As long as we were One, and were the Only One There Is, we could not experience One Self in any way in particular, for the precise reason that there was No One and No Thing Else with which to compare Oneself to—and in the absence of That Which We Are Not, that which We Are . . . *is not*.

That is, it is not experienceable.

Once more, so that you may know it by heart: You cannot experience Light without Dark. If there is nothing but Light, then Light itself is not experienced. You cannot experience Big without Small. If there is nothing but Big, then Big itself has no meaning. You cannot experience Fast without Slow. If there is nothing but Fast, then Fast itself is not "fast" at all.

You cannot experience God without that which is Not God. If there is nothing but God (in Its Absolute Form), then God Itself is not experienced. Yet God chose to be experienced. So God divided Its Absolute Form into many parts, creating what humans have perceived as Not God.

In Ultimate Reality, there can be no such thing as "Not God," for God is all there is. However, parts of God can forget they are parts of God, and using this shift in awareness, with this gift and with this device, God can know Itself again and again in Its own experience, through the process of the Part of Itself remembering the Whole from which it has sprung, and of which it is an individual expression.

Life is God knowing Itself again and again in Its own experience.

Yet must it be so hard? Must the process be such a struggle and include such suffering?

No. God has promised us that the answer is no. (See *Happier Than God*, second edition, Emnin Books, distributed by Hay House, 2011). All we need do is remember. All we need do is reclaim and acclaim our true identity, our real nature, our actual and only characteristic: Divinity.

This is all that Jesus did.

This is all that Buddha did.

This is all that Lao Tzu did.

No one who we have called a Master has ever done anything

else. Not one has done a single thing other than this. Once more, even as you have read before, it is placed here for you to read again.

God is talking to you all the time, and saying the same thing over and over again. Sooner or later you will hear this. Truly hear it. And sooner or later you will lead a God-centered life. All sentient beings ultimately do.

When you do, everything for you will change.

Applying This Message to Everyday Life

Listening to the innermost part of oneself takes practice. In a world where so many outer events and experiences are vying for attention, going within can be challenging. Yet it is possible to do so, at will and on command, by a variety of means. Meditation, of course, is one. So is prayer. So is visualization or guided imagery. So is ecstatic dance. So is chanting or quietly repeating a mantra. And there are other ways as well. Reading is one. Writing is another.

So we do not lack for ways to experience that God is talking to us all the time. We do not lack for ways to remember that God and we are One, that there is no separation whatsoever, and that the voice for which we yearn is the voice of our own soul, which is God In Us.

I have been asked many times by people all over the world, "How can I have my own conversations with God?" I have looked at how I have done it and broken that down into seven steps:

1. Acknowledge that there *is* a God.

2. Acknowledge that it is possible for human beings to have a conversation with God.

3. Acknowledge that it is possible for *you* to have a conversation with God. (This has to do with your own sense of worthiness.)

4. Acknowledge that you *are* having a conversation with God all the time and simply calling it something else.

5. Call *everything* a conversation with God, and see what God is saying to you.

6. Choose to have a *specific* conversation with God, and then *watch for it*. Observe closely what and where life is sending you.

7. After you have the conversation, don't deny it or dismiss it. Believe it, embrace it, and respond to it.

Here are some practical applications of this:

• The next time you find yourself in any kind of situation where the very best advice would be welcome, stop whatever you are doing, close your eyes, take in a very deep breath, exhale it slowly and joyfully, and then imagine that God is communicating with you then and there. The message may come in the form of a feeling, as a picture or image, or in words. Receive it in whatever form it takes.

- Keep a small pad and a pen on your nightstand, and on any night that it pleases you to do so, write a question for God on the paper. Immediately set it aside, and do not try to answer it. Go to sleep. In the morning, let the very first thing you do be to reach for the paper, pick up the pen, read the question, and write *the first thing that comes to you.* Do not question it, do not "try" to compose an answer, just write the first thing that comes to you. It may be one word, it may be one sentence, it may be one paragraph, or it may be a much longer message. Keep writing until your nonthinking self stops supplying you with words. Then take a look at what has "come through." Place this message with others in a special box or location where you can find them easily and look at them later. Do not be surprised if you are surprised by their wisdom and clarity.

- Be in this world but not of it. Pay attention to everything that the world is placing before you in any given moment, but do not comment to anyone on it in that moment. When you comment on it, you take your mind off of it and onto what you are saying about it. The energy of life is flowing *from* you. Let the energy of life flow *to* you. If you want to comment on it, comment on it later.

- Be "on the lookout" for God's communications. Listen to the lyrics of the next song you hear. Consider the words on the next billboard you see. Read in fullness the next article you encounter in a magazine or on the Internet. You will know immediately by its vibration whether it is something that the unknowing, unaware part of the world is carrying to you, or something that the Totally Knowing, Completely Aware part of you is placing before you as an aspect of its Every Moment Declaration of Divinity.

• Begin stepping into, rather than away from, any and every circumstance, condition, or event that Life is presenting you. Use all moments and what they present to you as a means of moving into the recreating of the remembering of Who You Really Are. Let each moment be a moment when you are born again into the expression, the experience, and the demonstration of Divinity in you, through you, as you.

28

Now that you've gotten the hang of having your own conversation with God, be sure to follow the seventh step in that process very carefully. Do not allow yourself to deny what you're hearing as you communicate with Deity, even if what you're hearing seems improbable or unbelievable. Because often it will.

My experience has been that nearly all of my conversations with God have yielded statements, commentaries, and observations that directly contradict what I have been taught and told by my elders and my religions and my society and my global culture. So you're going to have to become accustomed to hearing things you're not used to hearing if you're intent on having regular conversations with God.

And a prime example of this would be . . .

CWG CORE MESSAGE #3

There's nothing you have to do. There is much you *will* do, but nothing you are *required* to do. God wants nothing, needs nothing, demands nothing, commands nothing.

Of all the things we've been told about God, this may be near the top of our list of the Unbelievable. Everything we've ever heard about God tells us that exactly the opposite of this Core Message is true.

There *are* things that we have to do. There *are* requirements that God has of us. It may be true that God needs nothing, but it is certainly not true that God *wants* nothing or *demands* nothing or *commands* nothing. In fact, there's a *list* of commandments that we have received from God. And anyone who thinks that such a list does not exist or that we do not need to adhere to these commands is trafficking with the Devil.

So we've been told.

Yet the new theology in *Conversations with God* tells us something else consistently throughout: Because God is the source of everything, the creator of everything, and the expression of everything, it is impossible for God to need anything. And since God needs nothing, God has no reason to demand anything or to command anything.

God Did Not Send Us Away

When we say that God needs nothing, we are not referring merely to objects, but also to experiences. Emotional content is not something that God lacks and, therefore, needs to acquire from us. God does not need to be adored or obeyed or honored or somehow appeased by us undertaking certain behaviors and avoiding others.

The idea that Deity is something we have to appease in order to keep It on our side is a primitive notion arising out of the earliest thought of the earliest human beings on our planet: That God is just like us, and since *we* need to be appeased in order to find another pleasing, so must God.

This has all been explained before. If it starts to seem as if this narrative is going around and around in circles, that's because it is. All of life is a circle. And the reasoning that supports all of life being exactly what it is is circular as well. So you will hear the same thing said over and over again, sometimes in different ways and sometimes in exactly the same way, throughout this theology.

Thus we are reiterating here that because God is everything that God could possibly need, there is nothing you could possibly be, do, or have that God needs or requires.

God did not send us away from Her in order for us to struggle to find our way back to Him.

That's right, it is exactly the opposite of what we have been told. God never discarded us from Oneness with God. It is *we* who have discarded God from Oneness with *us*. We threw God out of the temple of our being. We threw God out of the place of unity with us. We did so through our belief systems, thinking that we were doing the right thing by never allowing ourselves to hold the idea that God and we are One.

Yet it is this very idea that God has invited us to hold from the beginning of time, and has been demonstrating to us by every manner and means to this very moment.

We Shouldn't Be Surprised

It is, however, understandable that, given the elementary understanding that the human mind was capable of embracing in the earliest stages of its development, we might come to false conclusions about the nature of life and the nature of Deity. What we may think is astonishing is not that we reached such false conclusions, but that we have *clung to them for thousands of years.*

We probably shouldn't be astonished, however, because this delay in development is merely the process of evolution among a species of sentient beings. Actually, on the scale of the age of the universe, we have come to a place of larger awareness and greater understanding in a remarkably short period of time. Indeed, on the cosmic clock, in a matter of seconds.

Life blooms and blossoms and fulfills itself very quickly in cosmic terms. And so, humanity has now reached a point where it is able to comprehend and accept, embrace and express the notion that there is nothing we have to do, no requirement that has been placed before us by some Larger Force in the universe, which we must obey "or else."

Now we face a larger dilemma than one posed by a demanding Deity. Now we have to decide, if there is nothing we *have* to do, then what *shall* we do and *why* shall we do it? What will be the new reason behind our actions? What will be the new moral code that supports our decisions and choices?

If God's punishment is not what we seek to avoid and God's reward is not what we seek to acquire, then for those who believe in an afterlife (which amounts to the largest amount of us on the planet by far), what code calls us to particular behaviors?

Thankfully, that question is answered in the *Conversations with God* theology. We have looked at the answer before. Now we see the basis for that answer in this Core Message. Looking backward from the Core Messages we've already discussed to those from which they emerged, we see the platform on which those later declarations stand.

A Wonderful New Direction for Us All

We've been told in this theology that there is no such thing as right or wrong, there is only what works and what does not work, given what it is we are trying to do. And *that* becomes the measure by which we will decide what we choose to do next.

We see here that God has given us a great freedom—another point that has been made repeatedly in this narrative. There is nothing we "have to" do. And yet there is always something that we are doing (the mind never stops, and the body is in constant motion even during our sleep).

So we see that "doingness" is a constant in our lives. The question is not *whether* we'll be doing something, but *why*. What is the motivation behind our action? And the *Conversations with God* theology suggests that the only motivation that makes sense to our Soul is the goal of experiencing, expressing, and demonstrating Divinity. So we will, as enlightened beings, seek to do "what works" to produce that experience from moment to moment.

This is the only thing that matters, and the whole complex and wonderfully sophisticated process and cosmology that supports this outcome is described in the book of the same title, *The Only Thing That Matters*.

It's wonderful to have a new reason for living, a grander reason, a more wonderful reason that makes complete sense to our Heart and our Mind and our Soul. It's wonderful to have a whole new direction in which to take our lives, knowing that life itself is not about profit and loss, win or lose, take it or leave it. It's wonderful to know that even the least among us can rise to the highest expression of who we are without necessarily having to achieve any of the goals and objectives that we imagined to be important and vital in our everyday life.

Isn't it astonishing to consider that nothing that we once *told* ourselves is important and vital is *really* important and vital? Isn't it even more astonishing to come to understand that nothing we have been told is important and vital to *God*, in terms of what we are supposed to be doing or are required to do, is anything of the sort? What freedom! And yet, what are we to *do* with this extraordinary, breathtaking freedom?

That becomes the central inquiry of life itself.

It is what the master and the student both ask themselves at every crossroad, at every intersection, at every juncture in every moment of life. It is what you are invited to ask yourself now. Again. Yet one more time.

What now, my love? What now shall we be, do, and have? What now shall we express and experience? What of God shall we now allow ourselves to know in, through, and as us? And what of God shall we now allow others to know of themselves because of *us*, because of the way we touched their lives?

Can there be better questions to ask and to answer? Can there be a better way to move through our days and nights than to live into these questions?

Applying This Message to Everyday Life

This is the most wonderful time of our journey, this moment in which we look at the questions above. Seldom do we feel this sense of expansiveness and freedom. Seldom do we feel this openness to life and its every possibility. And so it is with eagerness and hunger, with excitement and anticipation that we embark on the practical application of this wonderful Core Message.

Since there is nothing you have to do, you don't even have to do *this*! That's the fun of it, and that's the joy of it!

If you wish to do a few things to apply this message in your life, try these:

- Celebrate your freedom by giving yourself things to do rather than demanding of yourself things that you think that you "have to" do. And the first thing that you may choose to do is to express your fundamental freedom as a human being and as an individuation of God to say "no." You can say no to things that come your way in the next week that you really and truly don't want to do.

- Allow yourself to start a Seven-Day Request Diary and write down in that diary every request that is made of you, either explicit or implicit, to which you would like to say no, but to which you are tempted to say yes because it feels like something that you "should" do. Write a paragraph or two under each of those items that you've listed—the requests that have come to you in the seven days following the beginning of your diary—and in your narrative, explain to yourself why you feel that you "should" do these things and why you feel that you really have no desire to do them.

- Now talk to each of the people who have made these requests of you—even if they are your employers—and explain truthfully, gently, and with authentic sincerity why you feel that you cannot or do not wish to do these things. There may be some consequences to this, but it could be one of the most important steps to personal freedom that you will ever take. So let this be your first intentional exercise in self-direction, self-care, and self-discovery. If you are like most people, you will discover things about yourself as you embark on this process.

- Make a list of at least three things that have been asked of you in the past. It could be in the past week or the past month or the past year, or in the far distant past. Look to see if any of these three things are things that you did not really want to do, and still do not want to do as you consider them today. If any of those items fall into this category, give yourself permission to step into the Five Levels of Truth Telling, and tell your truth to another about all of this. Remember the admonition: Speak your truth, but soothe your words with peace.

- Remember, too, that your highest value should require you to keep your word. Therefore, if you have made a promise to do something and now simply don't want to keep that promise, ask yourself if your awareness that you do not want to do this should give you an automatic "pass" in this situation. See if it feels comfortable for you to release yourself from this promise without the other person's acquiescence and permission. Remember that every act is an act of self-definition.

- On a daily basis, conduct the "Why Exercise." This is a process in which we ask ourselves (and it works very well if one does this process in writing) why we are doing anything at all. In this exercise, you are invited to write down five things you've done in the last hour and notate your reasons for doing them. Be specific and be very clear. Keep a notebook that you can take with you wherever you are. Something that will fit easily in your pocket or handbag. Once an hour for the next two weeks take the notebook out and review all of the

actions, choices, and decisions you've taken in the previous sixty minutes. These could be large or small.
Don't make a value judgment as to their importance,
just notice that it was something you did. Then make a
notation as to why you did it.

• At the end of the day, take a look at your notebook and
the reasons that you have given for doing all things you
have done that day. Again, these could be big things or
small things. These could be items such as combing
your hair, taking a shower, wearing the blue shirt rather
than the green shirt, or large things like postponing a
major project or undertaking a major project, agreeing
to a particular interaction with another or choosing not
to enter into that interaction, deciding to eat this or
deciding to eat that, taking the call or ignoring the call,
entering the relationship or not entering the relationship. Whether large or small, every action has a judgment behind it that you have made—a reason for doing
it. These reasons are important—more important, perhaps, than you might realize—and the aggregate effect
of all the reasons tends to be greater on your state of
mind and well-being than you might at first glance
imagine.

• Because there is nothing that you have to do, ask yourself life's most important question before doing anything. That question is: *What does this have to do with
the Agenda of my Soul?* Let this be your guiding light,
your measuring stick, your criterion in every situation
in every moment. Do this for ninety days and watch

your life change dramatically. But first, of course, you must know what the Agenda of your Soul is. All that is covered in the *Conversations with God* theology, and all of it is explained in wonderful detail in *The Only Thing That Matters*.

29

There comes a time in the life of most people when the central question of life can no longer go unanswered. That central question is a recurring theme throughout this book because it is a recurring theme throughout the days and nights of all of us on this planet. The question: Who are we, and what are we doing here?

I have observed that the reasons many human beings do things are most often disconnected from this question. That is, our reasons and motivations for choices and actions do not reflect our answers to this inquiry (if, indeed, we have even asked ourselves the question). The result is that we are going around thinking things, saying things, and doing things that ignore both the Agenda of the Soul and what I refer to as the Ultimate Reality.

If this has led us to a good and wonderful life, free of strife, free of stress, free of emotional turmoil and major day-to-day problems, then there may be no reason for us as individuals, or humanity as a collective, to explore or discuss this any further.

On the other hand, if this has not led us to the life of which we have dreamt—or if, like me, you feel there must be more to life than simply "getting through it" with the least amount of pain and the most amount of fun—it becomes important for us to really have a deep understanding of what we are all experiencing here and how it all works. It is essential that we really comprehend this physical reality and what is true about it, and the reason and the purpose for life itself, both here on Earth and in every realm and dimension in which it is expressed.

The wonder and beauty of the *Conversations with God* theology is that it offers us answers to so many of Life's larger questions. Not *the* answers, but some answers. God has made it clear to us that the final answers are our own answers, and must always be, or we will have missed the point of our whole experience on this Earth, which is to both create and express who we are and who we choose to be, as only true Individuations of Divinity have the ability to do.

In fact, most of us who have inhabited the Earth *have* missed the point, which is why life on our planet is the way it is: constant turmoil, constant competition, constant struggle, and constant war. (An anthropologist—honestly, I forgot who—once made the point that there has scarcely been a day across all of human history when one party has not been warring against another for some reason. I'm not sure whether that's factually true, but it sure seems as though it has been true through all the days of *my* lifetime, at least.)

Humans apparently do not believe that their purpose is to create and express who they are and who they choose to be—or else they *do* believe it, but find themselves utterly incapable of accomplishing the task, even after thousands of years of trying.

Or . . . worse yet . . . humans have decided that who they actually *want* to be is a race of savagely primitive beings who kill each other when they don't get what they want, deprive each other in *order* to get what they want, and ignore the plight of each other when they *get* what they want.

I don't believe it is the latter. Nor do I believe that our species wants something that it is simply unable, by its very nature, to create. I think there is a third reason that humanity has not been able to produce that for which it yearns. I think it just does not have all the data that it needs to create it. The species has not fully developed yet. There's more to be remembered here.

Can we admit this? That is the question. Is our ego so huge, so uncontrollable, like that of a willful two-year-old, that we cannot acknowledge that there may be something we don't know here, the knowing of which would change everything—something we don't fully understand about life, the understanding of which would alter our experience forever?

Yes, I know, I know. I keep saying the same things over and over again. I warned you early on that I was going to do that. But honestly, that's the only way to get through to humanity at this point. We are all on sensory overload. You, me, all of us. We are being inundated with data. Pictures flashing, music blasting, voices raising, all to get our attention. So God is using the device of Repetition to get through to us.

Through the *CWG* dialogue She has brought us face-to-face with ideas and thoughts about every aspect of life—thoughts that He intends to send us over and over again to stimulate our own inner search for our own innermost truth, creating from our Source Within a sense of deep clarity about who we are and why we are here and how it all works.

And I found no particular idea or thought more stimulating, more igniting of my own search for a wonderful way to live and to express my true nature, than . . .

CWG CORE MESSAGE #2

There's enough. It is not necessary to compete for, much less fight over, your resources. All you have to do is share.

When we consider the above message, it is critical that we judge not by appearances. If we're not careful, it could look as we glance around us as if there is anything *but* "enough" in this world.

Even in your own life, it may feel right now as if there is not enough time, not enough money, not enough love, and perhaps an insufficiency of other things as well. And certainly as we look at the world at large we see evidence that this is true for some others even more than it may be for us. So to have God come along and tell us in a dialogue with humanity that "there's enough" seems almost to be the height of insensitivity.

How can God be so distant and so aloof, so unaware of and so detached from the human condition as to not be able to see how difficult life is for so many people? How can God say "there's enough" when billions of people experience just the opposite? What kind of a message is that? What truth is now being unveiled? Clearly, it must be hidden, or most of the people on the planet would not be living their lives the way they are.

Uncovering the Secret

What is hidden from us is the accuracy of the statement itself, which is revealed when we look deeply into exactly what it means.

The statement "There's enough" does not mean "everyone *has* enough." Yet this is not a word game, sure to produce I-thought-there-was-a-catch cynicism. It is a statement meant to reveal an absolute fact—and to let the human race see that it is humanity's *behaviors* that make it feel that it is *not* a fact.

It is clear to anyone even casually observing our world that many, many people do not experience having enough to live life with dignity, security, and happiness. Many do not even have enough to survive.

It is the supreme irony of the human story that we create insufficiency in abundance through insufficiency of will to demonstrate
our abundance.

Worried that there is somehow not enough of everything, we
create economic systems, political systems, social systems, ecological systems, and even spiritual systems that seek to protect us from
the insufficiencies we imagine exist—but that do not protect us at
all, doing instead *exactly the opposite.*

We have already pointed out in this narrative that none of the
systems we have put into place to make life better on this planet
have done so. They have made life worse. All of them. Every single
one, without exception. So because humans have *worried* about
insufficiency, they have *created* insufficiency with systems that *produce* it and behaviors that *guarantee* it, rather than eliminate it.

Presently, many humans use or hoard whatever of life's stuff
they can get their hands on, announcing as justification their imagining that these things are in short supply. Thus, they keep these
things from others or make them available to others only in minis-
cule proportion.

Yet the worst of human behavior goes beyond this. It is not simply
that some humans are using more than they need and hoarding more
than they could ever use. They are actually *wasting* more of these
resources than would be required to *fill the needs of everyone else.*

As an example, more food is discarded in *one day* as "leftovers"
in the world's restaurants and homes than would be required to
feed all the world's starving children *for a week.* Thus, we have the
illusion on this planet that there is not enough food to go around,
when all that we would have to do to *make* what we *have* go around
is to *stop wasting it.*

More energy is wasted in *one week* through unintelligent, in-
different, or careless consumption by the world's top energy-using
nations than would be required to supply all the energy needs of the

rest of the world *for a month.* Thus, we have created the illusion on this planet that there is not enough energy to go around, when all that we would have to do to *make* what we *have* go around is to *stop wasting it.*

More money is wasted in *one year* on inefficient, ineffective programs by government agencies and on unneeded products and services by private companies than would be required to finance assistance programs for the poor *for a decade.* Thus, we have the illusion on this planet that there is not enough money to go around, when all that we would have to do to *make* what we *have* go around is to *stop wasting it.*

There is more than enough of everything that we imagine we need than we imagine we have. Yet sufficiency is not experienced through *wasting,* but through *sharing.*

No Exaggeration

Now you might think I am embellishing just a bit or inflating facts here just a little in order to make a point, so let's see if that's true. Let's just look at one case in particular.

A report by Andrea Germanos, staff writer for the online website Common Dreams, was published on January 10, 2013, under the headline: "Food System Fail: Up to Half of World's Food Wasted."

The subhead said this: "'Staggering' amount of food waste squanders 'precious resources, including land, water and energy.'"

And Dana Gunders, project scientist/Food and Agriculture and blogger for the Natural Resources Defense Council, posted this the same month:

People all around the world are investing time, land, water, energy, and loads of other resources to grow, store, process, and

transport food, only for nearly half of that food to be thrown
away . . . In the United States today, about 40 percent of all
food goes uneaten . . . Food is lost all along the supply chain—
on farms, during processing and distribution, in retail stores
and restaurants, and in our homes. The reasons for these losses
vary.

At the farm level, crops can be left on the field because the
price at the time of harvest is too low for farmers to recuperate
even the costs of labor to harvest. Inventory can be left over at
distribution centers.

Retail stores often overbuy produce in the hopes that creating the illusion of abundance in food displays will sell more.
With offerings that are two to eight times government recommended serving sizes, large portions and extensive menus can
lead to food loss in restaurants.

And then there are consumers at the end of the supply
chain. You and me, tossing half a sandwich simply because we
don't feel like carrying it home.[*]

Gunder then notes that "the resources consumed to grow food
that is never eaten take a staggering toll on the environment, including a full 25 percent of freshwater consumption, 4 percent of
oil, and about 23 percent of all U.S. methane production once food
scraps arrive at the landfill. Yes, landfill. Only about 3 percent of
food scraps in the U.S. are composted."

And the trend in this wasteful behavior is *in*creasing, not *de*-
creasing, as one would hope in an evolutionarily advancing society. In the United States, Gunder's blog reports, "we're discarding
50 percent more food than we did in the 1970s."

---

[*] Reprinted with permission from the Natural Resources Defense Council.

With a simple Internet search I could find equally compelling evidence of energy and money waste. I won't bother filling this book with it. We all understand the nature of the problem. It's about self-indulgence and willpower. We want what we want when we want it, and we want to be able to throw away what we don't want when we don't want it. And this situation is getting worse, not better.

It is within this context that we are invited to consider Core Message #2. God is telling us that there is enough of everything we imagine ourselves to need. All we have to do is distribute it and use it differently. What there is *not* enough of is the simple determination to demonstrate our sufficiency. There is insufficient will to decrease the wasting and increase the sharing of "the stuff of which there's not enough."

An Aphorism That's True

Our sharing is our declaring. The more we share with others, the more we declare we have. The universe gives *to* us what we choose to have flow *through* us. We are, in fact, a flow-through mechanism, and nothing more.

When we allow the energy of life in any form to stop with us, we stop any more of it coming *to* us, because the entire process of life is circular. Or, as some have put it, "What goes around comes around."

This is one of those aphorisms that happens to be true in the absolute literal sense. It is a *fact* that what goes around comes around—and that what does *not* go around because we have *stopped* it from going around does not come back around to *us*.

This is easily observable as we look at our collective experience upon the Earth. Humanity, acting as a whole, has stopped what's going around from *continuing* to go around. Therefore, it is not coming around as it was intended to. As a species we've stopped love from going around to everyone, we've stopped abundance from going around to everyone, we've stopped opportunity from going around to everyone, we've stopped just about every good thing there is from going around to every*one* there is—not because we are greedy and selfish, but because we're survivalists.

We sincerely, truly, and honestly think that there is not enough. Of anything. Certainly, of anything that we need to survive and to be happy. And so we do whatever we can to gather as much as we can and hold on to all that we can in hopes of experiencing life as best we can.

Even those who have plenty believe they must gather more—and then more and more, and even more after that. Then they hoard what they have gathered, so that they and their families and inner circle never run out. Meanwhile, millions starve to death and millions more live in abject poverty and utter misery simply trying to survive.

A statement from chapter 8 is worth repeating here: Less than 5 percent of the world's people own or control more than 95 percent of the world's wealth and resources.

It's going to sound like I'm talking in circles here, but I'm going to do it. I can't say it enough and it won't be *said* enough until enough people hear it and do enough about it: The way to expand our experience of abundance and sufficiency is to expand the abundance and sufficiency of another.

Here is the golden rule of the Universe: In all things, what you wish to experience within yourself, cause another to experience.

Conversations with God says that what flows through you sticks to you. Ever it has been, ever it shall be.

Knowing this and *applying* this changes one's entire life.

The First to Have Control

The world was not made, and life was not constructed, in a way that renders it impossible to sustain itself. Life will sustain itself whether we interfere with its natural process or not. No matter what we do, life will remain functional by adapting however it must to what we are doing in order to sustain itself.

Whether we think there is enough of the stuff that we imagine we need to go on or not, *life will go on*. The only question is whether life will go on in a way that we call agreeable, hospitable, and favorable to our particular species. And that is up to us.

We are the first species on this planet for whom that is true. We can literally *decide for ourselves* how we want life to go on in many, many respects. Ours is a very important role in that process. Okay, maybe we can't stop a meteor from hitting us (unless we can!) or a "sun storm" from interfering with our global communications, or molten lava from erupting beneath us, but we can sure change our individual and collective human expression upon the Earth.

That we can do.

The question is not whether we can but whether we will.

APPLYING THIS MESSAGE TO EVERYDAY LIFE

I can think of nothing that brings more joy and produces more fun in life than practicing abundance, sufficiency, and "enoughness" on a daily basis. Here are some ways that you might find it very enjoyable to do that:

* Make a list of three things you think you do not have enough of in your life right now. Then walk through life in the next seven days with your sensitivity turned way up and your antenna collecting all the data around you. See if you can find anyone who has less of what you imagine yourself to not have enough of. As little as you imagine yourself to now possess, find someone who does not have even that. Immediately give that person what you wish you had more of. Do this at least once a day for three months. At the end of ninety days, make an assessment of how much you have of whatever it is you once thought you did not have enough of. Do not be surprised if you will find that your experience of insufficiency regarding those items has disappeared.

* If you want to *increase* something that you already experience yourself having enough of, increase the amount of it that you are giving away to others. This includes time, energy, money, love, or anything at all that you wish to experience in greater fullness. Move through your life and when you observe someone else who is not experiencing those things in fullness, cause them to do so, at least in that moment, because you were there. Decide to Be the Source. You may well find yourself expanding and enlarging your own experience of sufficiency to levels and to degrees that you may never have thought possible.

* As a specific exercise in moving the above into your reality, take a stack of paper money (dollar bills, fives, tens, or twenties) once a week and walk down the street handing those bills out to people who imagine them-

selves to need them. Notice at the end of the week and at the end of the month that you hardly missed them at all. You will discover that it's just paper and that it does, in fact, grow on trees. And it's when you discover that you don't miss it that you'll have the direct experience of how much of it you've had.

- As another exercise in implementing some of the above ideas and making them real in your life, go to a store and see if you can find carton containers with lids on them for storage or carrying of food and liquids. Purchase a bunch of them, and then each night when your family finishes dinner, fill the cartons with whatever leftovers there may be. If you can, take a little walk or a little outing right after dinner to where some homeless people are sitting or standing around wondering what they will eat tonight. Hand these cartons out with some plastic utensils and watch their faces light up. If you can't do it right after eating, put the cartons in the refrigerator, and when you gather two or three, rather than having these leftovers for yourself in the next day or two, drive to where you can expect to find people who are hungry and give these cartons away. Then take a look at the hunger this satisfies inside of you.

- Go to your closet tomorrow and remove anything that you haven't worn in the past three months (except for obvious seasonal clothing and celebratory garments, such as evening gowns and tuxedos). Remove the items from your closet immediately, make sure they are clean, and take them to any church or charitable organization that makes clothing available at little or no cost to others. Many cities and towns have placed so-called free boxes at strategic locations where unused items—from toasters to old boots to scrap lumber from a building project—may be dropped off. (I practically lived out of free boxes during a period of time in my life.) Make a trip to the free box or your Goodwill store one of your favorite ways to empty out your house of those thousand things you no longer use.

• Get up sixty or ninety minutes earlier every day and do those things that you have felt there was not enough time to do. Like write that book. Finish that project. Compose that song. Clean that back room. Organize that garage. Or meditate.

30

And so we wind up where we began. We find with these Core Messages of this New Theology that the end is the beginning and the beginning is the end—as is true in the great circle of life itself.

When the clock strikes midnight, what has happened at that exact moment? At the precise stroke of twelve, has a new day begun or has an old day ended? Which is it? *Or could it be both?*

Ah! It seems that *all* endings are beginnings!

That is more than a philosophical nicety. It happens to be what is actually so. It happens to be how the Universe works. It happens to be how the process of life functions.

And so we come full circle in this wonderful excursion into the 25 most important messages of *Conversations with God*. We come to . . .

CWG CORE MESSAGE #1

We are all One. All things are One Thing. There is only One Thing, and all things are part of the One Thing There Is. This means that you are Divine. You are not your body, you are not your mind, and you are not your soul. You are the unique combination of all three, which comprises the Totality Of You. You are an individuation of Divinity, an expression of God on Earth.

Most of us who have been taught about a God at all have been taught that God is the *All-in-All*, the *Unmoved Mover*, the *Alpha and the Omega*.

God, we are told, is All-Knowing, All-Powerful, and Everywhere Present.

If we accept these teachings—that is, if we embrace the thought that what has been said above is true—then we are led to two immediate conclusions:

1. We are all *a part of God* and cannot be separate from God.

2. We are all also *a part of each other* and cannot be separate from each other.

Logical as they may be, both of these conclusions, it turns out, have become highly controversial—largely because our idea of separation from each other and from our Deity has been so long lodged in our ancient story.

Where Our Idea of Separation Came From

It was in the earliest days of our development as a sentient species that we had our first experience of what we conceived of as "another"—and of our "separation" from that other.

I believe that the early story of separation may have had its origin in the first attempts of our species to understand the life we were experiencing. Something like this is what happened—or likely happened.

What we now call "self-consciousness" arose when we began to see or know ourselves individually. Perhaps it was seeing our reflection in a cave-side pool that sparked this perception. We raised a hand to scratch our head and saw the "man in the pool" doing the same thing . . . and soon we began to conceive of "The Self."

The next step in producing the perception of separation came, perhaps, as we sat around the campfire of our clan and found ourselves startled by a sudden flash of lightning in the night sky, followed by a booming clap of thunder. We looked anxiously around the campfire and asked, with whatever facial and verbal expressions we'd developed, "Did *you* do that?" When everyone in the clan shook their head in a panicked "No!," we came to a startling awareness: *There is something Other Than Us.*

This Something Other also seemed, as subsequent events appeared to prove, far more *powerful* than us. It could cause wind and rain and violent storms; heat and dry spells that lasted, it seemed, forever; a frightening shaking and even an opening of the very ground on which we walked. It could even start fires in the woods all by Itself.

It became clear to us that we needed to find a way to *control* this Something Other, or our lives would forever be at Its mercy. Yet we could not conceive of or imagine a way that we could do this. We tried everything. We knew we had to find a way to appease the gods.

We didn't call the elements of life "gods," of course. That word came along at a much later time. But we did think of this Something Other as an aspect of our existence that was both powerful and uncontrollable.

We knew some members of our own clan in exactly the same way. The biggest and the strongest and the most brutish ran rampant through the collective life of the clan, and efforts were continually made to appease them. They were brought offerings of every kind, from nubile virgins to plentiful food to beautiful things from the richness of the earth.

Once, when the most brutish became more sullen and angry than usual because of an unending drought and the sacrifices it imposed on them and the whole clan, we joined others in our small group to do whatever we could think of to calm them, lest they take out their anger on us—which they had done before.

We threw a campside "party" for them, sang and did dances for them. Someone in the group tore a dying branch from a nearby tree and shook it as part of his dance, its dry leaves making a rhythmic sound matching his gyrations as he twirled around the fire.

As it happened, at that exact moment the skies opened up and a sudden hard rain drenched the site. Everyone was shocked! And, given the limited intellectual development of the clan at that time, the Dance With The Branch was credited with having produced the water from the sky.

A way had been found to please and appease Something Other! A way had been found to get that Something Other to do what we had been hoping for! All of us were so excited! The "rain man" was elevated to a position of highest status. Ritual, and a class within the clan of Those Who Performed It, was created.

The clan believed that the Dance With The Branch by the Rain

Man created rain, and so it *did* in the future more often than not. And this was not by coincidence. Metaphysics being was it is, the formula worked. For the metaphysical process—whether modern or ancient—produces in physicality whatever it is fervently believed it will produce.

In that first instance, it was no doubt the ongoing, fervent hope, the deeply earnest wish, of the clan that the drought would end that generated the result. But the coincidence of the rain falling at the exact moment the noisy dance was performed could not be ignored.

The narrative above is, of course, all of my imagining. It was an insight—call it an inspiration, if you choose—that I received at the time of my Conversations with God. The entire story could be inaccurate . . . but I believe that either this, or something very similar to this, is what occurred in the early life of human beings, and what produced our sense of separation, our sense of Something Other, and our sense that there might be, after all, a way of controlling—or at least *influencing*—that Something Other.

Earliest humans were dealing with the alchemy of the universe, without knowing it. Thus was born what later became known as Religion.

As Man became more sophisticated in his understandings, the species sought a more sophisticated way of seeking to "appease the gods" . . . and, later, the single God that humans ultimately decided must surely exist.

We were right about that.

There *is* the thing we now call God. Yet our idea of God—that it is "Something Other"—is what has been inaccurate. This idea is a carryover from the earliest story we told ourselves about The Power Greater Than Us. That first idea is what created what I earlier here called Separation Theology.

Science Brings Us a New Story

We have developed, of course, since our caveman days. Not, perhaps, as much as we would like, given some of our continuing barbaric behaviors, but we are now moving more rapidly than ever before in our evolution—egged on by our own growing knowledge of life itself.

It wasn't long ago that astronomer and author Carl Sagan shared with the world the fascinating fact that analysis showed rocks brought back from the moon and debris falling to Earth from much farther out in space (meteors, space dust, etc.) all contained the same fundamental elements found on this planet. Not only in the rocks and dust of this planet, but in *everything*—including birds, animals, trees . . . and *people*.

The same chemical and mineral building blocks are apparently present in all the objects of the cosmos. *We're all made of the same stuff,* Sagan smilingly declared. Everything is One Thing, simply manifested in different combinations and constructions.

Take these elements and mix them in one proportion and you have a tree. Mix them in another way and you have a human. A third combination produces an aardvark. Or a moon rock.

The combining and adjusting of these elements in varying proportions takes place over a period of thousands and hundreds of thousands of years. We call those varying combinations *adaptations,* and we've labeled the entire process *evolution.*

I know that the idea that all of Life has evolved from the same primordial soup is a controversial subject. There are those who want to believe that humans were produced in a single stroke, all at once and as a separate (and special) creation of the Divine, disconnected from the development of any other living thing.

Yet science—and now space science—seems to be confirming

Darwin's theory at every turn. Life is energy, emerging in endless variation from a single Essential Essence.

There are, then, only two questions remaining regarding this birthing energy: (1) What is its quality? (2) What is its capacity or capability?

The Answer to Question #1

The fundamental quality of the Essential Essence is that it is ever moving and ever present. It is simple undifferentiated energy in its purest expression. It could be called the Stem Cell of Reality.

A stem cell in your body, as you know, is defined as "an undifferentiated cell of a multicellular organism that is capable of giving rise to indefinitely more cells of the same type, and from which certain other kinds of cell arise by differentiation."

I am given to understand that by employing the analogy of all that exists as a single entity, the Essential Essence could then be understood to be its "stem cell."

What is being described here is a single unit—which I have taken to call The Singularity (a phrase borrowed from Gene Roddenberry)—whose chief quality or prime force is *vibration*. It is constantly in motion, oscillating at particular frequencies, and It is present wherever there is what we call "life"—for It is Life Itself, in its purest or most undiluted, unaltered form.

Human beings and all other life-forms are *Singularizations of The Singularity*. That is, we are altered, diluted forms of the Essential Essence. We are differentiations of the Undifferentiated Energy that I call God.

You can call this Undifferentiated Energy whatever you wish. Call it the Prime Force, the Unmoved Mover, That Which Is, the Essential Essence—or by more personal names if it pleases you, such as Adonai, Akshar, Allah, Brahma, Deus, Divinity, Divine Mother, Ekankar, Elohim, God, Hari, Indra, Jehovah, Krishna, Lord, Mahesh, Manitou, Ormuzd, Parameshwar, Purush, Purush-ottam, Radha Soami, Ram, Rama, Theos, Thor, Varuna, Vishnu, Yahweh, and others.

One More Once: A Final Explanation

This Essential Essence has one other quality that it is important to describe. It is Self-Conscious. That is, It is aware of Itself *as* Itself. Yet while It knows Itself to be Exactly What It Is, It cannot *experience* Itself *as* that in the absence of something else.

We have discussed this before, and here offer one more explanation of this foundational condition, so that it may be clearly understood and always remembered.

There is nothing else in existence except That Which Exists. This is All That Is. So if All That Is wished to know Itself experientially (which It did, because simply *being* something was not enough), It would have to create something other than Itself. Yet such a thing is impossible, because that which begets is always part of the begotten. Every offspring or manifestation of life is part of that from which it emerged.

Because All That Is could not create something Other Than Itself, that which is Pure Existence was presented with its first question: How to experience Itself when there was nothing *but* Itself? The solution was simple: Allow Itself to forget Itself, so that it would *seem* like Something Else.

This would allow Essential Essence to know Itself experientially as the Creator, through the expression of Itself in forgetfulness of the fact that *everything has already been created*. Thus, forgetfulness is the greatest gift that Life ever gave to Life. As is its companion: remembrance. For when Life remembers Itself as What It Really Is, the Cycle of Life is complete, with Pure Being manifesting as Knowing manifesting as Experiencing manifesting as Pure Being once again.

And, as noted above, this can be accomplished at any time on the Cycle of Life. Death is merely our *assurance* that it occurs.

People have asked, "Why must we die?" "Why is death inevitable?" And now you know the answer! What you call "death" is the greatest gift of life! It is God making *sure* that your forgetfulness does not last forever. It is God reclaiming you as part of Itself by reuniting you *with* Itself, and then releasing you *from* nondifferentiation with Itself, that It might know Itself again in experience, *through you*.

And the ways in which you may experience the part of God that is you are unlimited. You may even return to physicality in the exact same form in which you exited. You can return as your Present Self as many times as you wish, as many times as it serves you to do so, given your built-in, cellular-encoded desire to experience yourself as who you truly are.

People who come back again and again as the Same Self are often called, in their later repeated incarnations, avatars or sages or even saints.

Or even . . . God.

(*"Is it not written, 'Ye are gods'?"*)

The Answer to Question #2

The chief capability of the Essential Essence is that It has the power to impact upon Itself. That is, It is self-sourcing and self-referencing.

An example of this might be water vapor that turns to liquid water droplets that turn to snow that turns to ice that turns to liquid water that turns to vapor once again. Here we see four distinctive expressions of the selfsame element, manifesting in variations created by the way other aspects of the Essential Essence are impacting upon it.

This illustration is simplistic, I understand—yet perhaps not so simple as you may think. Ask the people who live in Beijing. (More on that in just a bit.) Simplistic or not, the metaphor may be useful in assisting us in comprehending how the entire system called Life works—because if we could learn how to *deliberately* impact one or another of the aspects of the Essential Essence, we could potentially cause *particular manifestations* to occur.

That is, if we could turn the life energy back *upon* itself in some controlled way, we could presumably use that birthing energy to our purpose.

If true, this would not be a small matter. Indeed, it would turn us into gods, able to mix and match the colors of Creation's palette to paint the picture of our desire on the canvas of our lives.

God is telling us in *Conversations with God* that this is precisely what is true about the Essential Essence and how it may be used, and this is exactly what our species is doing—albeit without most of us knowing it, and without enough of us who do know it yet able to produce collective agreement on the outcomes we wish to collaboratively produce.

Think This Is All Nonsense?

If you are tempted to classify all this as nothing but wishful thinking, consider this: We have already learned how to seed clouds to modify weather, offering us one striking example of how we can manipulate life's energy to affect life's energy.

Getting back to what may have appeared to be a simplistic metaphor . . .

It has been widely reported that in February 2009 China seeded clouds over Beijing to artificially induce snowfall after four months of drought. Here was an actual case of humans deliberately turning life's energy upon itself in a controlled way to cause life itself to produce a desired and predictable outcome in one of life's most *un*predictable expressions. Namely, *the weather*.

Did it work?

Reports have it that snow fell in Beijing for most of three days. It was said to be the earliest snowfall in that city since the late '80s. And it wasn't just a light flurry. We're talking about snow that slowed traffic to a standstill and actually shut down many of the main thoroughfares in and out of the metropolitan area.

Now if life's energies can be impacted so effectively physically, can they be impacted just as effectively metaphysically?

What *Conversations with God* tells us is that the impact that Essential Essence has upon itself is magnified exponentially by the *amount* of it that is turned upon itself in a particular and specific way. The harder the wind blows, the more the tree will bend. Or, as someone else far more conversant with these energies than I has observed, "Wherever two or more are gathered . . ."

Humanity's most beneficial undertaking, then—its greatest experiment, investigation, exploration, and expansion in this, the first quarter of the twenty-first century—would seem to be to learn how to utilize the deliberate focusing of this birthing energy to produce consistent and predictable results.

Is there something to this business of *guided imagery*, or *visualization*? Was Norman Vincent Peale right about *The Power of Positive Thinking*? Did Émile Coué have something when he proposed his ideas about *autosuggestion*? More contemporarily, are the teachings of Esther and Jerry Hicks in *Ask and It Is Given* about the Law of Attraction, or the insights offered us in *Happier Than God* about the Process of Personal Creation, the golden keys that unlock the doors of deliberate manifestation?

This truly is the Final Frontier. Yet we are hardly paying attention to it. When we do, we will discover (that is, remember) that we are One with the Divine, and that the Essential Essence and we are the Same.

A Holy Trinity Indeed

Like all the other things in existence, human beings are not simply one single expression or element of That Which Is. When we "migrate" from the Realm of the Spiritual to the Realm of the Physical as part of the Cycle of Life, we divide ourselves into three parts. Thus, you are not only your Body, you are not only your Mind, and you are not only your Soul, you are all three.

(A description of this Holy Trinity can be found in *The Only Thing That Matters*.)

All three parts of your being live forever, traveling jointly through all eternity, rebirthing and reforming and re-expressing themselves in countless varieties through the endlessness of Time/No Time in the Always Here/Ever Now of Ultimate Reality.

The highest promise of God is that you are an individuation of Divinity, an expression of God on Earth. We have said this now a number of times. What we have not made note of before is that, fascinatingly, most of the world's religions agree. They have told us that we are made "in the image and likeness of God." The only difference between this belief and the message of *Conversations with God* is in the fine print.

Does being made in the image and likeness of God mean that we are beings who look an awful lot like God? Does it mean that God is just a Big Human living in some other realm, having total control over us and our ultimate destiny? Or does this enigmatic phrase about being made "in the image and likeness of God" mean that we are extractions of the Essential Essence, the Foundational Energy, and the Prime Force from which Life Itself emerged and which Life Itself *is* at its basis?

If we choose to believe the former, we may imagine ourselves to be isolated and alone, fending for ourselves and fighting for our survival in an earthly experience that is complex beyond comprehension and a universe that is huge beyond our imagining. We could think of ourselves as adrift in this endless sea of matter and energy, no bigger or more important in comparison to all the rest of that which exists than a grain of sand on a beach, washed over by the never-ending tide of events, drowned in its sorrows, swept away by its currents, to find ourselves floating on waves to nowhere.

Yet is that all we are? Is that the sum and substance of it? Or is it possible that there is something more going on here, something bigger happening, something larger than our just-emerging understanding has been able to heretofore comprehend? Is there more here than meets the eye? And if there is, what would that be?

What This All Means

Many people make the mistake of assuming that because *Conversations with God* says, "God and we are One" that it is saying that God and we are the same thing. Of course, no one could agree with such a statement, any more than anyone could agree that because the ocean and a drop of water are the same "stuff," the drop and the ocean are the same thing!

We are the "stuff" that God is, and God is the "stuff" that we are—but God is the sum total of all the "stuff" that exists, while we are a single *individuation* of it.

Our essence is Divine, and it is important to know all that this means. Yet we also need to know what it does not mean.

It does not mean for instance, that we can jump off a building and fly. It does not mean that we can never be hurt or injured in any way. It does not mean that we are like Superman.

It does mean that God is always present within us, to offer us help and guidance along the way as we live each day. It does mean that we have been given the same Tools of Creation that God uses, and that if we learn to use them, we can produce wonderful outcomes in our own lives. It does mean that even if we are hurt or injured in some way, or find ourselves in some kind of trouble or difficulty, that if we ask God's help we can find our way out of it.

Essentially, it means that we are not "alone" in life. Even when it feels as if we are alone—perhaps especially when it feels this way—God's presence can heal us of our loneliness and provide us with the gentle companionship and the quiet courage to go on.

The Implications Here Are Staggering

"We are all one" means that we are One with each other, One with all of Life, and One with God. There is no other way to interpret it, as I see it.

The implications of this for the human race are staggering. If we believed this was true, everything in our lives would change. Everything in our religions, in our politics, in our economics, in our education, and in our social constructions. And everything in our personal lives as well.

In our religions, we would see the end of their seemingly endless competitions for human souls. Religions would stop insisting on portraying themselves as the One and Only Path to God. They would assist us on our own personal path, but they would not claim to *be* The Path. And they would cease using Fear as the chief tool in their arsenal.

NEALE DONALD WALSCH

They would stop teaching that unless we follow their doctrines, we are going to spend eternity in the everlasting fires of Hell. They would be a source of comfort and guidance, of ever-present help, and of strength in times of need. Thus, religion would serve its highest purpose and its grandest function.

In our politics, we would see the end of hidden agendas, and of power plays, and of the demonization of those with opposing points of view. Political parties would stop claiming that their way was the only way. And they would work together to find solutions to the most pressing problems, and to move society forward by seeking common ground.

They would seek to blend the most workable of their ideas with the most workable of the ideas of their opponents. Thus, politics would serve its highest purpose and its grandest function.

In our economics, we would see the end of Bigger-Better-More as the international yardstick of Success. We would create a New Bottom Line, in which "maximum productivity" was redefined, and in which our endless drive for profits-profits-*profits* was replaced with a sense of awe and wonder in the universe, a reverence for all of life, and a dedication to creating a world in which each person can live in dignity, with basic needs being met. Thus, economics would serve its highest purpose and its grandest function.

In our education, we would see the end of propaganda substituting for history and of subject-driven curricula, where emphasis is placed on memorization of facts, rather than on the fundamental concepts of life that we want our children to understand: awareness, honesty, and responsibility.

We would see a democratic school in which children have as much to say about what they are to learn and how they will learn it as teachers, and in which we do not use the environment to *pour knowledge into* children, but to *draw wisdom out* of them. Thus, education would serve its highest purpose and its grandest function.

What "We Are All One" Does *Not* Mean

"We are all one" does *not* mean that what's mine is yours and what's yours is mine. The concept of Oneness does not eliminate the possibility of personal possessions or individual expressions.

We may find ourselves experiencing a higher level of desire than ever before to *share* our personal possessions with others when we realize that there really are no "others," but merely Additional Versions of the Self—yet we are not *required* to give our possessions away or take another's possessions from them.

Each human expression of The Singularization that we call "God" may experience Itself exactly the way It chooses—and what it gathers and what it shares becomes a striking part of that individual expression.

I believe that *Conversations with God* and the new theology that it brings to humanity offers us food for thought in response to eternal questions such as those explored on these pages. And I believe that our active discussion of these ideas could produce an extraordinary, perhaps even a life-changing, exchange of the very energy we have been talking about here.

In short, I believe such a discussion could produce the Conversation of the Century.

APPLYING THIS MESSAGE TO EVERYDAY LIFE

I wrote an entire book offering practical suggestions on how Core Message #1 could be applied to daily life. The suggestions cover all areas of our experience—political, economic, and cultural (includes spiritual)—and I consider it to be the definitive statement on how to apply *CWG* to life on Earth.

The book is titled *The Storm Before the Calm*, and it discusses what I have called the Overhaul of Humanity, which is now occurring with or without our participation. If you truly wish to look closely and seriously at how the idea that We Are All One could be made to *work* in our individual and in humanity's collective experience, you may find this useful reading.

I realize that I have mentioned other books of my authorship several times throughout the present volume. I suspect that there may be criticism of this in some quarters, yet I believe that the writing in the *Conversations with God* body of work and in the several texts attendant to it offer valuable insight into the human experience—and where we can all go with it from here. I should like to note that additional books I have mentioned here have all been made available (and continue to be) free for the reading on the Internet.

I bring your attention to them because I experience that the messages in these books have been inspired by the same Source that inspired contributions to the quality of our life on this planet such as Mozart's music and Michelangelo's art, Lincoln's leadership, Gandhi's politics, and the work and words of Martin Luther King Jr.

As well, I believe this to be the same Source that inspires you, daily, with your own highest thoughts, uplifting inspirations, and most useful ideas and solutions. We are all here *trading ideas*, and if we have what we feel might be a good one, it brings no one any benefit at all if you hide your light under a bushel.

31

Thank you for coming here. And thank you for remaining here until the end of this journey. I appreciate you very much for having the courage to explore ideas that may be very new to you, or to more deeply examine ideas that you've heard before, and had before, and explored before—but perhaps never quite at this level.

The New Theology presented here offers humanity another way of looking at things. It says that life is not a series of random events, occurring without rhyme or reason, but rather, an intricately designed and deliberately set-into-motion sequence of occurrences *collaboratively and spontaneously created* by all the Souls in existence, for the purpose of giving that Total Collection of Souls a direct experience of Itself, both *as* a collection and as individuals *within* the collection.

We are here on Earth, *Conversations with God* suggests, to do more than just live and die and make the best of the experience. We are also here to do more than simply find a way to "get back to heaven"—or, at least, avoid going to hell. Those are simplistic views of the reason and purpose for human existence.

We are here to advance a larger agenda. We are here to move forward an eternal evolutionary process through which each individual Soul (and everything in existence) experiences its True Identity fully, and by which Life Itself, through its individuated expressions, expands awareness of itself, thereby reflecting the wonder of its ultimate and true nature.

A Key Statement

The basic tenet of this New Theology is that we don't "have to" do any of this. The process is going on with or without our intentional or conscious participation. It is not a question of whether God's process (for that is what it is) is proceeding, but of how we choose to experience it.

Some of us may choose to experience it as if we were *at the effect* of it, and some of us may choose to experience it as if we are *at cause* in the matter. We alone can decide if life is happening *to* us or *through* us. Indeed, this has become the central question of our time. Are we ready, willing, and able to now take control of our lives, or shall we remain hostage to it?

We have an endless number of lifetimes, and nothing is specifically demanded, commanded, or required of us in any given passage through this physical encounter. Because our incarnations never end, with the soul moving from one physical expression to another on an eternal journey, it is not necessary for a particular lifetime to produce a particular outcome. God says we have all the time in the world—*literally.*

To allow your mind to grasp this, imagine that after forty years of going to a job every day, you have finally retired, are in wonderful health, possess ample financial resources, and can now look forward to years of doing whatever you please. Would you feel required to play golf next Thursday, as opposed to doing so a week later? And would you feel that your idea of fun had *better* be golf, and not tennis—*or else*?

Other than for the sheer joy of it, what would be the reason to do any particular thing on any particular day in any particular way?

The Heaven We've Been Told About

The beauty of retirement, of course, is *freedom*—the joy and the liberty to do what you want, when you want, in the way that you want. You are said to have "earned it."

This is also the beauty of Life Itself. And its freedom, too, you have "earned." By the very act of coming into physicality (not an insignificant decision) and living day-to-day in the Realm of Relativity (not a small task), you have earned the freedom to do what you want, when you want, in the way that you want.

Freedom is God's prerogative—and you are nothing less than Divine.

Life itself is the "heaven" you have been told about. The *whole* of life, not just part of it—the experience *between* physical lifetimes, yes, and the experience *of* each lifetime. "Heaven" for the Soul is the ability to know and to express Divinity in you, through you, as you . . . in the way and at the time that you wish.

In truth, Divinity is expressed through you no matter what you do. It is impossible for you *not* to express Divinity, since Divinity is Who You Are. It is simply a matter of how you want to *define* Divinity in this moment right now.

Put another way, God is what you say God is, locally expressed by how you are being in any given situation or circumstance. And Life Itself, expressed throughout the multiple universes, is the totality of God in the act of defining Itself as It wishes to know Itself through the here-and-now expression and experience *of* Itself.

The greatest gift we have is Free Will. We *can* express our Selves in any way that we desire, and we *are* still God demonstrating Divinity. This idea might lead some to scoff, saying, "How can the way human beings are behaving be an expression of Divinity?" Yet the real question is, "Why would human beings choose for Divinity to be expressed in this way?"

Indeed, why would we? Could it be because we got the story wrong? The story of what God is and what God wants and what we're all doing here?

More transformatively, we might ask: "What could cause us to define Who We Are, and Divinity Itself, in another way? A grander way? A more glorious way?"

Could it be a *new* story of what God is and what God wants and what we're all doing here?

Our answer to these questions will determine the future of humanity.

Is *CWG* the Truth?

Now let's move to the most important question we could ask about the *CWG* theology. Are we to take it as "holy scripture"? Is it the inviolable Word of God?

Humanity has been asking for a very long time, "Which scriptures *are* 'Holy Scriptures'? What scripture contains the One and Only, True Word of God?"

I wrote a piece about this a few years ago. I observed that the answer to that question depends upon to whom one is speaking.

Many say the Bible is the Holy Scripture. Others say, no, God's word is found in the Hebrew Bible. Others say, no, God's truth is found in the Qur'an. Others say, no, it's in the Torah. Others say, no, in the Mishna. Others say the Talmud. Others, the Bhagavad Gita. Others, the Rig Veda. Others, the Brahmanas. Others, the Upanishads. Others, the Mahabharta and the Ramayana. Others, the Puranas. Others, the Tantras. Others, the Tao Te Ching. Others, the Buddha-Dharma. Others, the Dhammapada. Others, The Master of Huainan. Others, the Shih-chi. Others, the Pali Canon. Others, the Book of Mormon.

Others . . .

Well, the point is, many people believe that Direct Revelation—that is, God speaking directly to Man—has not occurred since the Holy Scriptures with which *they feel comfortable* were written.

And while few of those who cite these sources agree with each other theologically, many agree on one thing emphatically: *Their* Word of God is *the* Word of God; *their* way to paradise is *the* way to paradise; *their* communication from Deity is *the only* communication from Deity.

By this measure, *Conversations with God* would have to be heresy, would by definition be blasphemy. Some of the adherents of the Old Books may not be clear about *which* old book contains the Truth, but they *are* clear that no *new book* does.

And so at the very outset (indeed, by its very title) *Conversations with God* presents a challenge, upsets the apple cart, turns much of present-day theology on its ear. Yet, interestingly, few people who have read *CWG* seem to have any quarrel with the possibility, at least, that God has revealed Himself once more through the written word.

Indeed, I'll go further. An astonishing number of people have come forward to say that *they, too, have experienced such communications*. And so it turns out that my conversation with God may not be such an "uncommon dialogue" after all.

An Invitation, Not a Declaration

What is most important to understand now is that, however it came to be written, *CWG* is a *theology*, not a dogma or doctrine. It is a study of God.

Please let me be clear. I believe the words to have come from God, directly. Yet whence does all true inspiration originate? What is the source of the experience that we call creativity, inventiveness, innovation, ingenuity, genius, imagination, originality, artistry, insight, vision, and yes, revelation?

The intent of this book has been simply to invite you deeply inside the *CWG* material, so that you may understand it thoroughly and thus be led to your own highest truth. That is, in fact and in short, *what God said*. God said, "The truth is within you." And God intended the extensive dialogue in *Conversations with God* to *lead* you to your truth, not to *become* your truth.

Yet if the truth you are led to is in concert with some or many of the constructs in *Conversations with God*, so be it. If, on the other hand, you wind up discarding the words in the dialogue altogether, they will have served you still—by bringing you to greater clarity about your own experience, so that you may live it even more richly.

This is the purpose of every form of art, is it not? Be it literature or drama, music or dance, painting or poetry, is this not what all creative expression seeks to do? And is this not the magic of every real communication from the Divine? For God would not have you follow God, but rather, *lead* God to the next grandest experience of who *You* are.

In this do you demonstrate yourself to be the Creator. In this is the greatest promise of God—that you *are* made in God's image and likeness—redeemed. And your own Soul, as well.

And So, Therefore . . . ?

What does any of this have to do with our lives right now, or our future—much less the future of our planet? Well, our history has shown that we keep repeating ourselves. We keep acting in the same ways, doing the same things, telling and believing the same stories about God, about life, about everything. Indeed, it has been said that the sins of the father shall be visited upon the sons, even unto the seventh generation.

Yet we have the opportunity now to end the cycle, to put a stop to that repetition, to put a period on the last sentence of the last paragraph of the last chapter of humanity's old and no longer fully useful cultural story. Not, then, to throw that story away, but to write *beyond* the last period. To hold on to all that is good within our old story, but to be willing, as well, to embrace that which is good that may be outside of it, that may be *new*.

Let us now declare ourselves to be the Eighth Generation, and let us be the first ones who shall visit upon future generations the grandest ideas that humanity has ever had about itself, the grandest notions that philosophers have ever proposed, the grandest thoughts that God has ever inspired.

Let us present to our children the beginning of a New Cultural Story, a new idea about human beings and who we are, a new thought about our potential and our promise and our purpose.

Let us bring to each other as well a new hope, a new under-standing, a new awareness, a new expression, a new experience of life and of God and of each other, the likes of which will make how we have lived our lives in the past a forgotten dream; a nightmarish way of being that we will never take up again.

Ever.

* * *

You can take up this New Way right now, today. You do not have to wait for the rest of your world to catch up to you. You can *bring* it up to you by how it is you are being in every moment, in every situation, in every encounter. You can do this by choosing to be Divine.

This is not impossible. All you need is a little help along the way. Some companionship, perhaps. Some support. Maybe a little guidance now and then, some suggestions on how you might go about it.

It is my hope that you have found a touch of that here. You decide.

As in all things, you decide.

Afterword

Evolution is not about *becoming* something, it is about remembering, and then demonstrating, what we already are. It is not about moving forward, it is about being right where we are, *fully*. It is not about *advancing* in our awareness, it is about enhancing our *present* awareness.

What is the difference? The first is about seeking something that we imagine we do not now have, the second is about expressing completely what we already possess. The first is about trying to find a bigger ocean, the second is about diving deeper into the ocean *in which we now swim*. It is about becoming fully submerged and completely immersed, not simply floating on the surface.

The point: We need nothing more than what is already present. But we must become fully present *to* it.

We can do this in a moment. In a split second.

Evolution does not take Time, it takes Will.

In the end, this is about our children, of course. And our children's children. If we see the gift and the wonder that life in human form has given us, we must ask: What can we do to give our children, and theirs, an even more wondrous experience than we have had?

Even if our own life has been one of constant struggle and too much suffering (perhaps *especially* if it has been), we will surely wish to ask the same question: What can we do to give our children, and theirs, a more wondrous experience than we have had, and how can we leave them a better world?

To me the answer to that pressing question seems clear. *We can give them the tools with which to create it.*

Millions of young people to whom we will be turning over the world in the decades just ahead are being educated and trained right now, *this very day.* They are being told and shown by our own actions what is true about life, what is true about who they are, and what is true about God. They are being taught how life works, what it's all about, what it means to have a "good life," and how to get it.

How are we doing with that . . . ? As you see what we are teaching our children about their world these days, how does it feel to you that humanity is doing? Do you think we might do better? If so, to whom can we turn to offer us an improved curriculum?

I want to suggest that we turn to God.

In the book *Communion with God*, here is what God said:

Teach your children that they need nothing exterior to themselves to be happy—neither person, place, nor thing—and that true happiness is found within. Teach them that they are *sufficient unto themselves.*

Teach them this, and you will have taught them grandly.

Teach your children that failure is a fiction, that every trying is a success, and that every effort is what achieves the victory, with the first no less honorable than the last.

Teach them this, and you will have taught them grandly.

Teach your children that they are deeply connected to all of life, that they are one with all people, and that they are never separate from God.

Teach them this, and you will have taught them grandly.

Teach your children that they live in a world of magnificent abundance, that there is enough for everyone, and that it is in *sharing* the most, not in *gathering* the most, that the most is received.

Teach them this, and you will have taught them grandly.

Teach your children that there is nothing that they are required to be or to do to be eligible for a life of dignity and fulfillment, that they need not compete with anyone for anything, and that God's blessings are meant for everyone.

Teach them this, and you will have taught them grandly.

Teach your children that they will never be judged, that they need not worry about always getting it right, and that they do not have to change anything, or "get better," to be seen as Perfect and Beautiful in the eyes of God.

Teach them this, and you will have taught them grandly.

Teach your children that consequences and punishment are not the same thing, that death does not exist, and that God would never condemn anyone.

Teach them this, and you will have taught them grandly.

Teach your children that there are no conditions to love, that they need not worry about ever losing your love, or God's, and that their own love, unconditionally shared, is the greatest gift they can give to the world.

Teach them this, and you will have taught them grandly.

Teach your children that being special does not mean being better, that claiming superiority over someone is not seeing them for who they really are, and that there is great healing in acknowledging, "Mine is not a better way, mine is merely another way."

Teach them this, and you will have taught them grandly.

Teach your children that there is nothing that they cannot do, that the illusion of ignorance can be eradicated from the Earth, and that all anyone really needs is to be given back to themselves by being reminded of Who They Really Are.

Teach them this, and you will have taught them grandly.

Teach these things not with your words, but with your actions; not with discussion, but with demonstration. For it is what you do that your children will emulate, and how you are that they will become.

Go now and teach these things not only to your children, but to all people and all nations. For all people are your children, and all nations are your home, when you set out on the Journey to Mastery.

This is the journey on which you embarked many centuries and many lifetimes ago. It is the journey for which you have long prepared, and which has brought you here, to this Time and Place.

This is the journey which calls you more urgently now than ever before; on which you feel yourself proceeding with ever increasing speed.

This is the inevitable outcome of the yearning of your soul. It is the speaking of your heart, in the language of your body. It is the expression of Divinity within you, and it calls to you now as it has never called before—because you are hearing it now as it was never heard before.

It is time to share with the world a glorious vision. It is the vision of all minds that have ever truly searched, of all hearts that have ever truly loved, of all souls that have ever truly felt the Oneness of Life.

Once you have felt this, you can never be satisfied with anything less. Once you have experienced it, you will want nothing but to share it with all those whose lives you touch.

It Is Time for a New Human

Conversations with God says that the purpose of life is to "re-create yourself anew in the next grandest version of the greatest vision ever you held about Who You Are." That is the most powerful statement of purpose I have ever read. And I am now clear that it is when we present our species with a New Cultural Story—a new idea of who we are, who God is, what God wants, and why we are all here on the Earth—that we give ourselves the chance we have been waiting for: the chance to begin again, to give birth to a new tomorrow.

The work begins not just with our children, but with those who would lead them and who would teach them. That means us, today.

It is time for a New Human to arise, a new kind of species to emerge. It is time now to create a Civil Rights Movement for the Soul, freeing humanity at last from the oppression of its beliefs in a violent, angry, and vindictive God. We have it in our power to release our species from ancient spiritual doctrines that have created nothing but separation, fear, and dysfunction around the world.

The time for this long-awaited shift in humanity's expression and experience of itself is at hand. I urge you to assist in replacing old dogmas, finally, with an ethos of unity and cooperation, understanding and compassion, generosity and love.

This will not take a huge life change or a major, time-consuming commitment on your part. Each of us has our own life to live—and some days it is enough just to get through *that*. Yet if you are willing to use the very process by which you meet your own daily challenges in a new way, as part of humanity's larger effort to change what it means to be human, your personal life can take on a meaning grander than you might ever have imagined.

The books in the *Conversations with God* cosmology are one human being's very best effort, one person's honest, pure, and earnest attempt, to convey messages believed to have been inspired by God. But I want you to be clear that *I* am very clear that everything I've written is open to question—and should be. As I have said from the beginning, let CWG be your inspiration to search deeply within.

I hope you find that you can use the messages you found here as a starting point on that new excursion. Share with those close to you—and with all those whose life you touch, if it feels good to do so—the awareness and the understandings to which your own inner and highest self has led you. There is no greater gift you can give.

And so I close with this sweet and gentle invitation, from the book *Home Remembers Me: Medicine Poems from Em Claire* . . .

Speak in a Soul Language
so that Everyone can hear.
Unwind This Story of Humanity
with a
presence so precious,
even God cannot give it definition.
Practice loving so deeply
that the word for tears
becomes
"ocean"
and
the School of Compassion
is the
World's Greatest Institution.
Let no one walk alone
on this journey that is
Ours
to share:
Speak in a Soul Language,
so that Everyone can hear.

Additional Resources

Many people inquire about further reading or supplementary materials attendant to the *Conversations with God* books. Some have expressed great surprise that there are more books in the original series than they thought.

For this reason we have listed here all of the titles in the dialogue series itself, plus the newest writings further explaining and expanding on the messages. As well, you will find below some information on educational programs for children and adults. We trust you will find this listing of resources useful.

TITLES IN THE *CONVERSATIONS WITH GOD* SERIES
Conversations with God (Book 1)
Conversations with God (Book 2)
Conversations with God (Book 3)
Friendship with God
Communion with God
The New Revelations
Tomorrow's God
What God Wants
Home with God

ADDITIONAL WRITINGS

When Everything Changes, Change Everything
The Storm Before the Calm
The Only Thing That Matters

EDUCATION PROGRAMS FOR ADULTS

The CWG Online School offers a series of six four-week courses for persons wishing to learn how to share the message of *Conversations with God* with others in teaching and helping ways. The courses were written and are presented by CWG Life Coach Annie Sims, who has worked closely with Neale Donald Walsch for more than ten years. Participants interact one-on-one with the instructor as she works to ensure that every person in the program totally comprehends the concepts of this new understanding of God and Life.

Four spiritual and personal growth retreats are privately presented each year by Neale Donald Walsch, with the Conversations with God Foundation also providing online and on-site spiritual education activities and resources of a wide variety, including programs for addiction recovery and spiritual renewal.

EDUCATION PROGRAMS FOR CHILDREN

The School of the New Spirituality offers a homeschooling kit through its CWG for Parents Program that reframes the messages of *Conversations with God* in fifty-two age-appropriate, bite-size lessons for children, one a week for a year. The "school in a box" may be used with one's own children and also as a Teacher's Guide in providing regular learning opportunities for the children of friends and neighbors. The CWG for Parents Program also includes a separate unit for teenagers.

SPIRITUAL OUTREACH

CWG Connect is the Internet-based global community for those who wish to more deeply explore the messages of *Conversations with God*. This subscription service provides opportunities to connect with the material every day through weekly video, audio, and written content, including monthly meditations, conversations with Neale, and a social networking platform to give like-minded people a place to stay connected with and be supported by each other.

The *Global Conversation* is an Internet newspaper offering commentary on world events and a platform allowing readers from around the world to share ideas about how to transform the global reality in one generation.

The Changing Change Network is a spiritual assistance outreach with a team of volunteer Spiritual Helpers responding to anyone facing unexpected and unwelcome changes in life. The program's purpose is to "change the way change changes you."

Humanity's Team, a global organization basing its mission on the *Conversations with God* messages, was founded by Neale Donald Walsch and gathers support for the idea of the Oneness of all of humanity. Its spiritual activist project, the Evolution Revolution, invites people around the world to help change the world's mind about God, the purpose of life, and our relationship with each other.

All of these resources may be accessed through a single Internet gateway site: www.CWGPortal.com.

THE POETRY

The poetry in this book is from *Home Remembers Me: Medicine Poems from Em Claire,* distributed by Hay House. Her work in written and audio form may be found at www.EmClairePoet.com.

Amy Venley.
        630 - 247 - 9964

Kareen Kippida.
       630 - 774 - 1588

Andrea Redfearn -
     312 - 316 - 7975

Lisa -
     708 - 204 - 7355

Pam Pozek

Sarah Schrage

Julie Carpenter

Amy Wilson

Candi Eistadt.

Jenny Tr

If ever these words do not sit well
at your heart's table
You can always invite them to leave
and they will go so peacefully . . .
Instead, You and God might sit together
at your own Heart-table.
In the candlelight. And the quiet. And create:
new Heartwords
no one has ever before heard!
God wants nothing more than to be

Your Heartscribe

If *What God Said* has touched your life in a positive way, you may wish to read the first of the nine texts on which it is based, *Conversations with God: Book One*, a two-way dialogue that its author, Neale Donald Walsch, says he had with God. This is the original book that startled the world and remained on the *New York Times* bestseller list for more than two and a half years, ultimately selling well over two million copies and being translated into more than thirty languages, creating a global spiritual renaissance. The back-and-forth exchanges between one man and God found on these pages are mind-bending and heart-opening, and will surely aid readers of *What God Said* in understanding the nuance and the context of the remarkable, life-changing material that has touched the world entire.

www.CWGPortal.com